D0554866

Lefty Kreh's Ultimate Guide to Fly Fishing

Lefty Kreh

LEFTY KREH'S ULTIMATE GUIDE TO FLY FISHING

Lefty Kreh

*Illustrations by Rod Walinchus
Mark Susinno
and Bill Bishop Jr.*

The Lyons Press
Guilford, CT
An imprint of The Globe Pequot Press

Copyright © 2003 by Lefty Kreh

ALL RIGHTS RESERVED. No part of this book may be reproduced or transmitted in any form by any means, electronic or mechanical, including photocopying and recording, or by any information storage and retrieval system, except as may be expressly permitted in writing from the publisher. Requests for permission should be addressed to The Lyons Press, Attn: Rights and Permissions Department, P. O. Box 480, Guilford, Connecticut 06437.

The Lyons Press is an imprint of the Globe Pequot Press

ISBN 1–59228–111–7

Printed in the United States of America
Text design by Compset, Inc.

   3 5 7 9 10 8 6 4 2

The Library of Congress Cataloging-in-Publication Data is available on file.

CONTENTS

FOREWORD

Let me begin by saying that I disagree with my mentor Lefty Kreh when he says in Chapter One that mastering fly fishing for trout is not complicated. I can disagree with our sport's greatest teacher because I have spent over four decades trying to master it, and I still have much to learn. What I think he means is that the introductory steps can be fairly easy, assuming that you have qualified instructors to help you learn essentially what is in this book. On the other hand, to reach the level of *master* you will need the decades of experience and commitment that animate the lives of the truly possessed fly fishers of the world. There is no one like Lefty Kreh, but there are many professional fly fishers whom I would describe as true masters. They all have one thing in common: a professional attitude, as professional as the most committed pro baseball, basketball, soccer, or football players. They pay their dues with practice, study, fishing, and more practice. They are all master casters—or more importantly *presenters of the fly*.

This book is a synthesis of Lefty Kreh's life as a fisher: more correctly, it is a distillation of what he has *learned* in over seventy years of fishing, most of it in the field of fishing that he loves most—fly fishing. Much of this information appears in his other books on fly fishing, and anyone committed to this sport should read them all. But this book should be the overview, the first reading as you set forth in a lifelong journey that will take you to the most mind-expanding experiences that you can have in the outdoors.

In reading this book I was constantly reminded of the lessons that I have learned from Lefty over the past twenty-six years that I have known him. He has been consistent in his teaching, though his methods in instructing fly casting have been modified though the years. One of the first things Lefty ever said to me as an editor of a magazine on fly fishing was this: "Writers on our sport should convey helpful knowledge directly to the reader. They should not attempt to *display knowledge*. That talks down to the reader." In his writing and teaching, Lefty conveys practical and helpful knowledge.

A newcomer's first introduction (he may have many) to fly fishing can be an inhibiting, even terrifying, experience. This is especially true if the student is a woman and the instructor is a man. The introduction is terrifying because the skills of fly fishing are so specialized and seemingly arcane. The best instructors introduce the students in a close one-on-one, gentle relationship and they simplify what seems complex. The toughest job the professionals have in introducing their students to our sport is the teaching of casting. This job is important, for if you cannot learn basic casting, you cannot fly fish successfully. (The fly-casting stroke and the golf swing are directly parallel in athletic movements.) Lefty Kreh is one of the best instructors of fly casting, although his teaching techniques depart from traditional methods. I am a Kreh casting student, and I can testify that his casting technique is absolutely essential to good casting on the flats and large rivers of the world, especially if you want to cast relatively heavy lines all day in the wind. Bad casting motions in these settings can lead to extreme arm fatigue and forearm tendinitis or shoulder problems. Good Kreh technique helps to forestall or eliminate those problems.

Casting is the *sine qua non* of fly fishing. Learn it well and you will be halfway home to success in catching fish. The Kreh casting lessons in this book should provide an excellent means for novice to intermediate casters to groove or correct strokes. Let me explain this statement. As in learning any athletic technique, you must program muscle memories correctly (golf swing, basketball shots, baseball swing, etc.) to achieve success. If you groove the wrong casting stroke, you are doomed to failure—you simply cannot present the fly correctly the way the fish expect to see their food. For success you must reprogram those muscles to the correct memories. What makes these instructions so useful are Kreh's instructions combined with professional fly-fishing guide and illustrator Rod Walinchus's drawings. Walinchus has been illustrating the Kreh techniques in books and articles for decades. He shows the right hand positions and arm movements in the way that only an experienced fishing veteran and fly-casting illustrator can.

Kreh's explanations of causes for the caster's nightmare—the tailing loop—are essential reading for most fly fishers since most of us have experienced this problem at some point in our learning. The symptom of this casting problem is the "wind knot," which isn't caused by wind but by poor casting. Kreh's explanations of the tailing loop causes are new, and they are important because they describe the many different ways that tailing loops can be created and how to correct them. There are many lessons that could be described as essential reading in this book, but this section is the core of the Kreh philosophy, the part that all fly fishers should study and use for their casting practice and improvement.

The most important aspect of learning successful fly fishing in my experience has been the elimination of variables, in other words reducing the complex to the understandable and doable. That is what this book does for the reader: It takes Kreh's decades of learning and turns them into simple understandable truths that reduce fly fishing to the skills needed to hunt, locate, and catch fish on a fly—everywhere. Lefty gives an example of reducing the complex to its simplest form in his description of the fishing hermit who lived in a shack on the Monacacy Branch and caught big bass and trout. When asked how he did it, the man replied: "Fish early and late." I have learned the same lesson throughout my fishing life, as has every successful fisher. This is an example of what Lefty does in this book: He conveys hard-earned knowledge and lore without arcane description.

The section on flies is important. It allows you to reduce the estimated 30,000 known fly patterns of the world to a manageable handful to meet virtually all your needs on both fresh water and salt water. As Kreh points out, this is a floorplan, a basic dozen or so that should meet your needs. You may never proceed past these favorites; you may not need to. On the other hand, fly fishing in one way is like peeling an onion—you can enjoy the outer skin or you can keep peeling into inner layers, learning and progressively enjoying each level to the inner core, which may be matching the hatches of the world through the study of entomology and tying a vast array of fly patterns or simply exploring the rivers, streams, and oceans of the world for an ever-expanding life list of fish species, which Kreh describes. Fly fishing is what you make of it— a short, relaxed journey with few demands and large rewards or a long, energetic, far-ranging adventure in voyeurism of the natural world, one that will take you, literally, to the ends of the earth.

To be successful at any pursuit at a high level of performance one must be religiously devoted to its perfection, to the exclusion of all distractions. That describes a professional. Ted Williams was a professional obsessively devoted to becoming the best baseball hitter of all time. Lefty Kreh has devoted himself to the learning and teaching of successful fly fishing throughout his entire life (at this writing he is now seventy-seven). He may be the all-around best sport fisherman who ever lived. This book is his *vade mecum* to fly fishing.

—JOHN RANDOLPH
JUNE 2003

INTRODUCTION

Fly fishing is one of the world's great pleasures. Whether it involves our first attempts to fool fish with an artificial fly or more advanced skills that allow us to catch and return them unharmed to their wild environment, this is a glorious pastime that involves skill and sportsmanship. I am one of those anglers, however, who believes there is very little luck involved in successful fly fishing. You make your own luck—good or bad. To successfully catch fish—especially large fish—on fly tackle means properly attending to a number of things between the time you decide to make a trip and the final release of your fish.

Many surveys reveal that 10 percent of fly fishermen catch 90 percent of the fish, and I endorse this finding. In the twelve chapters that follow, you will find a general survey of important techniques and tactics for increasing your chances of success. Even though some of the concepts I will be sharing are fairly sophisticated, they will give you a broad and solid foundation. At the same time I would not presume that the information in these pages is all you are going to need to become a fly-fishing master. But I do believe that I have selected material that is sound, practical, and informative. And you can use it to become more effective right now, on your next fishing trip, no matter where you are going or what species you will be fishing to, in fresh or salt water.

I will look at a number of important topics: properly preparing your tackle, being at the right place at the best time, knowing how to approach and position yourself in relation to the fish (whether you are on shore, wading or approaching from a boat or canoe), casting effectively, making the right presentation and retrieve, then striking, fighting, landing, and releasing the fish. These are not matters of luck, but learned skills. They are the essential techniques and tactics of fly fishing. Ultimately they will help you properly present the fly, which is the most important factor in luring a fish to your offering. It is not even a matter of always having the perfect fly for the occasion, for I know anglers who carry only three or four patterns in their fly box. It is a matter of realizing all of the factors that govern this ancient art of landing a fly on the water.

1

On this subject, those of you who have met me know that I am not a traditionalist. I have nothing against the history of our sport; in fly fishing we have a great tradition. And I get as much pleasure as any purist from making upstream presentations to trout with a bamboo rod, light tippet, and dry fly. But the world of fly fishing has changed. Convenient air travel has opened up the entire world to us: We can adventure in fishing hot spots and for fish species unknown to us a generation ago. Many of these new opportunities can be met only with newly developed techniques and tactics. Modern tackle technology—particularly in the area of rods and lines—makes possible some casting feats that were previously beyond the reach of all except the serious professional. It continues to amaze me, for example, what a moderately proficient fly caster can accomplish today on big water with a state-of-the-art graphite rod and a specialized fly line.

Also, more anglers are discovering the special pleasures of saltwater fly fishing. Saltwater wisdom has many freshwater applications. My own experience fishing in the ocean has substantially improved my technique for all other types of fishing. Casting into heavy ocean breezes and at extremely long distances are just two of the skills I have honed in salt water. Bonefish, tarpon, and permit can give a fly fisherman a thrill equal to any trout or salmon.

It is my hope and belief that not only will this book bring you more pleasure from the sport, but you will become a better all-around fly fisherman—an advanced practitioner in the art of catching fish on a fly.

1

FRESHWATER FISH

For most anglers who tempt trout, catching them on a dry fly is considered the ultimate method. And there is no denying that seeing a large rainbow or brown break the surface and accept your offering is one of the thrills of fly fishing not soon forgotten. It's probably true that no one ever got a heart attack from fighting a trout. But it is not the battle that excites most of us who enjoy this kind of fly fishing. It is solving all of the problems and finally getting the fish to accept the offering. This is the pleasure in fishing for trout.

Unfortunately, you will find more mystique and more misconceptions about fishing for trout than any other area of fly fishing. I think I know the reason. Some people who are not fully experienced in the sport have tried to suggest that this is a very difficult sport to master. This simply is not accurate. Learning to catch trout on dry flies is not complicated. The truth is that it may be one of the easier methods to master for taking fish on flies. What works on one stretch of water often works on many others, too. Learn the basics of trout presentation and you can likely do well almost anywhere these fish are found in North America. What is needed, I think, is an understanding of how a trout feeds on the surface. Once this is clear, much of the simple technique needed to become a proficient dry-fly angler is easy to conquer.

We need to remember a few basics about this fish. A trout does not have a brain the size of a gallon bucket. It does not have a computer in its head to identify and catalog thousands of insects. Trout also do not have to speak Latin. And neither do you. Trout and almost all other fish need and desire only three things out of life. They need a place to hide from predators, a good spot to rest, and preferably both of the above near a constant source of the essentials: food and well-oxygenated water. These three simple factors govern a trout's life.

3

Here is my own concept of how trout feed on the surface in flowing water. If you are driving a station wagon on a dirt road, the dust will come in the rear of the car—but only if the back window is open. Otherwise, most of the dust will remain behind the car. But some of the dust that the car kicks up is swirling so that it travels in the same direction as your car. You can equate this with the currents on the bottom of a stream. If a current is flowing strongly and there are boulders and rocks lying on the bottom, some of the currents downstream of the rocks will actually be going upstream, or there may be no current at all. In other words, behind these rocks the current will be flowing slower, be going opposite the main current, or actually form a quiet eddy. This is true even in a fast riffle, where overhead the water is sweeping by.

This concept is very important if you want to understand how trout feed on dry flies in running water. Dr. Robert Bachman wrote his doctoral thesis at Pennsylvania State University on how native brown trout feed in a flowing stream. He determined through the use of video and film footage that each trout had what he called "a specific seat in a restaurant." In other words, each fish in the pool has its own particular feeding place. This observation can be verified by the experience of good trout fishermen who have caught and kept large fish from a specific location. Returning later to the same pool, they may catch and keep another trout from the same spot. But it will not be quite as large as the first. And each succeeding trout caught will be smaller than the last one. The biggest or strongest trout in the pool controls the most desirable feeding

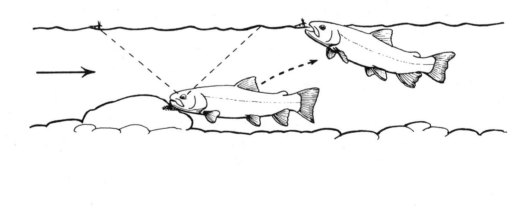

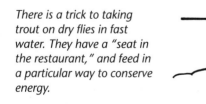

There is a trick to taking trout on dry flies in fast water. They have a "seat in the restaurant," and feed in a particular way to conserve energy.

location. Remove this fish, and the second strongest fish will occupy the location. (I would add that this is not as often the case in still waters such as lakes, but in streams I believe this is almost always true.)

The question is: Why do the trout behave this way? No large trout can afford to swim up through two or three feet of water, take a minute insect from the surface, and then return to its former position. The fish would actually consume more energy than it received by eating the insect. But if the trout can take the insect without expending energy—in other words, not being forced to swim to the surface and return—then it will do so. And that is what I believe such trout do in flowing water.

Holding its position, the trout sees an insect floating toward it on the surface. As the insect comes into the trout's window, the fish decides whether it can take the insect or not. If the trout elects to consume the insect, it tilts its fins so that they lift its body up and back with the current. The fish actually glides to the surface. Once there, it sucks in the insect. It then tilts its fins again, and with the subtle flick of its tail the trout changes its attitude and the current forces it to dive, allowing it to plane down and back to its holding position.

All of this is similar to a glider, which has no motor yet can rise against the flow of air, maneuver, and return to port. The trout does the same thing. If you think about it for a moment, you realize that any trout that you see taking insects from the surface in flowing water always lifts up and back, with its head tilted a little to the rear. Reaching the surface, the fish sucks in the insect, then tilts downward and returns to the bottom upstream from the point where the fly was taken.

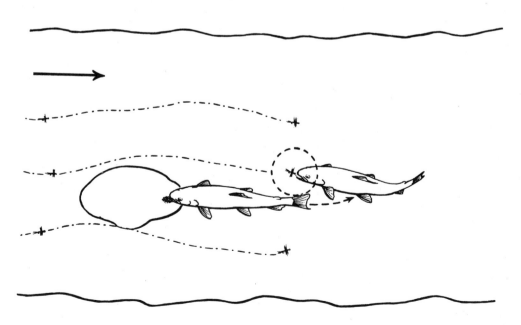

Trout cannot afford to chase small dry flies in swift water. Accuracy in placing the fly is vital to success.

Let's pursue this idea a little farther to see how trout take insects off the surface. The fish looks through a window, which is similar to a cone. Anything outside this cone that is on or above the surface, scientists tell us, the trout cannot see. Only when the fly comes into the cone can the trout see it. The fish sees the fly enter its vision only a short distance upstream from its holding position. The fish rises if it decides to take the fly. The actual distance the fly drifts while it is under the trout's observation is short. And over this short distance the currents are going to be the same. Thus, every insect that floats to this trout is going to come along the same path. For example, if a drifting insect is swept slightly to the right, and then back to the left before it is taken by the trout, every other insect will follow the same path. This is critically important. The trout does not have to know all of the currents in a pool. But it thoroughly understands exactly the currents that deliver each fly to it.

This means that over the short distance a dry fly floats on the surface while the trout is inspecting it, the fly must travel exactly the same path as a natural insect. If it does not behave this way, the fish will refuse it. Most fishermen know that a fly floating unnaturally is said to be dragging. Currents pulling against the leader are what drag the fly unnaturally. But drag is important only for that short distance that each trout

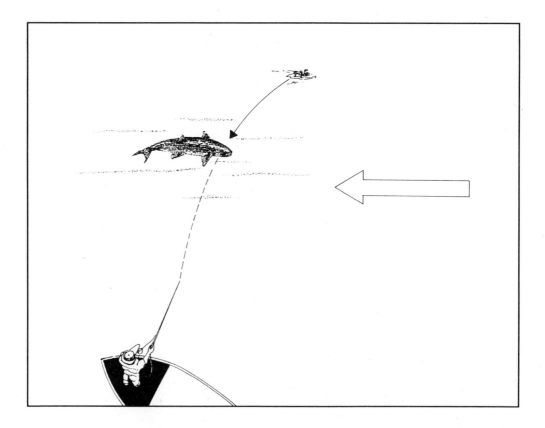

Fly swimming at fish—incorrect presentation.

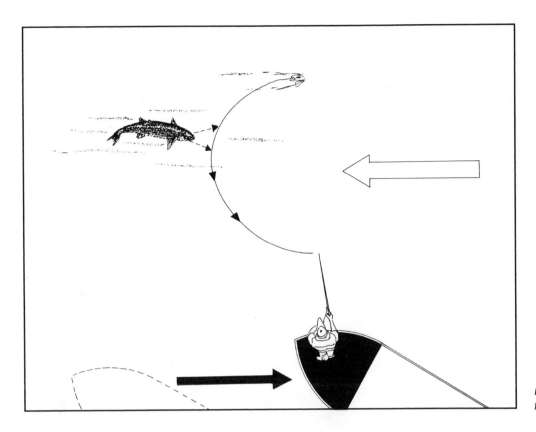

Fly swimming in front of fish—correct presentation.

sees the fly. So it is vital to use a leader that will allow the fly to float drag-free during the brief inspection period.

There is obviously a little more to doing the right things to catch a trout on a dry fly. Not only must the fly float drag-free, but it must also be cast accurately. As the trout sees the fly come into its cone of vision, it has to glide up, take the fly, and return with the aid of the current. It has to take the fly at a *specific* position on the surface. If it takes the fly too far downstream, it cannot glide back to its holding position, but must swim back to it. If the fish takes the fly too far to the right or left, then it would also have to swim to return. This the trout is not willing to do, since it would use more energy than it consumes.

You may wonder why, after you have made a series of casts with the same fly to a trout and gotten many refusals, the fish suddenly inhales the fly. I believe that all the casts but the one that scored were either not passing through the trout's cone of vision or were just a little too far to the right or left for the fish to take it without burning up too much energy. So to offer a trout your dry fly, you must first make it travel in such a manner on the surface that the fish sees it clearly. But it must also be floated drag-free and not too far to the right or left. This requires a great deal of accuracy, as well as a leader that is designed to deliver a drag-free float. As

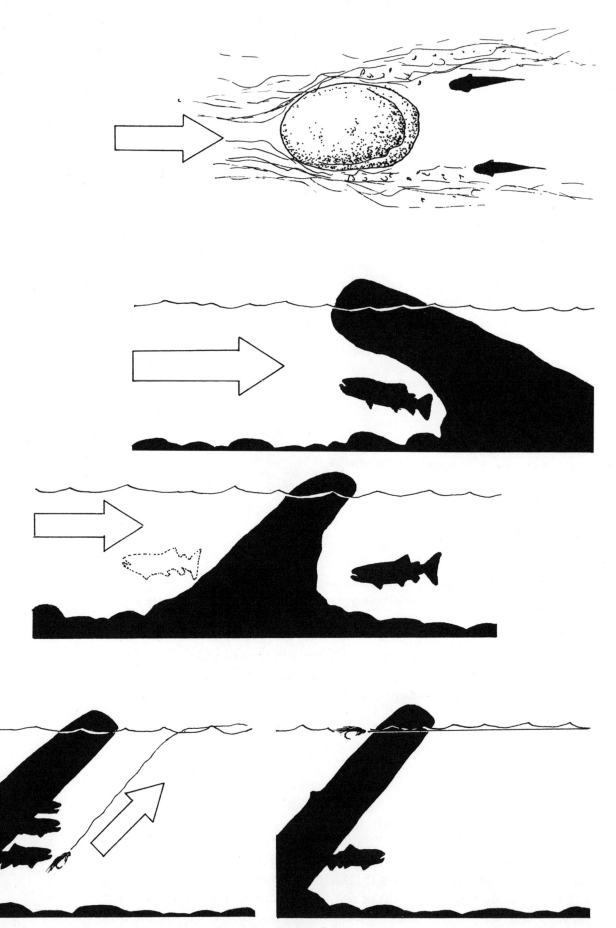

Various structures.

most designers and retailers will tell you, presentation is everything. For trout, you have a split second to make a good impression with your fly.

Trout live in a variety of environments: deep cold lakes, fast-running mountain streams, gentle ponds, limestone-fed creeks, and other interesting places. Because of this, their food supply varies from locality to locality. Unlike most of the other species that fly fishermen seek, trout are often regulated by these specific food sources in their environment, many of which arrive and disappear on a fairly reliable time schedule. Northern pike, bass, and other freshwater fish we like to catch are opportunistic and eat a great variety of foods. Trout are not roamers. They usually live in a home pool and are forced to eat what lives with them in that pool—or what happens to float through it.

Most of the trout's food is aquatic insects, usually in the form of nymphs. There may be mayflies, caddis, and stoneflies in their pool. These flies live most of their lives underwater, then for a brief moment they rise to the surface and become airborne. They lay their eggs on the water and then they die. Each species lives underwater in a unique manner, swims to the surface in a very special way, lays its eggs uniquely, and looks different after falling to the surface to die.

All of this demands that the trout fisherman know a little about these insects. As I suggested earlier, you do not have to be a Latin scholar, but it does help to be able to name the family of every insect—whether it is a caddis, a stonefly, or a mayfly. It may not even be necessary to know how to spot a quill gordon. If you can identify it as a little gray gnat that can be imitated on a No. 16 hook, you will usually get the job done. As long as your presentation is convincing.

Trout are coldwater fish, and for good reason. They will die in the same waters that are comfortable for bass. Understanding how critical water temperature is to trout will help you catch more of them. While trout can live in exceedingly chilly water, they do have a temperature range in which they feed more and are most active. The brook trout prefers the coldest waters of all North American trout: fifty-two to about fifty-six degrees. Rainbows do well from about fifty-five to sixty degrees, while brown trout are probably the most active at sixty to sixty-five degrees. Trout will feed at temperatures below these, but the cooler it gets, the less they feed. They will also react more slowly when temperatures rise above the optimum. If the temperature gets too high, they simply die. Brook trout, for example, cannot survive if temperatures rise above the mid-seventies.

Why is this important to the fly fisherman? During summer months, especially on small streams, the water temperature will often rise into the dangerous level for trout. Two things happen: The trout stop feeding and seek deep holes where the temperature is lower, or they migrate to spots where underwater springs bring cooler water into the stream. It follows that the best time to fish most smaller rivers and streams in midsummer is in the morning, when water temperatures are lower. Sometimes the temperature drops into a good fishing range again in the late evening. A wise trout fisherman will carry a little thermometer to constantly check the stream's temperature. When it rises a few degrees above what's desirable for the species you seek, your results will probably decline. At this point it's better to find a tailwater fishery or a spring-fed stream that holds a more consistently low temperature.

What I've described above is more the "science" of trout fishing. But I learned some of these lessons informally when I was very young. As a young boy, I worshiped an old man who lived along the Monocacy River, a seventy-five-yard-wide stream in central Maryland close by my home. He lived alone in a shack, which is the only word I can think of to describe it. No one caught as many catfish and smallmouth bass as he did, nor as big. These were the only two species he sought. I wanted to know how he did it, so I spent a lot of time with him, hoping to win his friendship and confidence. And to get the information I needed to catch the same kind of trophy fish he did, especially the smallmouths.

It took several enjoyable years before I screwed up enough courage to pose the question. Then I watched and waited for the answer, as he sat there looking at the river. Finally he said, "Fish very early and late." I waited for him to say more—to tell me where to fish, what to use, how to approach the fish, all his other pearls of wisdom. But he said nothing. He just got up, walked to the river, and started fishing. I followed, wanting to ask more questions, but his manner indicated that the subject was closed.

It took me several years of fishing before I really understood what he had said. If you are after trophy fish, usually the key factor is to fish very early in the morning and very late in the evening. Often these wary creatures only feed at those times. Experienced anglers who chase big rainbow or brown trout in shallow waters soon learn that just at dawn and at dusk, the chances that these wary fish will take a fly increase greatly. During summer months I have certainly found that smaller trout streams heat up in the daytime to the point that the trout become lethargic.

Here is more of the science behind this theory. Fish have no eyelids and bright sunlight must cause them some discomfort, for they seem to seek shade or other cover from it. This is especially true where the waters are clear. In fact, the clearer the lake, stream, or body of water, the better your chances of scoring on its trophy fish early and late in the day. Many anglers will also tell you how poor the fishing is after a weather front moves through and high barometric pressure occurs. (A high is usually associated with bright sunny days.) I believe it is not the pressure that causes the fish to go off their feeding—or to feed well as the front moves in. Instead, I'm convinced that fish feed well as the front approaches because the light level drops. They stop feeding as the high takes over mainly because the light intensity increases.

If you can't fish very early or late in the day, then certainly the best times to go are when the conditions are overcast. Many old-timers used to say that rainy days produced their best fishing. Once again, light levels are low during rainy periods, and I believe this is why the fish are on the feed. Remember also that when you are fishing at these times, the noise and surrounding disturbances are at a minimum. This is why it is vital to make as silent an approach as possible. Wading too quickly, clanking the oars, or running a motor close to fish are all unnatural noises and commotion that will reduce your chances of catching a fish. This also applies to presenting your fly early or late in the day. The fish are often in shallow water or near the surface, where they are easily spooked. If possible, try to locate a fish before making a cast. Then use a fly that, when cast correctly, will fall to the water without alarming the fish.

Catching trout on dry flies requires the ability to read the water, locate the fish, determine the correct leader–fly combination, and make an accurate cast that produces a drag-free drift. Fortunately, most of the time you can do all of this with only a little effort. I have already noted the three basic elements that "motivate" a trout: shelter from predators, a place to rest, and food and oxygen. And we know that their brains are not very sophisticated, so we do not have to take elaborate measures in order to entice them. If you add in a little knowledge of entomology, you have all the essential knowledge. The key, then, is in the presentation. An experienced trout fisherman using the "wrong" fly pattern will probably catch more fish than one correctly matching the hatch. Presentation, above all else, is vital to success.

Bass

Many books about fly fishing in North America focus on trout, but the most sought-after species by all anglers is actually the bass—either the largemouth or the smallmouth. One or both of these species live in almost every state or province across the continent. And they have been caught by fly fishermen for years. It was writer James A. Henshall who in 1881 wrote, "Pound for pound, it is the strongest fish that swims." I confess that my favorite of all the freshwater species I've boated around the world is the smallmouth bass. Perhaps it's because I grew up fishing for them. A smallmouth was the first fish I caught on a fly rod, and I simply love to fish for them.

Bass live in lakes, rivers, and small streams, as well as Texas watering tanks, farm ponds, and virtually anywhere there is fresh clean water. Largemouth bass can also tolerate the brackish waters of tidal creeks. Both species are structure oriented. Largemouths will use vegetation, old boat docks, stumps, and many man-made structures as resting places and

A nice smallmouth bass and an assortment of flies that appeal to these great gamefish.

Early fall is a great time to fish fast-moving poppers for smallmouth bass, like this five-pounder from the Susquehanna River.

ambush spots. In lakes, the rocks and aquatic vegetation are the keys to catching smallmouths, although they may use the same structures as the largemouth. In rivers, the most popular smallmouth hideout areas are around rocks, but logs and drowned timber are often good locations to find these fish as well.

Smallmouths prefer cooler waters than their larger cousins, which is a major reason why you usually don't find them in the shallow lakes and rivers of the Deep South. They do exist in the large impoundments there, however, mainly because the water is cooler in summer. Water temperature is critical to successful bass fly fishing. I do not subscribe to the idea that bass are more comfortable at certain temperatures. All fish take on the temperature of the water they swim in. Unless it is near freezing or very hot, fish are not uncomfortable because they are not attempting to maintain a specific body temperature.

But water temperature does have an effect on how bass feed. At precise temperatures the metabolism of a bass or any other fish operates at its fastest, and thus requires the most food. This means that at optimum temperatures, bass will feed more often, giving fly fishermen improved opportunities to catch them. If the temperature falls below or rises above the optimum range, the bass's metabolism slows down and requires less food, so the chances of catching them decrease.

Biologists have determined the temperatures at which both species feed the most. Smallmouth bass are most active in temperatures from about sixty-seven to seventy-one degrees. (Interestingly, bass smaller than twelve inches seem to stop feeding altogether when temperatures fall to fifty degrees.) Yet from about forty to eighty degrees, some size of smallmouth can be caught on flies—although the action slows as temperatures fall into the lower range or rise near the upper levels. Largemouth bass feed best in water from about sixty-five to seventy-eight degrees. They are much more tolerant of higher temperatures and, while they can be caught frequently in waters reaching even the mid-eighties, larger bass seem to slow their feeding once water temperatures get into the low eighties. The exception to this pattern is once again in the Deep South. Here, largemouths have over the centuries developed a resistance to higher temperatures. I have caught some big bass when the water temperatures were in the high eighties.

A major reason why smallmouths and largemouths in lakes will hold in twelve to twenty feet of water during summer months is that the water is much cooler there than at the surface. Here is another example of how water temperature can increase your catch rate. If you are fishing in midsummer when the water temperature is well above the optimum range, and you know where an underwater spring is located, you are in luck. Water exits springs at about fifty degrees, so the fish in the cooler water

Smallmouth bass favor rocky areas, but largemouths like this one prefer weeds. This bass came from Currituck Sound, North Carolina.

affected by the upwelling spring will have higher metabolic rates and thus be more likely to strike your flies. Conversely, in cooler weather you might want to fish the same spring again, because the water there may be warmer than what surrounds it. In spring, when lakes are starting to warm, look for shallow covers with dark bottoms to fish. A darker bottom will collect more heat from the sun and often have a water temperature five to ten degrees warmer than a nearby lake with a light-colored bottom.

There are two other differences between smallmouths and largemouths. Smallmouths are almost always found near a bottom that is rocky, sandy, or gravelly. While largemouths can also be found near such bottoms, they more often frequent muddy, marshy, or silty areas. The other difference is that smallmouths prefer clearer water than largemouths.

Basic Rules of Bass Fishing

There are some fundamental rules of fly fishing for bass. Both small-mouths and largemouths are structure oriented, as I just described. If there is one place you are likely to find smallmouth bass, for example, it is where there are rocks. They hold near sunken wood, too. Large-mouths prefer to hide in aquatic weed beds, or near stumps or drowned timber. In a lake they will often be found around boat docks and wharfs, as well as drop-offs from shallow to deep water.

You also have to remember that lakes are not a static environment, although they may seem so to a novice. There are many changes occurring. For example, lake waters can become dirty from muddy rivers that flow into them. The water can also lose much of its oxygen in certain areas during the hot summer months, and algae can build up and affect the water. Weeds furnish a natural cover that comes and goes with the seasons, too. While some lakes have a uniform bottom devoid of cover or undulations, most lakes have drop-offs—points of land that project into the water, and other similar features. These can erode and change over time. To be a successful lake bass fisherman, it pays to know something about the entire geography of the lake—both what is above the water and what is below it.

Here are some tips that may help you locate and catch both kinds of bass in lakes. If the water is very clean and transparent, then clear monofilament sinking lines and lighter tippets will catch more fish. Longer casts are often required. In fact, the farther you can stay from the bass, the better. When the water temperature is near sixty degrees and the lake is very clear, the best time to fish is when light levels are low. This could be on cloudy days, when it is raining, or at dawn and dusk. Gurgling your surface poppers slowly across the shallow flats on warm summer nights, for example, can be very effective.

In lakes where the water is exceptionally clear, your flies should be subdued, with little flash and lots of action on a slow retrieve. Excellent imitations of baitfish and crayfish will certainly give you an edge. Remember, crayfish are almost always the prime food of a lake bass, whether smallmouth or largemouth. Any fly that resembles this sizable meal will be an attractor.

Many lakes have areas that are not uniformly clear. For example, carp will root in some places, and strong currents and silt can also cause the water to get slightly dirty or tinted. Try fishing these areas. If a clear lake has a lot of vegetation, the feeding bass are usually more easily deceived when you fish for them in the grass.

If the lake water is dirty, your tactics need to change. Odd as it may sound, when lakes are discolored from high rains or other elements, there will often be some places that are much clearer. For example, coves that did not receive much of the dirty water may be less silty. Clear water may also be found where streams enter a lake, or where there are upwelling springs.

You will need special flies to fish dirty water, and you can usually expect a lower success rate. Flies that have bulky bodies and large heads will create small vibrations as they are retrieved, allowing the bass to better locate your offering. Some fly fishermen are big on rattlers, but I

A good assortment of largemouth bass flies. Top row, left to right: Dahlberg Diver, pencil popper, and Marabou Gerbubble Bug. Second row, left to right: Red & White Hackle Fly and a black Lefty's Deceiver. Third row, left to right: Half & Half and Clouser Minnow. Bottom row, left to right: Bend-Back and Dave's Hare Jig.

have never found them to be effective. (The Rat-L-Trap, I am told, is one of the best-selling casting plugs in the world.) When you retrieve a fly, it travels pretty much straight ahead, creating little noise. On several occasions I have fished in salt- and freshwater with a friend who used rattlers in his flies, while I did not. I never felt that one fly outfished another. However, in dirty water—especially if it is shallow—a slow-worked popping plug will often call you fish when nothing else seems successful.

Clear lakes with no visible cover provide other challenges. Here a depth finder is an extremely useful tool for a fly fisherman. Try locating grass beds, along with any structure in the lake that lies less than twelve feet deep. If no cover can be found, the bass will be difficult to catch. I recommend a shooting head, which lets you cast longer distances and search more water with each cast. Also, try fishing when it is raining or very overcast—or at night when the fish will be roaming and more likely to find your flies.

Lakes with lots of cover can be difficult, since the bass can be almost anywhere. This is the time to cast and move, cast and move. Do not stay in any one place for long unless you are getting strikes. The bass will generally be scattered, because food should be abundant throughout the lake. Look for openings in the vegetation and then use a sinking-tip line technique (see chapter 9, on casting, for more details).

Largemouths prefer lots of warm water filled with vegetation—such as here in the Everglades.

On bright sunny days, the bass will shun the light. So the key is to fish the shady areas. Try around or under boat docks, on the shady side of the shoreline, or around any structure (boulders, weed beds, or the like). You may have to locate spots where the bottom drops from five to eight feet and then descends into deeper water. Fish the side of the lake where the drop-off will be shaded for the best results.

On windy days I try something unorthodox. If it is possible, I fish the shoreline onto which the wind is piling. Do not fish the lee side, which is the natural tendency. This is especially true in summer, when the water is warmer and does not hold as much oxygen. The churned water will be much more highly oxygenated. On cooler days in spring and fall you can seek calm coves and lee shores, however, since the colder water will hold oxygen and bass will be comfortable there.

One sure bet is always to fish the underwater land points that slowly move away from shore into deeper water. Be sure to fish on top of an underwater shelf, as well as on both sides. Underwater projections of land are favorite hangouts of lake bass. And always fish weed beds when you find them. These are among the best places for bass to hide and ambush their prey. On sunny days fish the shady side. And try to work as close to the weeds as possible. When you can, it is best to fish along the edge of the weeds, rather than casting into the weeds and bringing your fly directly away from them. And in fall, when the weeds start turning brown, remember that they are no longer giving off oxygen; they are actually starting to decay. Bass will leave these aquatic weed beds as soon as they start turning brown.

Many lakes contain logs, with one end stuck in the bottom and the other end tilted up or close to the surface. Most anglers tend to cast at right angles to the log—which means they are usually fishing only the log's upper end. But the bass holding near the log will almost always be under it and fairly deep. Thus you should position your boat so that you can make a cast (a sinking line is almost always best for such work) where your fly will descend laterally along the log. On the retrieve, bring your fly back along the length of the log, instead of passing at right angles to its top.

And speaking of boats, your approach to any part of a lake is critical. Too often fishermen will roar into a quiet cove, throwing bow waves that wash up on shore. Instead, use an electric motor. This will allow you to get into position and within casting range of potential hot spots as quietly as possible. Remember that most noise travels about four and a half times as well through water as it does through air. Fish that are alarmed by noise and sudden disturbances are less likely to leave their cover and take your fly.

On some lakes, the most prevalent cover will actually be boat docks and anchored boats. It pays to fish these areas. If you are using a floating

The author's favorite fly-rod target—smallmouth bass. It brings a smile to his face each time he catches one.

line, try using the skip cast (see chapter 10), which allows you to get the fly well back under the dock where the best fish will be hiding. A low side-curve cast will also allow you to place your fly back in that area.

Early in the morning and late in the evening, when everything is quiet, a deer-hair popping plug with a weed guard is ideal for fishing

On the left is the conventional Gerbubble Bug; on the right a Marabou Gerbubble Bug. You can visualize how much more action is possible from the Marabou version.

boat docks. It is much better than a harder-bodied cork, balsa, or plastic popper. Get in position and throw your deer-hair popper right up onto the dock. A hard-bodied popper would make too much noise, but a deer-hair model drops silently onto the decking. And because you have a weed guard on the bug, you can tease it off the dock and drop it gently into the water. This can be extremely effective on an early-summer morning.

Because lakes are almost always clear or clearer in spring, it helps to know the spawning habits of bass. I do not believe, however, that you should be catching bass off spawning beds. If you do, return them to the bed area quickly. But if you are aware of the temperatures and times at which bass spawn, you can catch some great fish in spring as they move to spawning areas, or leave them when they are finished. Temperature, more than anything else, controls when bass spawn, so this information is important. The range is not large. Smallmouth bass spawn a little earlier than largemouths. The smallmouths like the water temperature when it ranges between fifty-five and seventy degrees; largemouths like it closer to sixty-four to seventy-five degrees. Remember, not all bass spawn at the same time. Bass start moving into spawning areas six to eight degrees before actual spawning occurs. And new fish continue to move in throughout the spawning temperature range.

Casting will be covered in more detail in a later chapter, but a few points are worth noting here. There are few chances to sight-fish for bass. You can cast around visible cover, but only rarely will you actu-

Bob Clouser, who invented the Clouser Minnow. You'd think he doesn't like to catch bass; look at the grin.

ally see the bass you are seeking, unless it is in the shallows of a clear lake. This means that much of your largemouth and smallmouth fishing consists of searching the water with your fly. The longer you can cast, the longer your retrieve will be and the more water you can probe. If you enjoy bass fishing, I urge you to practice until you can make long and effortless casts. It will certainly produce more fish for you.

If you backcast over land, you'll probably snag your line in trees and other obstructions—such as the tree behind the angler.

On farm ponds, casting over water reduces your chance of snagging the backcast.

Farm Ponds

Look at the lists of record fish and you will find that an amazing number have been taken from local farm ponds. This is especially true in the Midwest and the Northeast, where there are hundreds of these water holes. The best and most productive ones for bass fishing usually have several similarities. First, they are fairly clear. Ponds that remain constantly muddy are generally poor producers. Another criterion is size: Most ponds of less than a quarter acre will produce bluegills but few bass. Ponds surrounded by green pastures almost always fish better than those with mud banks where cattle walk, often roiling the waters.

Because these bass are aggressive, ponds can be fished out. Farm pond owners, if they want to continue to have good fishing, should insist that most bass be returned after being caught. Occasionally a pond gives up good fish for a number of years, and fishermen work its waters frequently. Then, because of the pressure, fewer bigger fish are caught, and anglers begin to believe the pond has been overfished—but a few bass remain. Anglers stop fishing because their success rate is so low. The few remaining bass, no longer pursued by anglers, grow fat and big. Then one day someone throws a bait, lure, or fly into the pond and hooks a real trophy. This happens more often than you might think.

Another reason ponds produce large crappies, bluegills, and bass is that so many contain a wonderful food supply. The bass grow fat on the abundant small bluegills, which in most areas produce two or three spawns, or

There's no better place than a farm pond to get a youngster started in fly fishing.

more, each season. Larger bluegills and crappies feed on their young—as well as on small bass. The tiny food also needed by young crappies, bass, and bluegills is plentiful in most ponds. They are great fish factories. In fact, it's generally recognized that farmers will have a better pond if they allow anglers to catch and remove many of the bluegills, which reproduce so effectively that they can create a problem of overpopulation. This results in thousands of small bluegills that will never reach appreciable size, simply because too many are eating the available food.

I learned one of the best lessons about catching bass back in the 1950s when I read a pamphlet produced by the U.S. Department of Agricul-

WRONG: Irv Swope demonstrates how not to fish a farm pond or lakeshore. A backcast thrown over the ground is bound to hit a tree or some other obstruction.

ture. It explained how you could use certain chemicals to poison and rid your pond of an overpopulation of bluegills.

The bass move in to feed along the shorelines mainly during the early and late hours of the day. From mid-morning until mid-afternoon the bass generally retreat to the greater depths of the pond. The bluegills move along the shoreline about the time the bass are departing for deeper water and leave as the bass return to the shallows. Therefore, you should spread your chemicals in the water near the shoreline about mid-morning on windy days. The wind helps to disperse the poison. The bluegills will then move into the treated area and be killed. If prescribed amounts

RIGHT: *Throwing his backcast over the water, Irv has a much better chance of success.*

are placed in the water on windy days, the chemicals will be dispersed by wave action before the bass return late in the afternoon.

Following the pamphlet's suggestions, I found that fishing early and late in the day along the shorelines indeed helped me make better catches of large bass. And of course, fishing the shallows during the middle portion of the day helped me score better on bluegills.

Because bass will always seek cover, in many ponds the only real refuge is deeper water. If a standpipe controls the level in the pond, it's usually located in one of the deepest parts of the water. This greater depth is desirable to bass, and the pipe also furnishes shade and a place to ambush whatever unsuspecting food swims by. Trees that overhang a pond can also be a hot spot. The shade is certainly an attractor, and insects fall off trees—another food supply. If there are rocks along the shoreline, these are always good spots to investigate with your fly, too.

Fishing Rivers for Bass

Fishing for both species of bass in rivers requires some particular techniques. In northern rivers, fly fishing really does not become effective until the temperature rises to at least fifty-five degrees, and it improves with every degree. Ideal temperatures are about sixty-two to eighty-two degrees. When temperatures are below or above that level, the fishing generally slows. The best time to fish in rivers in the Deep South is usually from December through March. While southern bass may feed in water as warm as ninety degrees, such temperatures do slow them down. From sometime in December until March, waters are cooler and contain more oxygen. This speeds up the largemouth's metabolism and it will feed more actively.

In the spring of the year on northern rivers, when water temperatures are in the high fifties, a unique opportunity occurs. Along many of these rivers, grass beds grow from late spring through summer. Where they die back, they leave only thick stubble. In spring the rivers usually run a little above their summer levels, covering these stubble patches. At this time minnows have few places to hide—there are no aquatic weed beds or lush shoreline weeds. But the stubble offers them some protection. I have had some great fly fishing in the spring of the year by drifting on a river that's a foot or so above normal and casting to the drowned stubble of the weed beds.

Cypress and other trees standing in the water furnish some of the best cover for bass in southern rivers. Learn to throw a curve cast and you will be able to fish around all sides of these trees. By using Bend-Back flies you can throw way back into areas that may hold some fine bass.

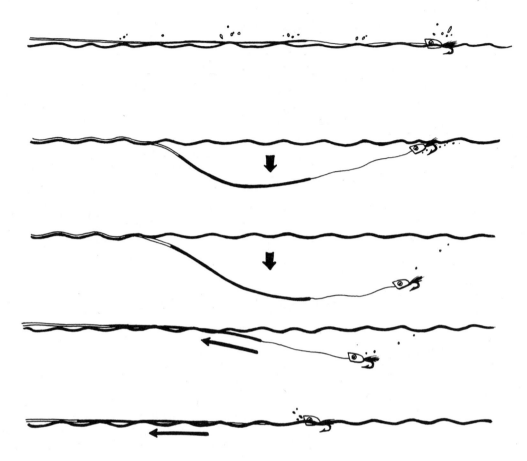

Here is an effective and fascinating way to tease bass with a sink-tip line, with the sinking portion shortened to five feet and a leader of about six or seven feet. Make a cast and allow the sink tip to drag the bug underwater. If you start to retrieve, the bug will swim underwater, but the retrieve also makes the line loft upward. Eventually the line and the bug will surface. Stop retrieving and the bug will sink again, and you can repeat the whole process.

At the same time, watch for southern rivers that may be discolored from tannic acid and plants. In these instances you should use flies with more than the normal amount of flash in them.

A good rule to remember when you are using streamer flies for river bass is to match the material the flies are made from to the water's clarity. I favor bucktail for most streamers; it has a lifelike action, and all fish seem to approve of flies tied with it. The exception is when I am fishing very clear water. Then I switch from using bucktail for streamer wings to the more translucent synthetic materials, such as Super Hair or Unique Hair. This applies to flies for other freshwater and saltwater species as well. Time and again I have had slow fishing in clear water, but when I changed to more translucent flies my ratio of strikes increased.

Bass in rivers, especially smallmouths, will be found near current-breaking structures. This can be broken-down dam rubble, single boulders, rock ledges, sunken logs, and similar underwater structures. If there is one good rule for smallmouths, it is that you should fish where there are rocks, ledges, and boulders.

The shape of the rock, however, has a lot to do with where the fish will be holding. If a rock slants downstream, the current rushes up the

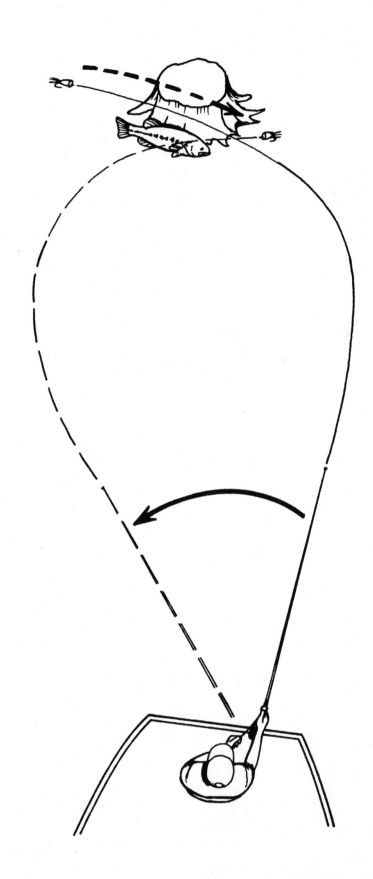

Flipping the rod back and forth is a great way to tease a bass holding in front of a stump or other obstruction.

slant and then swirls around the rock's downstream end. Bass will almost never hold in front of such a rock because they would have to fight the current. Instead, they lie in the water behind the rock. If the rock is very wide, they will usually be in the quiet water but near one of the seams formed by the meeting of the calmer water with the current. The best way to approach such a fish with your fly is not from downstream, or by casting into the quiet water and working the fly out into the current. These would be unnatural approaches. Instead, toss your fly upstream from the rock and retrieve it down past the rock, the way nature would carry any creature with the current.

During warmer weather, many insects hatch on rivers. This is especially true in the mid-Atlantic region. Often only bass of four to ten inches will feed on these emerging insects—but not always. In July and August there occurs in many northeastern bass rivers an insect hatch that no avid fly rodder should miss: the white miller hatch (genus *Ephoron*). On many rivers these mayflies emerge in near-blizzard numbers. The height of the hatch looks like a snowstorm because there are so many large white flies in the air. Usually the hatch begins on the lower portion of a river and, over a two-week period, progresses upriver. White millers begin coming off at about dusk. They are unusual mayflies so far as mating is concerned: The male nymphs shed their skins within minutes of emerging, and sometimes can be seen with a portion of this skin trailing along behind them in flight. The females do not molt at all. These *Ephoron* emerge from the water ready to mate.

The first two indications that this hatch is about to occur are tiny rings appearing on the surface where fish are quietly sipping on emerging nymphs, and a few white mayflies fluttering in the air. The total hatch time is short—from about sundown to no more than an hour after dark. Of all the bass-triggering insect hatches I have fished, the white miller is the most phenomenal. It is usually so intense that it causes large bass (some better than four pounds) to feed avidly. This is one of the rare times when you have a good chance of catching a very large bass on a dry fly.

To catch bass during a white miller hatch is easy once you know where the bugs are emerging, which is usually over a gravel bar. Use a floating line and a 7- or 8-weight rod, but you will be casting less than thirty feet, so an even lighter rod is okay if you prefer it. Many people tie large, buoyant white or Royal Wulff–type flies on No. 8 or 10 dry-fly hooks. Even small popping bugs will work. Here is my favorite fly. Attach a sparse, short tail of white deer hair to the shank of a No. 6 or 8 standard dry-fly hook. Then spin white deer hair onto the hook shank, being sure to pack it firmly. Trim the body to a rodlike shape approximately one-quarter to three-eighths of an inch in diameter. To make the

Here is an old photo of me with one of the first smallmouth bass I took on a popping bug. I got my start in fly fishing by chasing smallmouths on the large limestone rivers of the mid-Atlantic region.

fly float better, I grease it well with fly floatant. Locate a fish taking either nymphs or adult millers on the surface. Immediately cast a few inches above it. Bass will cruise, so your cast should be directed to the target area as soon as possible. Then watch the action.

If your river has carp that are rooting at the bottom, these spots can furnish some great trophy bass. Bob Clouser guides on the Susquehanna

River and explains that the carp are digging around on the bottom to get their food. He noticed that big bass were swimming right beside the carp as they rooted. When he located a bass following a carp, he dropped a fly just in front of the bass and was rewarded with an instant strike. Apparently the carp dislodge or frighten crayfish, which flee. The bass know this and follow the carp. In summer a good river bass caught with this technique will weigh three pounds. I recall taking my son and grandson on the Susquehanna River one August day. Using this method we managed to catch five bass of more than three pounds, two of them exceeding four pounds. We caught them all in less than three feet of water.

If it is possible, I recommend that you always carry two fly rods armed with different lines and fly patterns. Unless a bass river is very deep—and most of them aren't—I suggest carrying a weight-forward floating line, which is the one you will probably use the most. It is ideal for working popping bugs, for flies close to the shoreline, and in water depths not exceeding five feet. Incidentally, if you are fishing sinking flies on a floating line and you need to get a little deeper, you need to change to a fly with a bit more weight. Then you need to increase the length of your leader. A conventional leader will be buoyed by the floating fly line; with a longer one you will give the fly a better chance to swim in the water column.

I favor a brightly colored floating line for bass fishing. Much of the casting is done in the early morning and late evening, when light is low and things become difficult to see. Brightly colored (especially fluorescent) lines permit you to better monitor both your cast and your retrieve. Also, remember that floating lines fish better if they are clean and float high on the surface. If the front end sinks, it is a good idea to clean the line. I suggest using one of the fly-line manufacturer's products, not a commercial cleaner. These products were developed for this special purpose and will not only clean your line but also allow it to shoot through the guides better.

The other fly line I recommend for river fishing is not an intermediate (with an approximate sink rate of one inch per second), but a line that sinks faster. Use a Scientific Anglers Wet Cel II, which sinks about twice as fast. Even better, I think, is to cast one of the all-monofilament lines designed for coldwater fishing (lines designed for tropical fishing will tend to coil in cooler waters and make casting difficult). These lines cast superbly and will permit you to retrieve your fly several feet deeper than an intermediate line—often a decided advantage.

Unless you are casting to specific targets and you are a good caster who is trying to cover a lot of water, I suggest not using a bass-bug taper or conventional weight-forward taper. Instead, get one of the lines that has a longer belly and front and back taper. Such lines as the Scientific Anglers Steelhead Taper or Cortland Rocket Taper allow you to make longer casts than you normally could with a conventional weight-forward. If you cast well and have not tried these lines in situations when you need to make frequent long casts, you may be pleasantly surprised.

When it comes to popping bugs, I long ago decided that the color of any bug that's moved fairly quickly on a retrieve is unimportant. Eyes are put on poppers for anglers, not for fish. They are almost always located on top of the bug and above the water, and go unseen by the bass. However, I find that it is to my advantage to color the front or face of my popping bugs with bright yellow paint. This is the portion of the bug that faces me during the retrieve. It is important always to know the location of the bug, and a bright yellow face helps me see it better.

If you grease almost all of your leader with fly floatant (the exception is the tippet, when you are fishing midges), the leader floats or at least stays near the surface. This trick works well with popping bugs, too. This can be helpful in slick water, but where it really shines is when you are working vegetation, and especially in swift water. A greased leader stays on or near the top and allows the bug to be worked better. In swifter water, an ungreased leader often sinks. This tends to drown your popping bug, and it ruins your presentation.

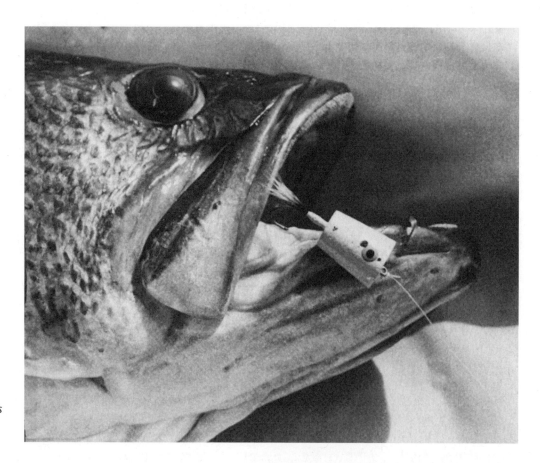

This nine-pound Georgia largemouth fell for a Lefty's Bug, one of my favorite poppers.

Fishing seams is important. A river rarely flows at the same speed throughout its width. Underwater obstructions slow the current or create eddies, big or small. Where the slower-moving water meets the faster-flowing current is what is called a seam. It is clearly visible to anyone looking for it. Bass will hold just within the quiet water, waiting for any food being swept downstream on the current. Seams can occur in the middle of a river or close to the shore. They are an important structure that you should constantly be looking for.

One of the most effective places in a river to fish bass is any barrier. Look for a small ledge, a little dam, or the head of a riffle that has a rock barrier with water flowing over. Such barriers form a dead flow of water immediately in front of them. They can be only a foot or two high, so long as the water slows as it approaches one and then flows over it. Bass can lie at rest in this dead water and watch for incoming food. I try to anchor upstream at an angle from the barrier. Then I make a cast several feet above the barrier and retrieve my fly across the current so that it swims immediately above the barrier. This is an exceptionally good way to take nice bass.

One of the finest of all rock structures that hold bass is a ledge slanting upstream, with a recess on its upstream side. A bass can lie in the dead water of the recess with the overhanging stone roof making it feel secure. It does not need to work in the current; it just watches the food approach. Cast upstream from the ledge and bring your fly back just the way Mother Nature would deliver prey to the bass.

Fishing Streams for Bass

The same techniques that work on rivers often also work on small streams, but there are a few subtle differences. Personally, some of the most enjoyable days I have ever spent fly fishing have been on small meadow streams. These usually run warm in summer, so they support few or no trout—but they do hold lots of scrappy sunfish, rock bass, and smallmouth bass. A big bass on most of these streams would weigh about two pounds; a true trophy would weigh close to three pounds. I wet-wade these streams, and on a warm summer day there is nothing finer than to be along with a light fly rod, sneaking up on these fish.

First, however, your tackle has to be scaled down. Panfish-sized popping bugs dressed on a No. 6 or 8 hook are the ticket. Streamers and nymphs dressed on No. 6 or smaller hooks are also recommended. Use a 4, 5, or 6 weight-forward line, just as you would for trout.

The next important difference between fishing a small stream and a bigger river is your approach. Because you are wading in rather thin, quiet water, your approach must be much more silent and careful. Most important, you should wade upstream. In a narrow, small stream, the wading fisherman flushes silt and mud downstream before him, which apparently alerts the fish. Make it a point to wade upstream.

In pools, bass will almost always be holding in one of three places. If there is a large rock in the pool, this will be the prime location to find bass. If there is no rock, the best spots are usually at the head of the pool, just below the riffle, or at the pool's tail. Finally, on small streams all flies should be worked gently, including popping bugs. These fish are not huge, and they aren't sure whether a fly will hurt them or they can hurt it. A gentle technique brings better results.

Peacock Bass

The peacock bass is becoming a prized quarry for fly rodders. They have lived in the canals of southern Florida for many years, because the state stocks them. There are now enough of these giants to warrant full-time guides to take you through the canals. But the best fishing for peacock bass is in Central and South America. I have fished for them in a number of places; the best trophies come from the upper Amazon basin of Brazil. Many of the waterways and rivers of this region have only been lightly fished, or not fished at all. On one trip we caught several bass that weighed in at just under twenty pounds. Colombia also has some fantastic peacock opportunities, although that country is considered less safe for travelers. Venezuela has some great peacock bass, too, but the lakes are frequently filled with drowned timber and it is difficult to fish among standing dead trees.

If you fish for peacocks in their home range in Central and South America, here are some useful tips. First, a peacock has a huge mouth in relation to its size. But you do not need large hooks for this fish. My biggest hook is a No. 2/0, and I have hooked many peacocks heavier than twelve pounds. Large hooks are more difficult to cast and to set properly on a strike; you simply do not need them. However, larger streamer flies will catch bigger fish. My favorite large peacock pattern is a modified Deceiver (I call it a Magnum Deceiver), which is actually nine inches long. But because it is tied on a 3X-long No. 2/0 hook, it can easily be cast with a 9-weight rod.

Popping bugs will catch peacock bass, although I urge you to use them only as a last resort. The favorite lure of spin and plug casters who seek monster peacock bass is the Woodchopper or a similar plug. These are huge wooden lures, as thick as a broom handle, with one or two propellers on them. They are thrown out and retrieved to create as much disturbance as possible. Some huge peacocks are caught on these monster plugs. But every time I have been at a camp with fishermen who used plugs, jigs, spinners, baits, or spoons, I have found that fly rodders outfished them. The anglers always caught bigger and more peacocks—providing they used large flies.

A nice peacock bass taken on a fly rod by the author in the north-central Amazon basin of Brazil.

Why does this happen? Much peacock fishing is done either in rivers, along banks, around fallen trees, in deep holes, or in lagoons (small lakes off to the side of a river). Visualize one or two anglers going into a quiet lagoon and making thirty or forty casts with those noisy lures. Any wise peacock will be alerted that something very abnormal is happening.

But if two fly fishermen using streamers move quietly into a lagoon, they can cast for an hour or more and cause little disturbance. Because of their silence, they will catch more and bigger peacocks. I have seen this occur time after time.

The best tackle for this kind of fishing is a 9-weight rod, even for a twenty-pounder, as long as you have decent fish-fighting skills. If you are in some doubt, then bring along a 10-weight—even though it might get tiresome to cast. You should have two lines. A weight-forward is ideal for fishing a popping bug, or when fish are in shallow water. There are times when peacock bass will either be spawning, or in one to three feet of water and cruising like bonefish. At such times, a long cast with a ten-foot or longer leader and a fly that drops quietly to the surface is ideal. Most of the time a floater and a Teeny 300 fast-sinking line are the ticket. You will probably use the Teeny 300 more than the floater. Peacock do not have big teeth, so a shock leader of twenty-pound test at the tippet is all that is needed.

Fortunately, fly patterns for these fish are simple. Several Lefty's Deceivers, in red, yellow-and-red, black-and-yellow, and—best of all—chartreuse-and-white, will all produce well. Put plenty of Flashabou or Krystal Flash in the wings. Large versions of Clouser Minnows dressed in chartreuse-and-white, yellow-and-black, or white with a touch of red at the front are also excellent. Add to these some Magnum Deceivers and you have all the fly patterns you will need for peacock bass.

And here is one last tip before you head off in search of these trophy fish. Native waters for peacock bass also contain all sorts of toothy fish: payara (which have two huge teeth protruding through their skulls), piranha, morocoto, jacunda, and other similar species. For these aggressive species, take along some smaller versions of the flies I have described—but be sure to bring along some braided thirty-pound-test wire as well. When you land any of these fish, you'll need to take extra care when you remove the fly, too!

Northern Pike

I caught my first northern pike on a fly rod in 1947. It was such a fine fish that I can still vividly remember it. For many years the northern was shunned by fly fishermen, but fortunately we have recently discovered what a wonderful fly-rod fish it is. A few years ago my friend Bill

Heavy rods are not necessary for big pike. The author landed this 16-pounder on an 8-weight and Teeny 300 line.

Anderson and I fished at Lake Maria in the North Seal River Preserve of Manitoba. In six days of fishing we caught more than fifty northerns of twelve pounds and up—and all on fly rods. Some were quite a bit bigger. It would be hard to match such fly-fishing fun.

There are many features about fishing for northern pike in the far north of Canada of interest to any fly rodder. First, longs casts are often unnecessary, because many of these fish can be caught with a cast of less than twenty-five feet. Also, much of this is sight-fishing. This is especially true in spring, when pike move into the shallows. And northerns are not selective when it comes to flies. Every fly rodder I know has several favorite patterns. Truth is, these fish, when in the mood—which seems to be most of the time—will eat anything you put in front of them.

For some years outdoor writers insisted you needed huge flies to encourage larger pike to hit. But I've found that a fly of five inches will draw as many strikes as a nine-inch fly. And the five-incher is so much easier to cast. I believe that four flies are all you need. Lefty's Deceivers in red-and-white, chartreuse-and-white, and olive-and-red are excellent. Also try orange-and-black and yellow-and-red. The same colors of Clouser Minnow do well, too. When pike are in deeper water, you'll want to add lead eyes.

Most northern pike lakes hold leeches. Pike must feed on these things, because the best fly on many occasions is so shabby looking that you wouldn't use it unless someone suggested it. Place a 2/0 hook in your tying vise. Cut a black rabbit-fur strip three inches long and a quarter inch wide. Attach it at the front end of the hook and finish the fly. Add a light coat of epoxy to the thread, and that's it. This fly looks like the devil, but tease it in front of a pike and you will almost always get a strike. When the pike are lying in shallow bays, drop the fly a few feet

Four patterns have worked wherever there are northern pike. Top: Rabbit Leech; middle: Clouser Minnow; bottom: Lefty's Deceiver and Bend-Back.

beyond one and retrieve it slowly up to the fish. If it shows interest but does not strike, let the fly go to the bottom, then slowly drag it through the silt. Few pike will resist this presentation. If the fish are in deeper water, I add a pair of one-twenty-fourth-ounce lead eyes and fish this deep and slow.

The final fly that you should always carry is a Bend-Back. I use a No. 2/0 long-shank hook and tie only a wing on the fly—with a lot of flash. Don't bother with any body material on the shank. This fly can be fished among sunken weed beds, lily pads, and drowned logs or rocks without fear of snagging. In fact, it is one of the most important flies you should carry for northern pike. The best colors are, once again, the ones mentioned for the Deceiver.

Tackle requirements are simple. An 8- or 9-weight rod is ample. Pike rarely make long runs, so a good freshwater bass reel is okay. What you do need is the right leader. Most of the time I use a straight piece of fifteen- or twenty-pound-test monofilament for the butt section. Leaders with many knots tend to tangle in the weeds that you will so often find in pike waters. For a floating line I use a leader of about seven or eight feet. For a sinking line, such as the Teeny 300, a leader of three to four

Many fish, such as this pike, are found in the weeds. One of the best flies for this is the Bend-Back.

feet is ample. What is important is the bite tippet. It should be thirty-pound-test braided wire (solid wire kinks too quickly).

Any pike has a big mouth, and a fifteen-pounder has a huge one. They frequently strike from the rear of the fly. Surging forward, they suck it in or deeply inhale it. Because they have sharp teeth—which also cover the roofs of their mouths—you need a long wire leader. I suggest starting with a fourteen-inch bite leader. As flies get destroyed, you will have to retie a number of times, which means shortening the wire. When it reaches ten inches or less, I replace it with another fourteen-inch length. Attaching the leader is simple. Clinch-knot the smallest barrel swivel you can find to the end of your monofilament leader. Then tie the braided wire to the other end of the swivel with a figure-8 knot. Then attach the fly with another figure-8 knot.

Just after ice-out in northern Canada (usually in late May), northern pike move into the shallows. They gather outside two- to five-foot coves and small bays when the water temperature rises above fifty-five degrees. As soon as it hits sixty degrees they move into the bays, where they will remain until the water reaches about seventy degrees. This is some of the most exciting fly rodding you will ever do. It is like fishing for freshwater barracudas. Your boat quietly moves into a bay and you search for the pike, which are usually lying motionless. Once you have located one, you place your cast so the fly is about five feet past and two or three feet in front of the fish. Begin a slow retrieve and get set for the action.

As soon as the water temperatures hit seventy degrees, most fish move out of the bays. At these times—and also when the bays are colder, in the high-fifty-degree range—pike can be found just outside the mouths of the bays and coves in deeper water of six to twelve feet. This is where the Teeny 300 line and a weighted Clouser are ideal. Since these lakes are so clear, much of the time you can still sight-fish. Pike can also be found where there is a profusion of lily pads.

During much of July and August the fish will gravitate to underwater weed beds, rocky shorelines, or spots where streams enter a lake. Again, you can still sight-fish, but usually you will be blind-casting. If you have not tried fly rodding for northern pike, you have missed one of the most thrilling aspects of our sport.

2

SALTWATER FISHING

The sea has always held a fascination for me, and the creatures in it offer some of the greatest challenges a fly rodder will ever encounter. The seclusion on a mountain brook is a taste of real solitude, but so is wading along the shore or on a shallow flat in search of trophy fish. In fact, saltwater fly fishing often combines the best qualities of hunting and fishing. You need good stalking skills if you are bonefishing, seeking permit or tarpon, searching for big cruising sharks on the flats, looking for heavy stripers that move up on the mudflats to feed, or trying to engage a big shark in shallow water. Sight-fishing for these species is one of the ultimate thrills for an angler.

Unlike fresh waters, the sea is wide open to anyone who has a boat or cares to wade. And while fresh waters are diminishing at an alarming rate, there has been only a slight decrease in the areas that are good for saltwater fly fishing. In fact, new saltwater fishing areas are being discovered all the time, as adventurous fishermen test new waters. There is a bonus thrill, too: fishing over huge schools of feeding fish. Anyone who has ever approached a school of savage bluefish or jacks tearing into frantic baitfish, and tossed a fly into the carnage, wants to keep repeating this experience forever. The excitement of the chase—getting there before the school goes down—and then catching as many as you can, is difficult to describe.

No stocked fish roam the seas. These are fish straight from God's hand in prime condition. There is little cover in the sea, and since almost every sea creature feeds upon something smaller than itself, the only way the pursued can escape is to go away fast. Species that did not learn to swim quickly disappeared. When a saltwater fish hits your fly, its speed is evident as it strains your tackle in its natural attempt to escape. Newcomers to saltwater fishing quickly learn that these species are much stronger than their freshwater counterparts. The freshwater fly rodder worries that a fish may break his leader; the saltwater fisherman occasionally wonders if he owns enough line to hold the fish streaking through the water with his fly in its mouth. No one can really describe the run of a bonefish, the slugging battle of a jack crevalle, or the mighty leap of a tarpon.

Similarly, anyone who has hooked a tarpon of more than a hundred pounds and seen it emerge from the surface like a silver rocket, throwing water like a broken fire hose, appreciates fly fishing at its best. To watch a billfish, enraged because it cannot get the teaser, suddenly charge your fly as it trails in blue water behind the transom will thrill you as no freshwater fishing moment can. I once hooked a fifty-pound Allison tuna in 150 feet of water on the Challenger Banks off Bermuda. Nothing, literally nothing, has ever stripped line from my reel with the speed of that fish. And when, twenty minutes later, I had that magnificent gamefish lying fifteen feet off the transom, exhausted but still beating its tail, I was completely overjoyed. Minutes later the line had somehow tangled in the rudder and the fish was lost, but the memory of that great fish and the battle it gave was worth the game. These things have to be experienced. And afterward the freshwater angler is never the same.

Where it is tailored to the fishing, as for bonefish, tarpon, and other fish that take flies well, the fly rod is really the most efficient tool for the

Tarpon can make spectacular leaps and runs.

sport. As an outdoor writer for more than forty years, I have fished for everything from giant tuna to bluegills, with anglers who have sampled every area of fishing. I have never met a single fisherman who did not prefer a fly rod to any other type of tackle. A ten-pound striped bass offers little resistance on a rugged surf-spinning stick, but that same fish on a light fly rod and leader is another experience. Somehow a sea fish caught on fly tackle is that much more rewarding.

Permit

The permit is regarded as the most difficult of the tropical flats species to catch on a fly rod. (Of course, a mutton snapper offers a greater challenge, but then so few are encountered on the flats.) For years we thought permit simply couldn't be caught regularly, but the last decade has seen a technique perfected that will allow you to catch permit with some confidence. Several factors account for this. First, a fly has finally been developed that appeals to this wary fish. Second, we've also perfected a technique that works—about one-third to one-half of the time. Know from the beginning that you'll scare a lot of permit, and still get a lot of refusals, with your offerings.

The important fly is a crab pattern. The best crab flies, in my opinion, are those with a soft base. Any crabs whose base is coated with epoxy or

Permit.

a similarly hard material will make a loud splash that spooks many permit. A crab pattern made from acrylic yarn, wool, or similar soft materials alights much more quietly and, I believe, enhances your chances of drawing a strike. Del Brown's Crab Fly (often called a Merkin) has probably produced more permit than any other.

When you make a crab pattern there are three factors that I feel are important. I believe that the crab should be weighted on one end: This way it enters the water, tilts to the side, and dives for the bottom at an angle, just as a swimming crab would. You should also have crabs in at least two or three colors. On light-colored flats there are ghost crabs, which are a creamy white color. On other flats the crabs are very dark; you'll also find many crabs of an olive color. I feel it's important to carry crabs that are unweighted, lightly weighted, and heavily weighted—in the same sizes and colors. I prefer lead eyes in the following weights: one-fiftieth of an ounce, one-thirty-sixth of an ounce, and one-twenty-fourth of an ounce. There are times when crabs will be swimming near the surface; it's not just permit but also all sorts of fish that will take them. When fishing in very skinny water, you need a lightly weighted fly. Of course, in water more than two feet deep, a more heavily weighted crab fly will often produce more strikes. While many people throw huge crab patterns to permit, I've found that you don't need one larger than a quarter in size. Just be sure you use a hook with large enough gap that when a permit grabs it, there's ample space for a hookup.

What's the retrieve technique for permit? You'll need a rod that throws at least a 9-weight line—and many experts prefer a 10. The reason is that many fish are cast to at short distances and to get a weighted crab fly into action quickly, you need a line heavy enough for the purpose. Many people use an intermediate line; others prefer a floater. The advantage of a floating line is that you can more quickly recast to a permit, if needed. Still, both lines work. Del Brown has caught more than 350 permit on a fly—more than any other angler. I've fished with Del several times and his technique is simple: When he sees a permit, he casts as close in front of it as he can. He scares the hell out of more than half of them, and they flee. The crab fly is allowed to drop to the bottom. Del believes that if you begin to strip-retrieve the fly you'll frighten the permit and rarely get a strike. Once the fly reaches the bottom, the permit will often circle it to see what's there. Del keeps the line taut. If the permit ignores the fly it may require a *very* gentle movement of the fly with your stripping hand. Don't make any sudden strips; give just enough life to the fly to get the fish believing that here is a live crab. Permit can pick up a fly and blow it out of their mouths quickly, so you have to be ready. If the fish takes the fly, Del simply strip-strikes by pulling back on the line in his hand. If the fish moves away and Del is certain that it's leaving, he picks up and casts again in front of the fish.

Almost all permit are released, as their numbers are not large.

This retrieve method is repeated as often as possible and has allowed Del to become the king of permit-hunting fly fishermen.

Here are some more tips for catching them. Permit action seems best when water temperatures are between seventy-two and seventy-five degrees. Permit can tolerate water temperatures a little lower and higher than bonefish. Small permit can often be found in a foot of water, but larger permit require a flat to be at least two feet deep. Of course, spring tides are better than neap tides for them, too. Many anglers fish the flats directly against the keys. But some of the best permit fishing is well away from shore, as much as a mile or more. Such distant flats may be dry on spring low tides, but carry several feet of water during high spring tides. Because they're less frequently fished, the permit on these flats are often more easily approached. Permit frequently follow low underwater ridges that can corral or trap bait. Look for a flat that's dry on a low tide, but well watered on a high one. If there's a shelf that drains the falling water into the depths, permit will prowl the deeper side of the shelf grabbing any foods that wash over. Many times a permit will swim with the same wobbling back-and-forth motion of a shark. Don't be fooled by this—as I have several times.

Because of their silvery sides, permit are often difficult to see. What's often most visible is the black line on the top of the body, or the edges of

Permit are relatively plentiful in the estuaries of the Yucatan Peninsula.

the tail. On a flat most permit will travel in the same direction during each tidal phase. If you see one or two swimming northward, chances are all the others will be doing the same thing. You can often locate permit in the shallows from a distance by watching low-flying birds, such as pelicans and cormorants. If these pass immediately over a permit, it

Del Brown with one of his world-record permit, taken on his crab pattern.

will spook and show itself. Yet this is a natural occurrence, and the permit will soon settle down so you can approach it. There are a number of locations where you can reliably catch small permit. But if you're seeking trophy permit on the flats then undoubtedly Key West, Florida offers you the best chance.

Bonefish

Known as *Albula vulpes* (gray wolf), the bonefish is found in the tropical and subtropical seas of the world. Most bonefish must die from their version of an ulcer. They feed and swim in a constant state of alarm. They can also be maddeningly difficult to approach and entice with a fly. Bonefish do not have lockjaw, supersensitive noses, or any sort of radar that can pick up an enemy angler from half a mile away. But all of these thoughts seem reasonable to a bonefisherman at some point during his career.

Bonefish are scattered throughout much of the world. Fly fishermen have pursued them in Central America, the Caribbean, Christmas Island, and the Florida Keys. Each year more places to catch bonefish are being discovered in the South Pacific. Christmas Island is one of the best places to learn how to catch bonefish. You'll cast to more bones in one day than you will in most other areas in a week. The fish are usually in schools, but you will also find them in singles or pairs—and there are

The bonefish—the author's favorite fly-rod quarry.

Nearly all bonefish flies are fished on the bottom. For this reason almost all are tied with the wing reversed, so that the hook point rides upright.

incredible numbers of them. There are bonefish in many other areas of the Pacific as well; some of the flats simply remain to be explored.

I have fished just about anywhere in the world you can find bonefish, and they are by far my favorite fish to catch on a fly. If I had to choose the best place for quality bonefishing, I would suggest the Bahamas. By *quality bonefishing,* I mean that there are a lot of fish—and you'll have a very good chance to catch large ones, too. There are certainly many other fine places to seek bonefish: the rest of the Bahamas, Los Roques (one of the best), parts of the Yucatan Peninsula, and Belize, to name a few.

Unfortunately bonefish have been drastically depleted in areas where they were once numerous. Some native peoples spread Clorox in the water, which chases the spooky fish off the flats and into their waiting nets. However, the bleach also kills much of the life on the flats, leaving it a virtual desert for a long time to come. Other areas allow netting of bonefish or, where it is illegal, the authorities simply turn their heads. The fish are then sold cheaply in local markets. Local governments have been extremely shortsighted. Not only do they deplete a natural resource, but they also lose the revenue generated by camps catering to tourists from across the world. These fly fishermen can bring more money in a week or two than is generated by all the sales of the netted bonefish. Perhaps some of these countries will make an effort to protect the bonefish, and it will surge back.

Finning bonefish.

In the Florida Keys, perhaps the best bonefishing occurs in Biscayne Bay. However, there are big bonefish from Key Largo all the way down to Key West. Oddly, the flats in the Key West area—which would appear to be excellent bonefish territory—have very few bones, but teem with the wily permit. Three locations in the world consistently produce the largest fly-caught bonefish. In late January huge bonefish, full of milt and roe, move onto the flats on the east side of Bimini in the Bahamas. These fish will remain there until sometime in late March or early April. The southern end of Biscayne Bay still holds some of the biggest bonefish you're likely to encounter as a fly fisherman. Shell Key, on the Florida Bay side of Islamorada, is another hot spot for trophy bonefish. But these are some of the toughest to catch anywhere. A fourth area where I have seen and caught huge bonefish is on the west side of Andros Island.

Bonefish also inhabit many of the flats fed by the Gulf of Mexico all the way down past Content and Sawyer into the Lower Keys. In Florida Bay you may locate some fish as far as Nine Mile Bank, but bonefish are not caught in Flamingo very often. There are, however, a few banks near Flamingo where some of the largest bonefish in Florida are taken each year. The Bahamas, of course, have some choice spots, including the Deep Water Cay area and throughout the island chain. Bermuda hosts a few bonefish along the deeper and somewhat sandy flats during the

A tailing bonefish—one of the most exciting sights in fly fishing.

summer months, and this seems to be the northern extent of their range. Bonefish are plentiful in parts of Mexico's Yucatan and through Belize. We are now finding some large bonefish in remote areas of the Pacific Ocean.

In April and May giant spawning bonefish invade the flats of Biscayne Bay. Captain Bill Curtis, who has perhaps the most productive record of all the bonefish guides who take fly rodders, works the flats of Biscayne Bay, within sight of the skyscrapers of downtown Miami. It's not unusual for one of his clients to catch six or more bonefish with a fly in a single day, and they consistently catch bonefish of from eight to twelve pounds. Fish caught in Biscayne Bay will range in weight from five to nine pounds. This is trophy size in many other areas. If I couldn't get to Bimini, and I was interested in catching a world record—or at least a trophy—on a fly, I'd probably fish in the southern end of Biscayne Bay or the Islamorada area. No one seems sure why. The fish have had to accommodate water-skiers, fast-traveling pleasure boats, and other invaders, but they have adjusted admirably well.

As with other kinds of angling, knowing the strong and weak points of the bonefish and using this knowledge to your advantage is the key to

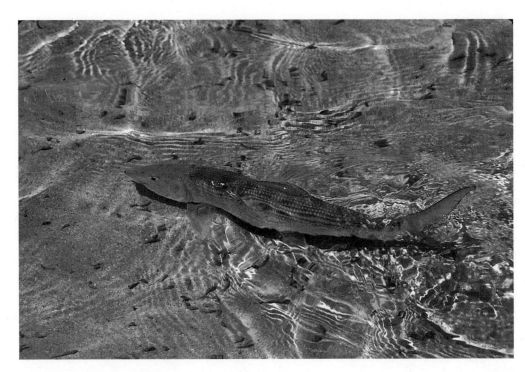

Bonefish are spooky and well camouflaged.

success. The bonefish is a tough quarry; it's hard to deceive, and it gives a good account of itself once it is hooked. When learning how to bonefish, there's no substitute for spending time with a guide or angler experienced at the art. Watch him, listen to everything he says, question him constantly about his techniques, and learn all you can about the habits of the bonefish. Just one day with a guide or good bonefisherman is worth a year of study on your own.

These experts can tell you about the fish's particular habits. For example, bonefish are very sensitive to water temperatures; you'll see almost none on a flat if waters are cooler than sixty-eight degrees. At seventy degrees a few fish will be around, but they'll be reluctant to strike, even at a tasty shrimp. Once the temperature rises above seventy-three, however, the fish become very active. After the temperature gets above eighty, some bones will desert the flats. I have experienced good bonefishing in water temperatures as high as the upper eighties. Scientists identify the twenty-degree Celsius isotherm as the dividing line. We know the threshold better as sixty-eight-degree Fahrenheit water. Guides may be able to find a fish or two in slightly cooler water, but to catch bonefish consistently, the water temperature must exceed seventy degrees Fahrenheit.

If you study their physical features, you recognize the marks of a fish originally built to feed on the bottom in deep water. They do just that in

Large bonefish such as this can be caught in mangroves as well as on the flats.

places such as Hawaii or off Angola in Africa. Where the tidal range is not great and there are expanses of flats, bonefish will come into the shallows to feed. Invariably, the better flats have turtle grass on them or some other form of marine growth. Bonefish often cross white sand flats and may feed in passing, but they seldom stay long. They will, however, sometimes look for food over coral or hard rock flats.

In Florida and the Bahamas during July, August, and September, bonefish feed best at dawn for an hour or two, and then very late in the evening. In the heat of summer or in winter, the best flats are those close

Women especially enjoy bonefishing. The tackle is light and the fishing is exciting. They usually do very well with it. This is a ten-pounder that Lynn Fuller landed at Andros, in the Bahamas.

to deep water. Here the environment is not heated by the sun or chilled by winter as much as the flats water. Each tide sweeps cooler water from the depths into the flats in summer, and warmer water in winter. Flats located far from deep water tend to be hotter in summer and cooler in winter than those close to deep water. This is something to consider when going on vacation to a distant place, or even when fishing local waters during these times of the year.

Bonefish travel in schools, in singles, and often in groups of two or three fish; the extra-large fish are almost always loners. Even if there are several on a flat, they seem to prefer being alone. Single bonefish are much more difficult to approach and less likely to strike a fly. School fish are apparently more competitive in their feeding habits and accept a fly more readily. Many people have caught bonefish on bare white sand, but in these cases the fish are usually crossing the sandy area either to get to a food source or to return to their sanctuary in deeper waters. When over light sand, the fish are almost always more easily frightened, so the fly must be cast much farther ahead than normal.

Bonefish are bottom feeders; their mouth is located on the lower portion of the head so they can easily suck up food. Here is a scientific description of a bonefish that, while accurate, is certainly unflattering: "The bonefish has an elongated, torpedo-shaped body with a slender head and a small inferior mouth." Bonefish feed on crabs, shrimp, varieties of sea worms, small minnows found on the flats, and almost any-

Catching bonefish requires patience and technique.

thing else they can swallow. Many good bonefish flats hold turtle grass. This plant resembles lawn grass, except that the stems are about three-eighths of an inch wide, from a foot to eighteen inches long, and dark green. Turtle grass is a breeding ground for small sea life, vital in the food chain.

For the fisherman coming from freshwater trout streams and salmon rivers, the bonefish was made to order. Frequently the same tackle is acceptable, and delicacy of presentation becomes paramount. Since the water ranges from a foot to perhaps three feet, you can wade for bonefish providing the bottom is hard enough to support the weight of a human being. Some flats are hard and firm enough to wade; others have a mushy bottom. Bonefish feed on both types, but if you prefer to wade it's a good idea to select a hard flat.

After an extensive study, Gerard Bruger of the Florida Department of Natural Resources has found that three-quarters of the typical bonefish diet consists of shrimp, crabs, and other crustaceans. Small fish and mollusks make up most of the balance. These facts can be interpreted to mean that bonefish are constantly searching the bottom for their food. In fact, their mouths are located on the underside of the head so the fish can dip down and pick up food—this is what scientists mean by the term *inferior*.

Wading for bonefish is one of the special joys of fly fishing.

Despite the general insistence that the first of the rising tide is prime time for bonefish, there is in fact no single best stage of the water. Optimum tidal conditions depend on the type of flat, its location, and where on the flat you are fishing. What the specialists are really saying is that

Use the comfort grip when releasing bonefish.

you can start at low slack water and follow the cycle of the tide through the rise and fall if you don't know the area. To do this effectively, you must find an ocean or Gulf flat. Usually the fish will come out of the deep water as the tide starts in. Never lose sight of the fact that there are places that produce fish on an incoming tide and those that become active when the water turns out.

I should warn you that bonefishing is addictive. The gray ghost of the flats may lack the bulk and brute force of the tarpon, but it makes up for it with a marked degree of wariness. A number of the world's leading anglers rank the bonefish as their all-time favorite species.

Redfish

If you are new to redfish, one or two days with a competent guide are more than worth the money. Redfish used to be less wary, but fishing pressure all along the coasts of Florida and the Gulf has made them as shy as bonefish. In fact, the techniques for the two species are essentially the same. Redfish will live on bonefish-type flats, but they are more frequently found where the bottom is softer and covered with grass and where the water is a little less clear. Both fish have small mouths located on the bottoms of their heads so that they can feed on

Redfish live in many of the same waters as bonefish.

Large redfish are caught among weedy flats.

the bottom. Flies longer than three inches are usually not as effective. Although redfish will try to take a surface fly such as a Dahlberg Diver or popping bug, underwater flies fished close to or on the bottom offer a better chance for a hookup.

You need to make a quiet approach. I cast the fly at least six to ten feet in front of a cruising redfish or bonefish and allow the fly to drop to the bottom. I usually make two long strips with the fly to give the fish the impression that prey has seen it, and it is trying to escape. If the fish acts as

A Dahlberg Diver fly fooled this nice redfish.

Captain Rod Smith guided Don Leyden to this thirty-eight-pound redfish taken near Cape Canaveral. It was recognized at the time as a new world record.

if it has spotted the fly, I then begin alternating in short strips. If the fish tracks the fly closely but doesn't strike, I do something different. Often two or three fast, long strips will trigger a strike. I use a slower retrieve for redfish but essentially the same technique. The flies you use for bonefish and redfish should match the color of the flat. If bones are found on light-colored flats, then a cream, light tan, or pink fly is a good choice to start with. Most redfish are found where there is an abundance of grass on the flats—usually olive or tan—so a fly matching this grass color is best to start with. The only exception to this is a pattern that contains chartreuse.

Bonefish and redfish can be tricky. Here is a typical fly-fishing scenario. A wading angler sees a redfish facing away from him. The angler has a three-inch shrimp imitation on his leader. He makes a careful and quiet cast, being sure not to drop the fly line on the fish. The fly settles to the water so gently that the redfish is not spooked, and the angler begins the retrieve. The fly approaches from directly in front of the redfish. It sees a three-inch shrimp attacking it. Naturally, it flushes away from something so unnatural. What should he have done instead?

Whenever presenting a fly to a fish, try to have the fly and the fish come together in a natural manner. Let me give an example. If you have ever fished a river or tidal current, you usually make a cast across and slightly downstream. A retrieve is begun. Most of your strikes will come at the end, when the fly swings in a curve just before the line straightens. Why? As your fly drifts downstream, it makes that looping curve just in front of predator fish holding in the current. I think this is natural to the fish. Any baitfish or food for the predator that is drifting in the current must look downstream from it. If it sees the predator, it will attempt to swim to the side and away from the predator. The looping curve of the final part of your retrieve imitates this action, which is why the fish strikes.

Let's take the redfish example cited earlier. Don't throw the fly so that when it is retrieved, it attacks the fish. Instead, if you cast the fly a little to the side and in front of the fish, then you can make a good retrieve. As the fly swims back toward you, it is off to the side as though it were trying to sneak past, and the redfish is tempted to strike.

Tarpon

If you ask a group of leading flats anglers to name their favorite fish, most will point to the tarpon without hesitation. Suggest that they then name the second most exciting fish and, to a man, they will have to pause and think. I was a striped bass addict for most of my early fly-fishing life. Then I caught a tarpon. I have boated nearly every species that will accept a fly, but my heartbeat races when I catch one of these exciting fish. Few species will offer me more fishing excitement than a big tarpon I have just put a hook into.

Tarpon come in many sizes. You can fish a canal ditch with a 4-weight fly rod and line for tarpon as small as freshwater trout. Or you can stake out on a tarpon flat in the Lower Keys in spring and toss a streamer to a

Tarpon are among the largest and most exciting saltwater gamefish.

150-pound giant. Few fishing experiences compare with standing on the casting platform of a skiff, armed with only a fly rod, and seeing a "log" of a tarpon coasting across the flats. The big ones, more than a hundred pounds, make you feel inept and foolish. You stand there, poised with a three-inch streamer fly in your hand, wondering how in the hell you are going to win over six feet of scale-encased muscle, so big that you can describe the fish by its width! Legs become rubber, arms inoperable; your eyes misjudge. If the fish actually takes the fly, you'll probably strike too hard. The tarpon then catapults from the water like a giant jack-in-the-box, sometimes throwing water over you.

Although the silver king is caught from Virginia to Texas, the most serious flats fishing takes place from lower Biscayne Bay in Miami down along the Florida Keys to Key West and the Dry Tortugas. Plenty of action occurs in Florida Bay, up through the Ten Thousand Islands, and along the west coast of Florida to the area around Homosassa. Outside the United States, tarpon fishing can be enjoyed along the Gulf side of Mexico and in several spots through the Caribbean and Central America. The ultimate sport takes place on those clear-water flats where you stalk the fish. The extra dimension of visibility has no parallel in blind-casting. Tarpon may battle just as hard in turbid water, but it is not the same game.

Even on the flats, tarpon fishing has several dimensions. Usually they will be in three to ten feet of water prowling alone, in pods of two or three, or in schools of several fish. Channels become the highways and

Costa Rica offers a brand of tarpon fishing that is unlike many other places. Here, in murky waters, giant tarpon are caught in good numbers by fly rodders.

resting points. Tarpon will work the downtide end of a channel before getting up on a flat or after coming off a flat. Very early in the morning they may lie motionless in the shallows with dorsal and tail puncturing the surface, or they may nestle on the bottom in the various basins. These are difficult fish to approach, but they will eat readily if a fly, lure, or bait is on target.

Most tarpon fishing is done from a skiff with a guide poling the anglers across a flat in search of fish, or staked out in a spot where tarpon are known to pass with regularity. No casting is done until the fish are seen. It is my experience that the Florida Keys boast some of the best shallow-water light-tackle guides in the world. All of them are quite capable of finding tarpon in season, and they are skilled at helping you catch them.

The water temperature on the flats must be seventy-five degrees or more before tarpon will leave the sanctuary of deeper water. As a result, the migratory run starts below Key West and moves up the chain of islands beginning in January or February, when three or four warm days in a row raise the temperature on the flats. Where the fish come from is a mystery, and it is even more baffling to speculate on how they know the shallow water is tolerable. Whatever the reason, anglers must be alert to these conditions.

The main run starts in March most years, and later if the weather has been particularly severe. It will last into July. This is not to say you cannot find the odd fish during other times, but the right season makes all the difference. On the lower west coast of Florida, May would have to be the prime month. May and June are the peaks of the season in the Keys. As a basic guideline anywhere within that range, look for the best tarpon fishing in the spring of the year.

Tarpon can often be seen rolling in the distance.

Lefty Kreh holds up a tarpon caught by Harold LeMaster. Hal and several other Clearwater anglers fished the Homosassa area of the west coast of Florida for years before it was discovered by the Florida Keys guides.

Tarpon tend to be slow-growing fish and it takes many years for one to exceed a hundred pounds. The largest recorded was a 350-pounder taken in nets off Hillsborough Inlet on Florida's southeast coast. Some exceptionally large fish are now being caught in parts of Africa, and there is unexplored tarpon action along the northern coast of Brazil. These places do not offer flats fishing.

Anyone who has seen a tarpon knows it can open its mouth wide enough to swallow a bowling ball. The inside of this cavern is as hard as a cinder block. Trying to set the hook can present problems for even the most determined fisherman. Unless you take the time to sharpen every hook, your percentage of hookups will drop dramatically. Veterans talk about "jumping tarpon" rather than landing them because so many fish are able to throw the lure. As they leap clear of the water, these massive fish shake their heads violently from side to side, rattling their gills with bone-jarring authority.

Although tarpon don't have teeth, their mouths are like coarse sandpaper. It is surprising how quickly they can fray through a leader. For this reason, you must use a shock leader of stout monofilament. If you intend to catch fish over seventy pounds, the shock leader should be ninety- to one-hundred-pound-test mono. Some anglers use wire, but you will get fewer strikes if you follow their example. For smaller fish, you may scale down the breaking strength of the shock leader accordingly. Along with the shock leader, you must also use a slightly lighter leader long enough to stretch across their backs to prevent fraying of the monofilament. After each fish, check both leaders and change them if they are the least bit worn. Many experts believe that fluorocarbon shock leader draws more strikes.

The key to catching these tough-mouthed monsters is the fly itself, or more specifically the hook. The marvelous thing in hook manufacturing, which relies on a metal stamping machine to fashion the product, is that there is any point at all. Hook makers do an excellent job consider-

For a few minutes, this baby tarpon in Mexico gave Jennifer Carley all the action she could handle.

ing their use of mass-production techniques. The points of all hooks, however, should be touched up by hand—especially those used in tarpon fishing. You can test any hook point by pulling it gently across your thumbnail. If it doesn't dig in immediately, the hook is not sharp enough. And the point is only one consideration. To achieve penetration, a hook must have cutting edges that slice the flesh and push it apart. Hook setting requires that the point hang up momentarily before the cutting edges take over to ensure entry.

Let me digress and explain the three basic methods of preparing hooks. The simplest is to lay a file or stone at right angles (first one side, then the other) opposite the barb and just behind the point. If you stroke

It surprises many fly rodders when they see how small a fly a giant tarpon will strike.

from the point of the hook back toward the bend, you will not bend the point or curl it. Avoid making a long, tapered point that may collapse when you try to drive it into a fish's mouth. With this method, you have put a cutting edge on the back side of the barb.

The second method is called triangulation, because you actually form three cutting edges in the shape of a triangle. Instead of putting a cutting edge behind the barb as you did in the first method, you file this area flat so that it becomes the base of the triangle. Then lay the file or stone inside the bend of the hook and file the area flat on either side of the barb from the edge of the base you created to the center of the barb. Each corner of the first flat area has a cutting edge, and the third one is right down the center front of the barb.

Finally, you can make a diamond-shaped point. This is a combination of the first two methods. Start as you would in the first technique to cre-

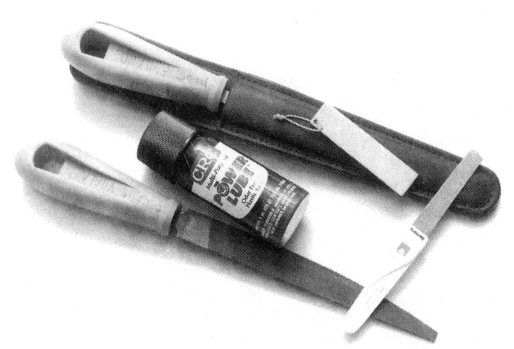

Pictured here are three good hook sharpening tools. At the top is a Nicholson 6-inch smooth file, stored in a leather case. By saturating the file with CRC or WD-40 and storing it in the case, the file can be used around salt water often for several years before it will rust.

Lying on the leather case is a white, ceramic stone sold by Tiemco. I don't usually use this for original sharpening. Because it will never rest, I carry it when wading in salt water, or on the boat, to touch up a dulled point.

The small tool at the right of the photo is a diamond dust (usually silicon carbide) fingernail file available in most drugstores. One side has a very fine grit and the other side slightly more coarse. The finer side will sharpen flies as small as No. 24. The more coarse side will work for hooks to about No. 2.

ate a cutting edge in back of the barb. Then do the same thing to put a cutting edge on the center front of the barb. If you make the angles correctly, additional cutting edges will be formed halfway between the front and back edges on either side. As you look at the point of the hook, you can actually see a diamond shape with four cutting edges.

Anglers believe that a treble hook or treble-hooked lure has enough barbs to snag anything. Unfortunately, this is not true. Each hook in a treble must be sharpened individually, and all trebles on a lure should receive equal attention. I cannot emphasize enough the importance of honing hooks. Your percentage of hookups will soar if you take the time to perform this routine task. In fact, it should be done before you ever leave home. Touch-ups can then be done on the water. A mill-smooth file will do a good job; there are several makes on the market from which to choose. I use this kind of file and believe that it will also work effectively for you.

Snook

The snook has made such an astounding comeback in Florida, due to new regulations managing the species, that it is now one of the most popular of all fly-rod fish in that area. There are several reasons why fly fishermen hold the snook in such high regard. The most important is that it acts so much like largemouth and smallmouth bass. Northern anglers visiting Florida (and the thousands of fly fishermen who have migrated from the North to the state) instinctively know how to fish for them.

Snook, like freshwater bass, hold in, or under, cover and then blast out to grab their prey. They will hide along undercut banks, back in myriad mangrove roots, close to bridge pilings, around channel markers and buoys, or wherever they can remain unseen by their prey. On the flats, snook often suspend in what fishermen call "white holes." These are depressions in a flat that is free of grass and light in color. Snook frequently suspend in such a hole, ambushing bait. Cast a fly across the white hole and retrieve it, and you stand a good chance of hooking up. Redfish will also frequent such white holes, though not so often as snook and seatrout.

Like freshwater bass, snook feed a lot at night. They are also very sensitive to drops in temperature. I remember back in the mid-1960s when the air temperature dropped to twenty-nine degrees during a spring-tide week and the flats at Flamingo in Florida Bay were exposed during the night. As the tide rose, it began to flow across these flats that had stood in the freezing air. The resulting water temperature, drastically chilled,

Snook inhabit areas that have a lot of structure and vegetation. Use a weedless fly to catch them.

killed many species. To my surprise the fish to die were sharks and jack crevalle, which I would have guessed to be among the least affected.

The other species that died by the hundreds was the snook. And just as surprising were the numbers of huge snook (more than twenty pounds) that had been living and prospering in the Flamingo marina area, where hundreds of boats traversed weekly. If there is a temperature drop, the snook will generally leave these shallows and head for deep water in creeks, channels, or bays. Most of these snook habitats have a dark bottom. As soon as the air temperature warms and the sun comes out, the water on these flats warms quickly and the fish, now hungry, will move back fast. This is a great opportunity for fishermen to reap a bonanza.

The best snook fishing in this country is in Florida, usually along the lower west coast and in the Ten Thousand Islands area that borders on Florida Bay. Almost all of it lies within the vast Everglades National Park. This is ideal habitat for snook. There are thousands of islands, channels, oyster bars, rivers, flats, and bays. These furnish mullets, crabs, shrimp, and a host of other foods that snook can eat. The standard fly-fishing method is from a boat poled along the shoreline. The flies are cast in among the mangrove roots. On a falling tide the snook will wait at the openings of small ditches to grab bait being carried to the main watershed. These will eagerly take your flies. Many snook are caught

Ned Brown caught this snook just off a marker during a slack tide.

Canoes are one of the best ways to penetrate the mangrove backcountry where many snook live.

when sight-fishing—perhaps the most thrilling way to tangle with this exciting species.

Bonito and Albacore

Bonito and albacore are two of the most energetic fish you can encounter in salt water. They are speedy and can rip line from your reel in a hurry. You will certainly be able to see and identify them from their quick leaps as they catapult into the air to chase baitfish. My advice is to use small and sleek flies for both of these species. Occasionally, large albacore will take flies like a Half & Half, but most of the time a fly from two and a half to four inches in length works best. Flies with synthetic wing materials seem to do better than more opaque materials like bucktail, because these fish have excellent eyesight and roam clear waters.

In most instances fly fishermen will need a boat to locate and catch bonito and albacore. Once you have found them, you race in front of the school and hope they will pass close by. Because they are usually pushing the bait to the surface, you don't have to fish deep. Just get the fly in

The grin on Sara Gardner's face tells you how much fun albacore can be on a fly rod. Photo by Tom Earnhardt.

front of them and retrieve quickly. Fly-fishing pros Bob Popovics and Lance Erwin developed a deadly technique for large numbers of albacore. Use a small popping bug with a Surf Candy or Clouser Minnow as a dropper below the bug. Get ahead of the fish, stop the boat, and cast the popper with the fly suspended about eighteen inches below if there is a chop. You don't need to retrieve. Simply hold the rod still, and the waves will cause the popper and Clouser to bob up and down. If the surface is calm, manipulate the popper gently. This technique will often outfish frequent casts and retrieves.

When the bonito or albacore are not breaking the surface very often, or when there are only scattered schools around your boat, you can resort to an old trick to keep them around you. Keep an ample supply of small frozen baitfish two to three inches in size. When albacore or bonito are surfacing, immediately throw a few handfuls of the bait out on the water. If you keep a constant but not overly heavy flow of chum in the water, the fish will usually remain, and you'll increase your chances.

The best albacore fishing occurs during the last part of October and most of November at Cape Lookout, North Carolina. Many years ago, Tom Earnhardt took me out fishing one day, and there were thousands of albacore (locally called albies, or Fat Alberts) roaming inside the bight and just outside. Scores of bottom fishermen were anchored everywhere, fishing for seatrout and croakers. Tom and I caught big albies until we simply gave up. As we fought and released the albacore, we could hear the locals commenting about how crazy we were to catch fish you couldn't eat, and then throw them back.

That first year Tom and I were the only fly fishermen in the area. The next year we saw two other boats with fly anglers. Then the word got out. Now Earnhardt and Donnie Jones have organized a gala albacore event in the first week of November, when several hundred fly fishermen descend on Harkers Island. Two years ago I counted 126 boats around the bight. There were so many albacore that almost every boat had at least one person fighting fish at any time. Not only are the albacore plentiful there at this time of year, but the average size is larger than elsewhere along the East Coast. It is not unusual to catch albies of sixteen or seventeen pounds; the largest I've seen taken on a fly weighed twenty-one pounds.

On rare occasions, when there aren't many albies thrashing the water at Cape Lookout, you can catch fish by following trawlers. The trawlers drag nets on the seafloor just outside the bight. Fly fishermen have found that by using fast-sinking lines and fishing deep behind the boat, they can often hook many albies. The nets must stir up considerable food. This is one place where a true trophy albie may be caught, and it is a good idea to use slightly larger flies in this situation. I recommend the Half & Half.

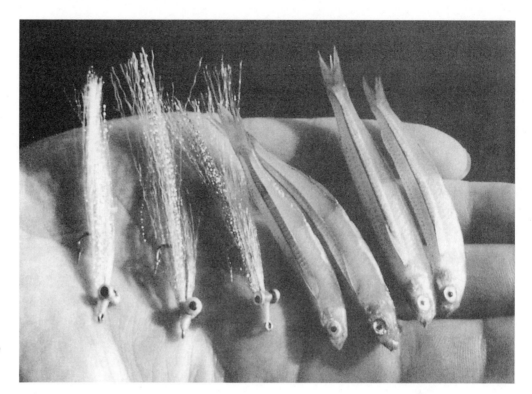

Here is Tom Earnhardt's version of the Clouser Minnow, which is deadly on albacore and other species feeding on small baitfish.

Tuna, bonito, and albacore need to be kept in the water if possible. Never keep them out of the water—even for a few minutes. When ready to release, don't just sit them in the water. Instead, their chances are much better if they are thrown in, as demonstrated by Tom Earnhardt.

Albacore are fast and catching them can be exhilarating.

Seatrout

There are two common species of what are called saltwater trout. Spotted seatrout are found in the East, generally from the Gulf Coast to Virginia. Gray trout, or weakfish, range from South Carolina to New England. These species are not actually trout, but are related to drum, and were in decline for many years. Both have bounced back. The spotted seatrout does not get as large as the weakfish. A trophy would weigh more than six pounds. I have caught weakfish to nine pounds, although most will average one to two pounds.

The spotted seatrout usually inhabits saltwater basins that are three to ten feet deep with a bottom containing a lot of grass. This vegetation will float on the surface because storms and the tide frequently tear it loose. This can interfere with your retrieve, so I recommend a weedless fly. The seatrout and weakfish species are not strong swimmers; they prefer to hold where food can be swept to them. Two surefire locations are where a slough drains water from a bay, or where a river enters a larger bay on the falling tide. Larger weakfish tend to be nocturnal feeders, but spotted seatrout usually do not. They will feed at night near lighted boat docks and bridges if there is a good flow of tide, or wherever tidal currents will funnel baitfish to them.

The gray trout, or weakfish.

During the colder seasons of the year, the fish either move into deep holes in marshes, rivers, and bays, or go offshore into the ocean. The best seasons tend to be spring and fall; there is also excellent summer fishing along the Gulf Coast. Spotted seatrout are taken in estuaries along the Atlantic Coast as far north as the Chesapeake Bay.

The same flies work well for both weakfish and spotted seatrout species. They are easily attracted to a noisy popping bug, and the combination of the popper with a Clouser Minnow is deadly. Good baitfish imitations such as squid flies, Lefty's Deceiver, and Surf Candy work well. I know of no other saltwater fish that responds as well to fluorescent-colored flies, especially chartreuse, orange, and yellow, or a combination of two of these colors. Seatrout also like a lot of flash in the flies. Remember that a sinking line is also advised for most fishing, unless the trout are in water less than four feet deep.

Spotted seatrout and *grass* are almost synonymous. If you want to locate seatrout, you must first find basins covered with turtle grass. The fish will be in three to ten feet of water, or even shallower. Plateaus with deeper water on the sides are prime areas. The trout forage in the shallow areas, and these are the best places to catch them. Fly fishermen often tie on a Bend-Back fly or create weedless patterns that can be worked through the grass. A 1/0 hook is about average, and the fly can be three inches or less. Again, bright colors tend to catch more fish. The fly should be worked slowly and just above the bottom. You will find that a sinking-tip line or a fast-sinking line will put your fly in the right zone.

Using a live shrimp and a popping cork is the most popular method and certainly an effective one. The cork is rigged a few feet up the line from the shrimp. As the rod is moved, the cork acts as a chugger, making a commotion. Trout come topside to see what is happening and eyeball the shrimp. The popping cork can also be used with jigs, flies, and other lures. It is nothing more than a noisemaker and attractor. Since seatrout respond to sound, small lures that pop, dart, or chug will catch their share of fish. Mirror-type plugs are a traditional favorite for this species. Leadheads with action tails have become increasingly popular. As noted earlier, these trout seem to prefer bright colors and anglers oblige with chartreuse, fluorescent red, fluorescent yellow, and other shades.

Seatrout prefer open areas and are seldom found around mangroves. If you are in a boat, the best technique is to drift over the flats, casting until you locate the fish. They usually move in schools; if you catch a couple of fish, you should be in the right place. Throw a marker buoy over the side so you can return to the spot, or drop an anchor and hold until the action dies down. Then start the search pattern once more. Most fish will school according to size because it is difficult for a small fish to keep up with a large one while swimming. Therefore, if you are catching trout of one size and want bigger fish, you must scout out another school. The chances are slim that huskier specimens will be mixed in with your current one.

Tuna

Chumming works exceptionally well for tuna. During summer and fall, various species of tuna move to the inshore waters of New England and the mid-Atlantic states. To keep them near the boat, cut fairly large pieces of fish (bonito are great, because they hold a lot of blood) and throw them overboard steadily. The tuna see the hunks of fish sinking in the water column and hang around for more. This very effective technique is called chunking, and it is also used in the tropical waters of Florida and the Bahamas to hold many excited and hungry species of fish near the boat. Small baitfish are effective as chum.

Blackfin and other tuna can easily be led into chum lines.

Barracudas

Many anglers thrill at the prospect of catching a barracuda because it has such a fierce reputation. Big barracudas invade the flats as though drawn by an unseen hand when the weather turns cold and the water temperature drops. You will find them in January, February, and March, particularly during the cold snaps that send bonefish and permit scurrying for the comfort of deeper water. Some of these fish look like logs in the water with dentures that resemble the blade of a buzz saw. This fish is so fast that once it attacks a prey, the baitfish rarely escapes. You can never retrieve a fly fast enough to deceive a 'cuda. So don't even try.

Barracuda are fast and ferocious predators.

If you see a long, green, indistinct, and motionless object on the flats, it just may be a big barracuda.

A barracuda is lurking in the foreground.

Bermuda boasts an abundance of barracudas during the summer months, but the water temperature inshore is not as hot as it is in Florida. There are times when the saber-toothed barracuda lies motionless on the surface and there are fish at every point on the compass. The barracuda provides a challenge throughout the Caribbean in channels, on the flats, and along the edges. Because water temperatures are more moderate there, sharks and barracudas may be found during most of the year.

I have used long, skinny patterns that resemble needlefish, a favorite food of 'cudas, for many years, but there are disadvantages to this fly. It frequently tangles during a cast, which can ruin an opportunity. It also offers such a thin profile that sometimes I think 'cudas never see it. When fishing for 'cudas, you must accept two facts: Perhaps half of all your presentations will be ignored or cause them to flee, and a 'cuda will almost never strike after it has been lured to a boat on a retrieve. I favor a fly that is red-over-orange, or chartreuse-over-white, or a popping bug. The underwater flies work about half the time if you make a special retrieve.

Once a 'cuda is located, approach close enough so you make a forward cast with a weight-forward line, but pick up all the line you cast. Toss the fly about six to ten feet in front of and just beyond the 'cuda. Lower the rod immediately, draw the fly through the water in front of the fish, and make a backcast. This will frighten at least half the 'cudas you throw to. But it seems to interest the rest, which apparently see something hit the water, streak past them, and disappear. Repeat the same cast two more times. On the fourth cast, begin an erratic retrieve of the fly. It does not have to be moving fast, but it does have to be moving at all times! I have found this to be the most effective underwater retrieve for 'cudas. Many times a popping bug worked with a never-stopping retrieve is very effective. Because 'cudas have such good eyesight, I prefer using single-strand wire, never more than ten inches in length, as a bite tippet.

Sharks

Barracudas and sharks have been maligned by anglers and guides who seek the more glamorous denizens of the shallow flats. They are usually relegated to the second-class role reserved for the so-called "day-savers" that you hope to catch when all else fails. To my way of thinking, this is a mistake. These toothy critters are underrated in skinny water. Not only are they tough to fool, but they put up spectacular battles complete with sizzling runs that leave a bonefish gasping in the shallows.

Small specimens of both species seem to be on the flats most of the time. And you are likely to see plenty of sharks and barracuda on the flats when you are bonefishing. In fact, it is a sign that at least some

Sharks are among the finest flats trophies a fly fisherman can catch.

moderate-sized bonefish are there, too. Of course, if you wish to tangle with trophy-sized fish, you must time the season closely. Sharks prefer warm weather; you will find consistently larger ones on the flats during summer months than at other times. This is not to say that you won't find six- or even eight-footers in winter, but there aren't as many and they are prone to leave when water temperatures fluctuate. March and April are excellent times around Key West for really big sharks.

Sharks are one of the most difficult fish to catch on a fly rod. Very small and blacktip sharks will attack almost any fly as they cruise bone-fish flats. But as they get bigger, they seem to get smarter. Fortunately there is a surefire way to get a shark to hit your fly. Catch several lady-fish (the best fish to use as a decoy) or a catfish (which is very tough)—though any small dead fish can be used. Attach the dead fish to a length of thin rope or line and let it drag behind the boat as you drift along in waters that sharks inhabit. The juices and scent from the fish are very apparent to any nearby shark, which will move in to grab your decoy. Remember to keep a careful watch on the fish or the shark may steal it!

When you see a shark near the decoy fish, get ready to cast. (Remove the decoy immediately before the cast is made.) Orange-and-red or yellow-and-red flies appeal most to sharks, and they are easy to see. Remember, a shark's eyes are located well back on its head. If you cast directly in front of the shark, even if it sees the fly, the shark's nose may push it aside as it tries to grab your fly. You must cast the fly so that it lands and is retrieved

Shark.

near the eye of the shark. Since the amount of time the fly remains near the shark's eye is crucial, the boat's position and your own prior to the cast are important. If you cast to a shark that is going away from you, the fly, no matter how well placed, will zip by so quickly that the shark will either not see it or miss it on the strike. You need to approach the shark at such an angle that it swims toward you. Then you can make your cast and maintain the fly near its eye. As the shark moves close to the boat you should also kneel, because despite its poor vision the shark can still see a silhouette. And in stalking a big shark, silence is vital.

Remember that a shark strikes by sweeping its head to the side, so be ready for this action. You will need about ten inches of wire connected to the fly or the shark's teeth will sever the leader. Don't use braided wire. Instead, use No. 5 or 6 solid stainless-steel trolling wire. Braided wire deteriorates during a battle as the shark goes through one strand and then another; finally enough are severed so that the wire breaks.

Another method to draw sharks is to slowly pour concentrated fish oil and ground-up fish parts on the water. If there are any sharks in the area, they will usually show. This method works well in most cases, but not on a slack tide, because you need some current to broadcast the scent to the sharks.

Flashabou or Krystal Flash built into the fly helps the shark locate it. Since it is also necessary for the angler to know the location of the fly and keep it near the shark's eye, a fly with a dash of bright orange or red is helpful, too. I like the same fly patterns that I use for barracudas.

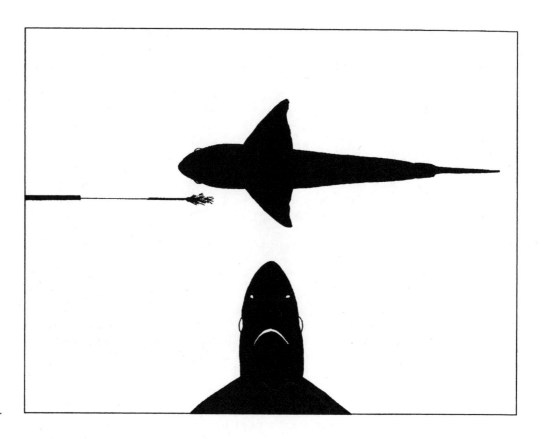

Cast to a shark near its eye.

Sharks take such a fly well, and you can see it easily. Sharks have powerful jaws that can crush a small hook easily. For sharks of more than forty pounds, hooks in the 3/0 to 5/0 size are recommended. Popping bugs will certainly draw strikes, but because the shark's mouth is located so far back on its underside, it has difficulty grabbing the bug. Too often the front of the fish's head just pushes the popper away.

Sometimes when stalking a shark you'll find that it is moving away at such a speed that you'll lose your chance for a cast. Stick the first two feet of the fly-rod tip under the water and swish it rapidly back and forth. The vibrations may attract the shark, which will often turn and approach the boat.

If you live in an area where the waters are slightly murky, or the water is deep enough that the sharks cannot be clearly seen, you can still take them on a fly. Establish your boat along a sod bank or other points sharks frequent. Set up a chum line of blood (hatcheries and slaughterhouses can supply it) or ground fish chum. The sharks will often be attracted enough to come within a few yards of the boat. Once hooked, sharks can provide terrific excitement on a fly rod.

There is a vast and unexplored world of sharks out there that is starting to get the attention of fly fishermen. These are the inshore waters of the South Pacific and Indian Ocean, and the waters off Africa. Some of us have fished these lightly. I have fished the exciting waters off northern Australia and New Guinea, and have talked to others who have fished many of the small islands that dot the South Pacific.

Barramundi

In the South Pacific a number of fish offer great potential for fly fishing. One of the most sought after by local anglers, and sure to become a coveted trophy for many fly fishermen from other parts of the world, is the barramundi. I am no scientist, so I can't say for sure that it is a first

Ed Givens strains to lift a huge barramundi caught in New Guinea. This fish is very similar to the snook in Florida.

cousin to the snook. But it has the same sloping head and sharp-edged cutting plate on its gill flap. It has the same basic overall shape, too, and a strong lateral line. And its flesh tastes like snook. It also seeks the same cover as snook, hiding under fallen trees, old stumps, and similar structures. It, too, can be found at the mouths of estuaries or miles upriver.

There are places in New Guinea, and other areas of the South Pacific, where no one has ever thrown a fly to these fish—and they can reach more than fifty pounds! I was with Ed Givens, the great saltwater fly fisherman from California, when he boated a thirty-pound barramundi on the Bensbach River in New Guinea. What a fish! Some of the most exciting action I have had with barramundi has been on rivers where I knew that few, if any, fly fishermen had ever cast to them.

Threadfin Salmon

In some of the same waters I described above roam two other fish. One is the threadfin salmon. This is a fish shaped much like a bonefish, with a powerful tail and silvery color. Few fish you'll catch on a fly could be confused with it: The threadfin has six long barbels dangling from its lower jaw, much like those of a catfish. Threadfins, which inhabit inshore tropical waters of northern Australia, can range up to forty pounds. They fight

This is a threadfin salmon, a wonderful flats fish found in Australian waters.

like hell and can be taken by sight-fishing, just as you would bonefish. They also hang around drainage areas on a falling tide when you can blind-fish for them. They will eagerly strike Lefty's Deceivers, Clouser Minnows, and Whistler patterns. They are a great flats or shallow-water fly-rod target.

Trevally

The jack crevalle is revered as a tough opponent. A big jack would be one of twenty pounds; a monster would be forty pounds. But in the South Pacific there roams a fish that looks exactly like a jack crevalle called a trevally. There are about three dozen different kinds of them; the one that can reach more than 150 pounds is the giant trevally. I saw two of these fish caught on fly rods at Christmas Island by Randi Swisher and Cary Marcus that were around the seventy-pound mark. Once, when I was offshore of Christmas Island at the mouth of Cook Island, there were huge groundswells—maybe thirty feet high. As one swell approached, a giant

Rod Harrison is releasing one of the toughest fighters in saltwater shallows—a giant trevally.

trevally ran across in front of us on its forward side. As that fish moved across the wall of water, it was like looking in a store window. I gasped and asked the boat captain how big he thought that trevally was. He looked and said, "I'd swear that fish approaches two hundred pounds!"

Trevally will attack flies, especially popping bugs, but it can sometimes be difficult to get them to strike. One method that has worked well for me is to make a cast with a popping bug and begin a fast retrieve. If the fish refuses to take it, I backcast quickly and start another retrieve. As the fish approaches, I lower the rod at the fish and, holding the line, sweep the rod so that the bug streaks through the water. This almost always draws a strike.

Niugini Black Bass

Some years ago I made a trip to New Guinea to be in a film that involved outdoor writers Rod Harrison and Dean Butler, and cinema photographer John Henke—all Australians with a great sense of humor. Rod and Dean began extolling the terrible ferocity of a fish they called the black bass or Niugini black bass. (*Niugini* is the way the people in Papua New Guinea spell *New Guinea*.) They told me I would need fifty-

Sam Talarico with a big Niugini black bass. Only a handful of fly fisherman have ever caught this fish or its cousin, the spot-tailed bass. This is perhaps the strongest fish that swims. It lives near river mouths that enter New Guinea seas. The Australians have a perfect name for it. They call it River Rambo.

pound-test leaders, and that the fish's tooth-filled mouth would destroy my flies. I could write an entire chapter on this great fish. All I will say is that it is the strongest fish for its size of anything I have ever hooked—and that includes yellowfin tuna.

If you seek this fish, which lives in the brackish river mouths of New Guinea, go prepared! Use at least a forty-pound-test leader straight off the fly line. Have extra-stout hooks and get a very good grip on the line when you set the hook. Up the same rivers is a cousin of the Niugini black bass called the spot-tailed bass. It is nearly as strong. Few fly fishermen have caught both of these species, and perhaps less than three dozen anglers have caught the Niugini bass on a fly rod. So the opportunity is there! Unfortunately, much of New Guinea is now hostile territory due to civil strife.

Milkfish

The final inshore South Pacific species I want to mention is the milkfish. It can be found through much of the Pacific, in places such as New Guinea, northern Australia, the Philippines, and Southeast Asia. This fish looks so much like a bonefish that few people can tell the difference. Years ago the International Game Fish Association recognized a world-record bonefish that was later determined to be a milkfish. But there are several differences. A monster bonefish would be one that topped eighteen pounds. A very large milkfish would be close to forty pounds! I have hooked only three, but others who have caught them agree with me that milkfish, pound for pound, are much stronger than bonefish. The major difference between bonefish and milkfish is their feeding habits. The milkfish is a vegetarian; I have watched it apparently eat algae.

Just as we faced a challenge when trying to discover how to effectively fish for permit, we face the same type of problem with milkfish. On my last trip to Christmas Island (where there are many milkfish), I tried a fly I had tied in an attempt to imitate the algae they feed on. To tie it, I made a loosely spun body of Antron, then palmer-hackled the entire fly. Hackle was trimmed from the top and bottom; I teased the Antron so it projected outward from the hook shank. It was then dressed with dry-fly oil, so it would float in the surface film. It worked fairly well (I hooked three fish, which all ran away and cut me off on sharp coral), but there is much experimenting to be done. Someone in the future will work out a formula for catching milkfish. When he does, we will be able to fish for one of the greatest inshore trophies in all salt water. Anglers in the Seychelles have developed a fly to take milkfish there, but I suspect that different flies and techniques will be required to take them elsewhere.

Rod Harrison holds up a milkfish, often confused with a bonefish. This South Pacific species is much stronger (and grows much larger) than a bonefish, and eventually we will figure out ways to take this vegetarian on fly rods.

Other Species

Both the inshore and near-offshore waters of the South Pacific are filled with a huge number of species that most fly rodders have never heard of. There are narrow-barred mackerels, which can weigh more than one hundred pounds and leap twenty-five feet through the air. These fish can be caught both close to land and well offshore. Dogtooth tuna prowl in big schools, as well as the biggest cobia I've ever seen. There is a great species called the queenfish that roam in packs, as do the bluefish on the northeastern coast of the United States. I never met one that wasn't hungry, and when hooked I've had them actually jump into the boat with me.

The narrow-backed mackerel, often called the Spaniard in the South Pacific, is similar to the king mackerel and abounds in these waters.

I have been lucky enough to catch most of the fish people would like to catch on the fly rod. The only fish I have not yet taken is the dorado (the natives call it the "golden fish") of the freshwater rivers of Peru. I have tried, but jungle rains roiled the rivers while I was there.

If you are looking for new frontiers, the South Pacific, the Indian Ocean, the waters off Africa, and a host of other locations are yet to be really tested by fly fishermen. Be one of the first!

3

TACKLE

Planning

A great fishing trip almost always begins at home. You need to think about what kind of clothing and sunglasses to wear, select the proper rod and line, choose your flies, and correctly build your leaders. At the same time, planning your travel arrangements is important, too. Even if you are only going to a regional trout stream fifty miles from home, it's worth getting up-to-date information. Call a tackle shop, outdoor writer, friend, fish or game warden, or someone who knows the local conditions. Find out if certain flies are hatching, if water levels are high or low, if the water is clear or silty, and how the phases of the moon are affecting the fishing. Too many anglers, especially those who are familiar with their local waters, will simply grab their tackle and drive to the scene—only to find they did not bring the right tackle, could not match the hatch, or arrived at the wrong time of day.

Whatever travel plans you have made, be sure to arrange for a local guide before you reach your destination if you are fishing in a foreign country or exotic locale. Experienced guides are not cheap, particularly those who have an international reputation and enjoy a number of repeat clients. But the cost of a knowledgeable guide will normally be far below the cost of your air travel, and usually a good guide will be the single most important factor contributing to the success or failure of your trip.

For all your trips, whether they are foreign or domestic, always make yourself a travel checklist. Mine is rather lengthy: It includes more than fifty items I would need whether I was making a trip to Alaska or the

Lefty's Trip List

Personal Items

Passport
Copies of passport pages
Visa (if needed)
Tickets
Letters and phone contacts
Reading materials
Notebooks—recorders—pens
Business cards
Thirty $1 bills
Extra money
Credit cards—checkbooks
Shaving kit and extra blades
Sunscreen
Lipshield
Fishing license
Sunglasses—spares
Spare reading glasses
Maps and charts
Wrist watch spare
Sewing kit
Pocketknife
Spare keys
Toothpicks
Ziploc bags, napkins, and rubber bands

Fishing and Camera Gear

Rods
Reels
Lines and extra lines
Flies and lures
Hip boots and shoulder harness for hip boots
Nail clippers
Pliers and hemostats
Wading vest
Band-Aids
Crazy glue
Cigarette lighter
Cortaid and Stingeeze
Any medicines
Camera and extra bodies
Film
Lenses
Protective camera case or bag
Extra camera batteries
Shooting list
Lens cleaning liquid
Tripod

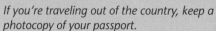

If you're traveling out of the country, keep a photocopy of your passport.

Clothing

Dress suit—shirts and pants
Light summer shirts and warm shirts
Dress socks and heavy socks
Light summer pants and warm pants
Light underwear and warm underwear
Spare belt
Sun gloves
Rain gear—two sets
Boat bag
Sneakers (two pairs)
Down vest
Fleece jacket
Hat and spare hat

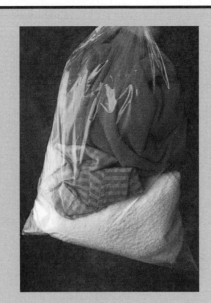

jungles of New Guinea. I make multiple copies, put them on a clipboard, and then modify them for each trip to match special requirements. If you use a checklist, you will rarely take a trip and forget something important.

Your fishing gear is the place to start. This is the equipment that will deliver your offering to the fish, hook it, and bring it close enough to land. Unfortunately many fly fishermen select their tackle improperly, because they start with the wrong premise. Usually they decide on a rod to buy, then a line to match it, then the reel they prefer, and finally the flies for fishing. Actually the flies should often be selected *first*, because they will determine what kind of fish you are likely to catch in your particular locale—or the area in which you plan to fish.

Flies

Selecting the proper flies, of course, is an essential part of getting ready to fish. (This subject will be covered in greater detail in later chapters.) Regardless of what other tackle you use, you must offer an artificial enticement that will be acceptable to the fish. This fly must be tailored to the fish species, and frequently it must be matched to the habitat. For example, coaxing a fish out of dense vegetation, such as a bass among lily pads or a redfish down in the turtle grass, demands the use of a fly with some sort of weedless device that allows you to fish there without snagging. In swift currents, when fish are lying deep, a fly designed to dive quickly is a necessity.

Generally flies are designed to imitate food that predatory fish feed upon—although not always. Those not designed to imitate a food source exactly are called attractor flies. These patterns do not resemble anything actually living in the water, but experience shows that fish really will strike such flies. Just about any predatory fish is at some time susceptible to them. (A Royal Wulff, for example, is a good fly to entice trout.) Attractor flies may be tied with vivid fluorescent colors or have a radical shape and design. There is another type of fly that has no special name or designation, so I call it a creature imitation. These flies do not fall easily into any category, but they often imitate such food sources as squid in the open ocean or crayfish in fresh water.

For most species we use either a surface fly or one that swims underwater. But for freshwater trout we have developed a number of specialty flies that range from those used on top of the water to those that creep and crawl along the bottom. These special flies have names that designate their unique design and purpose. In fact, there are more than a dozen special designs just in the category of trout dry flies. Among the most popular are the conventional dry, terrestrial, thorax, Paradun, parachute, Griffith's Gnat style, No-Hackle, spinner, Renegade or Fore-and-Aft style, skater, Variant, caddis, and stonefly.

If we disregard trout flies (dry and wet) for the moment, most other flies used to take fish fall easily into two categories. Poppers or popping bugs sit on the surface and can be designed to make a little noise or none at all. These are popular for bass fishing in particular. Many underwater flies are designed to imitate baitfish and are called streamers. These are particularly popular for saltwater fly fishing.

Sharp hooks are essential. The best way to check them is to drag the point across your fingernail under only slight pressure. If the hook doesn't dig in, it needs sharpening.

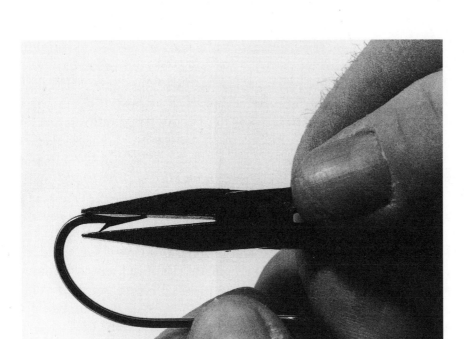

Crimp a barb in this manner and you'll never break another hook.

Regardless of the kind of fly you are using, it will never hook a fish if it is not kept in good condition. If there is any question about whether the hooks on your flies are sharp enough, touch them up with a file or hone. You might also want to consider removing the barb, particularly if you are fishing for trout in a catch-and-release area. If you are going to let a fish go after a fight, you certainly want to have it in hand rather than lose it because of a fly with a dull hook.

Backing

In almost all fishing situations a fly line is often not enough, especially if you have a long-running fish. You must use a thin, strong backing to battle such fish, but not just any line will do. Years ago we used monofilament as backing, and as the fish would make a long run, and we would pump the rod to recover line, the monofilament went back on the spool under tension. This stretched the monofilament and buried it deep into the coils of the backing underneath it. The result was that if the fish made another long run, and the reel paid out enough line to reach the section that was buried, the reel would stop, the line would jerk, and the leader would break.

Today we use basically two kinds of backing, either Dacron (or Micron, which is very similar) or the new, thinner and stronger gel-spun polyethylene braids, such as Spider Wire. Both line types offer advantages and disadvantages.

Dacron and Micron offer several advantages over braided nylon, which stretches quite a bit under tension. These lines stretch to about 10 percent above their usual length when exposed to extreme tension, but this doesn't pose a problem when fighting a fish. One of their best attributes is that they lie flat on a reel spool. This makes for a good, firm bedding for the fly line and any backing placed on top of it. However, they are relatively large in diameter, which restricts how much backing you can store on a saltwater fly reel. They also tend to fray under constant fish-fighting pressure, and should be checked regularly. A quick examination with a magnifying glass should suffice; if the line looks like a barbed wire fence, it's time to replace it.

Most saltwater fly fishermen select thirty-pound test as a universal choice. If you are fishing with small reels and fish that run less than 125 yards, you may want to use twenty-pound test. I compared the relative merits of twenty- and thirty-pound test with an experiment using two pieces of each about eighteen inches long. Someone held the lower portion of a fly rod while I inserted a piece of twenty-pound test through the stripping guide. Then I grasped the line firmly on each end and sawed it back and forth under tension about forty times. Then I looked at each through a magnifying glass. The thirty-pound test held up much better.

To connect fly line to Micron or Dacron, first make a whipped loop in the fly line. Then make a Bimini twist on the backing portion and loop the two lines together. This configuration allows you to quickly exchange fly lines on the spool, and the connection never hangs in the guides.

The new gel-spun lines are very thin and super strong. The main advantage of a gel-spun line is that you can put so much more line on the spool. For example, a gel-spun line of fifty-pound test is smaller than thirty-pound-test Dacron. Experience has taught us that for most saltwater situations, fifty-pound-test gel-spun is the best option. If you are using small reels for fish that won't run too far, you can use thirty-pound test.

There are two disadvantages, however; because gel-spun lines are so thin, it is vital to install the line under tension. I prefer to use a glove so I can grasp the line firmly when reeling it onto the spool. If you don't store gel-spun under tension, the backing isn't firm and you'll encounter the same problems as with nylon monofilament—that is, the line buries itself down into the backing during a fish-fight. When battling a fish, you must take extreme care to make sure the line doesn't pile up on one side of the spool. If it does, it may collapse into a tangled mess during the fight. Some claim that gel-spun line is less abrasive than Dacron or Micron, but that isn't true.

The color of your backing is important. The first concern is that it should be different from the fly line color. When fighting a fish, you need to know how much line the fish has taken. One of the most important factors in fighting stronger saltwater fish is to try to keep the fish as close as possible, with most of the fly line on the spool, if possible. If the backing is a different color than the fly line, you have an indicator telling you where your fly line is. The color of the backing should be fluorescent if possible, since you may be battling a fish under poor light conditions. If a long run occurs, you may have to chase the fish in a boat. The captain is less likely to run over a backing that is easily visible.

How much backing do you need? Many people recommend over two hundred yards. Forget it. Unless you are fishing for giant tarpon, where you often have to fight from an anchored boat—or you fish offshore for huge fish, such as billfish and tuna, you will almost never need more than two hundred yards of backing. Think about it. If you have an albacore on—which runs pretty well—and he rips 150 yards of backing from your reel, if you add 30 yards of more fly line and leader—that's one and two-thirds of a football field away! This will happen only in your dreams. I feel confident that if you have 150 yards of backing on your reel, almost any inshore fish can be subdued.

You should install enough backing so that when the fly line is added, the reel spool is full. The more backing on the reel, the fewer revolutions you'll have to make when reeling in line. Here is how to determine the exact amount of line for your reel, fly line, and backing combination. With an empty spool, attach the fly line to the spool and wind it on. Then wind on enough backing until the reel is properly filled. Then, reverse it so that the fly line is on top. This is extra work, but it's worth doing. Another tip is how you attach the backing to the spool shaft. Most anglers will wrap the line once around the shaft and then wind on the line. But under tension (should the fish run all the line off) this may slip and you will be unable to recover line. Instead, make two turns around the spool shaft and use a uniknot to firmly tighten the backing to the spool.

A last thought about backing: If you've fought a fish and it has taken out your backing, you've contaminated the backing with salt water. After your fishing trip, it's a good idea to fill a sink with warm soapy water and pull off all the backing you feel was soaked in the salt and wash it. Be sure to also wash the spool sides to prevent corrosion.

Fly-Line Selection

Most fishermen know that there are four basic types of fly lines: level taper, double-taper, weight-forward, and shooting taper. Lines are also given numbers from 1-weight to 15-weight, with the most commonly used lines ranging from 3 to 12. Approximately the first thirty feet of the line is weighted, and of course this must be matched to the rod for optimum casting. Many anglers have several tackle outfits, and each one will require a different weight of line to match the rod. In most fly-fishing situations, the line is one of the essential elements of a good presentation. The proper selection is based on two criteria: the size of the line and its design performance in the water—that is, the type of line as defined by its floating or sinking characteristics.

One well-known rule of line selection is that the size of the fly determines the size of the line. In other words, a big fly equals a big line. What is less understood by many anglers, however, is the design characteristics of the various types of fly lines that are available today, and when and where each type of line should be used. For example, many anglers fish their whole lives using only a floating line. This is okay, but they will not catch as many fish. There are a many situations in which another type of line—sinking tip, slow sinking, fast sinking, or shooting taper—will deliver a better presentation and increase fishing success.

In calm waters you should definitely use the lightest floating fly line that will deliver the fly. For dry-fly fishing to freshwater species, only rarely is a 6-weight or heavier line needed. Most of the time a 2-, 3-, or 4-weight line is best for these situations. Such light lines settle to the water almost silently. Unless it is very windy, the angler using dry flies will simply catch more fish by using these lighter lines.

When conditions are windy, you will need more weight in the line. For fishing at short distances (less than twenty-five to thirty feet), use a line one size larger. This allows you to load the rod with only a short amount of fly line outside the rod tip. If you are going to cast into the wind at long distances, use a line one size smaller, with at least forty feet of line extended beyond the rod tip for false-casting. This amount of extended line will allow you to load the lighter-weight line properly. And because you are false-casting a considerable length of line, your fly will be closer to the target when you finally release the line. Do not use the reverse tactic. In other words, do not use a heavier line than normal when attempting to false-cast a lot of line in a heavy wind. This will simply cause your rod to bow deeply, creating large open loops that will not drive well into a breeze.

Light floating lines should also be used on very calm days in salt water. I opt for a 6-weight line for bonefishing. These lines come to the water so softly that I can cast with a ten-foot leader to even very shy fish. But this light-line principle also applies to saltwater species other than nervous bonefish. The shark, a species that lately has become increasingly popular with saltwater fly fishermen, may seem a primitive and unemotional creature. However, in low clear water it can be easily alarmed. A heavy 12-weight or 13-weight line crashing to the surface on a calm day will spook a shark just as easily as it would a bonefish. In such conditions a 9- or 10-weight line would be much preferred.

When fishing for tarpon on a dead calm day, a 10-weight line that falls to the water relatively quietly gives you a much better chance than a heavy 12- to 14-weight line clunking down to the surface. These fish are often spooked by the line following immediately behind the leader. A clear monofilament fly line (or a conventional fly line with a long monofilament tip) is far less likely to alarm the tarpon. This is especially true when casting for these fish over a light sandy bottom.

Redfish are often maligned for having poor eyesight (an observation I don't necessarily agree with), but these wily fish certainly have keen hearing. So when possible, go no heavier than a 7- or 8-weight line on redfish, and only resort to a 9- or 10-weight when fishing conditions demand these heavier lines. Under calm conditions, make it a firm rule to use the lightest floating line possible and you will up your score considerably on most species in both fresh and salt water.

With the exception of trout fishing, sinking-tip lines are not good lines for most fishing situations. Of all the fly lines, these are the most difficult to cast and still make a quiet presentation. And with a sinking-tip line, every time you strip in some line, you cause the forward and submerged portion of the line to loft toward the surface, pulling the fly away from its intended course of travel. If your tactic requires that the

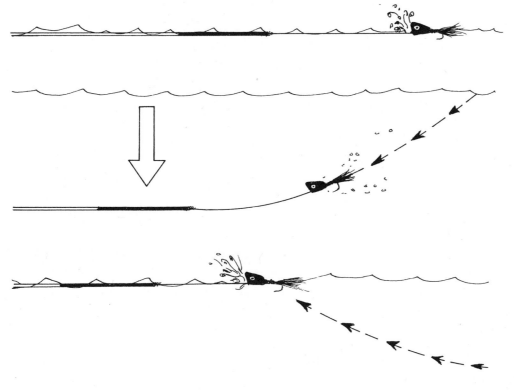

Fishing a popping bug with a sinking tip.

fly line travel at the same uniform depth throughout the water column, you need to use another type of sinking line, not a sinking tip.

There is one situation, however, in which the sinking-tip line is the perfect presentation tool: whenever you have to cast into a small open hole in vegetation, retrieve the line across the vegetation, and then make a backcast. This frequently occurs in fishing for largemouth bass in water where the surface is choked with lily pads, or when you are trying to get to a snook lying in a pothole on a saltwater flat. In such situations a floating line cannot be used successfully because it will not drive the fly deeply enough into the water.

But a sinking tip works very well if you use the following routine. First, cast and drop the fly on the far side of the hole. Then allow the fly to sink into the depths of the hole and begin your retrieve. When the fly nears the edge of the hole, make a backcast. In this situation the long, rear, floating portion of the sinking-tip line permits an easy backcast to be made. Conversely, a full-sinking line would tangle in the lily pads or grass as you attempt the backcast.

While we are on the subject of fly lines, here is a tip about their maintenance. If your fly line has been used frequently, it may be dirty. Some waters, especially large southern and mid-Atlantic rivers, will put enough dirt on a fly line in a single day to require cleaning. A dirty floating line will not sit well on the surface, and any type of line—floating or sinking—will not shoot any distance if it is covered in bits of minute debris collected from the water.

One solution is to use Glide, a commercial fly-line cleaner that removes the dirt quickly and gives a slick finish that permits the line to shoot better. To ensure that the slick surface it imparts to the line will remain for a long time, Glide should be applied several hours before using the line and allowed to dry thoroughly. Another method of cleaning a fly line is simply to wash it in warm water with a mild liquid soap, but not detergent. Pull the line through a sponge soaked with the mixture and then be sure to rinse the line with cold water so it will float properly.

At least five types of full-sinking lines are in general manufacture today. They are distinguished from each other by their sink rate in the water column, from slow sinking to extra-fast sinking. Let's look at the slow-sinking line first.

In salt water, the areas where you want to fish are often filled with floating grass, sometimes so thick that it makes fishing nearly impossible. At other times, often during the first few days after extra-high tidal conditions, the abnormally high water carries small pieces of grass and deposits them along shorelines and over the surface of the water where you are fishing. A floating line is useless in these conditions. It will simply lie on top of the grass that carpets the surface until you begin the re-

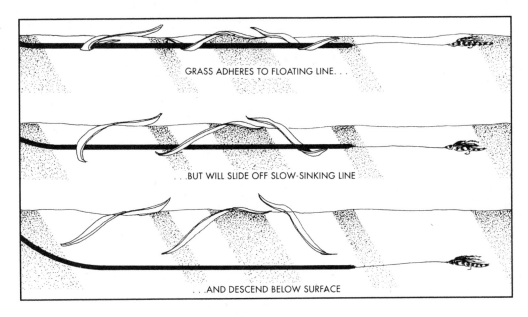

GRASS ADHERES TO FLOATING LINE. . .

. . .BUT WILL SLIDE OFF SLOW-SINKING LINE

. . .AND DESCEND BELOW SURFACE

Slow-sinking line in grass.

trieve, at which time the grass slides down the floating line, then over the leader and onto the fly, ruining your retrieve.

A slow-sinking line—often called an intermediate line—is a good choice when the fish are not too deep in the water column and you need to keep your fly tracking toward the surface. When you cast a slow-sinking line onto pieces of floating grass, it will slowly slide off to one side and descend an inch or two below the surface of the water, remaining in position quite a while before you begin your retrieve. Such a line gives you the advantage of being able to present your fly near the surface of the water, while eliminating the problems associated with grass.

Another common use for slow-sinking lines is in Atlantic salmon fishing with tube flies, which are often most effective when they are fished just below the surface of the water on the swing. In this form of streamer the body and wing of the fly are dressed on a tube made of plastic or metal. Depending on which material is used, the fly will need more weight to take it below the surface.

All sinking lines need to be evaluated based on how rapidly, deeply, and effectively they sink into the water column. Years ago, when I was researching the first edition of *Fly Fishing in Salt Water,* I asked a number of experts if an 8-weight fast-sinking fly line would sink faster than the same type of line in 10-weight. No one seemed to know, so I conducted some experiments and confirmed that the larger size definitely would sink more quickly. The heavier the sinking line, the faster it will descend in the water.

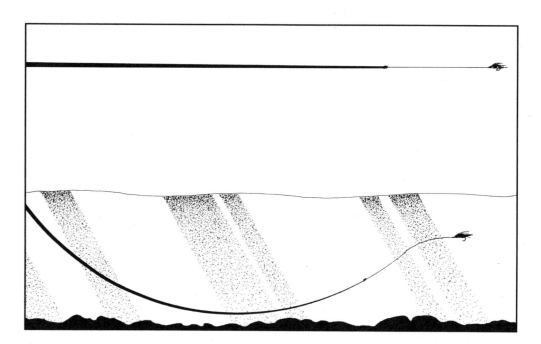

Profile of conventional sinking line.

How fast and how deep you want the fly to sink will therefore depend on selecting either a larger size of sinking line or one that has a faster sink rate. But the most important consideration about a sinking line is how well it sinks to the depth of water in the water column where you perceive the fish to be, and therefore where you want to present the fly. In this way, conventional sinking lines are simply not a good presentation instrument, and I do not recommend them, except in special situations.

The flaw in most commercially manufactured conventional sinking lines is that the front section of the line—usually the first ten feet—has been deliberately designed to taper in order to achieve a better turnover of the leader and fly on the cast. This means that in a conventional sinking line, the front ten feet or so will weigh less than the midsection of the line (the belly), and thus it will not sink as rapidly. In turn, this creates an underwater bow in the line. As you fish this type of line at a depth in the water column where you perceive the fish to be holding, the belly of the line may sink fast and deep enough to reach the fish, but the front section of the line, including the leader and the fly, has bowed up and is riding higher in the water column than you perceive the fish to be.

Fortunately, there is a way to overcome this problem by using a uniform-sinking line or one of the weights in the T-Series of Teeny Nymph lines. Uniform-sinking lines have almost a straight taper to the forward segment, which is weighted to conform to, and have the general casting characteristics of, a conventional weight-forward floating line. These lines are readily available from most of the large fly-line manufacturers,

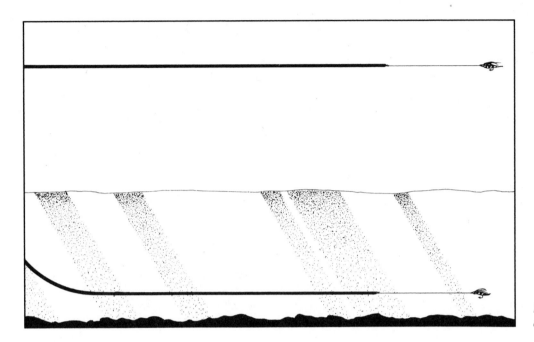

Profile of uniform-sinking and Teeny Nymph lines.

and they can be purchased in five or more sink rates, from slow sinking to extra-fast sinking.

There are several other advantages in using uniform-sinking lines. One of their principal qualities is that you feel the presence of the fish on your fly faster and more clearly, whether it is the delicate inhalation of a nymph or a slam dunk on a big streamer pattern. Instead of having the underwater bow in the line, which is created by the conventional sinking line, uniform-sinking lines travel straight through the water. Thus when a fish makes contact with the fly, you are immediately aware of it.

This same factor aids in striking more efficiently. Working with a conventional sinking line means that you have to get rid of the slack, or the bow, in the forward end of the line and leader before you can properly hook the fish. With the uniform-sinking lines, which travel straight at the fish, all you have to do is strike and the hook starts to bury itself inside the fish's mouth immediately.

Yet another advantage with these lines is their effectiveness in casting in strong winds. When I was fishing for sea-run brown trout in Tierra del Fuego, Argentina, I was often casting flies in winds that exceeded thirty miles per hour and sometimes reached fifty mph. It soon became apparent that if a good cast was to be made, there had to be a lot of weight in the forward portion of the line. The uniform-sinking lines, with no taper and more weight forward, tended to buck the breeze and turn the fly over much better than a conventional sinking line with its tapered and thinner front portion.

In offshore saltwater fishing, floating lines have a small niche for specialized applications. However, perhaps 90 percent of all offshore fishing is best practiced with sinking lines, because most offshore species—dolphin, wahoo, and all types of billfish—normally swim at some depth below the surface of the ocean. A slow-sinking and a fast-sinking line are the two mainstays for these types of presentations. So if you are stuck with only one line for offshore fly fishing, go for the faster-sinking line and adjust your retrieve. Or you may simply elect to use a sinking shooting head, as outlined below.

We now know that there are many fishing circumstances when the shooting head is the best tool available for presenting the fly to the fish. *Shooting taper* is the generic term for this type of fly line, even though *shooting head* (which was first adopted by one of our major fly-line manufacturers, Scientific Anglers) is now the term commonly used by most anglers to describe this type of specialized fly line. Most manufacturers continue to refer to the line as a shooting taper, and thus the technical designation that generally appears on retail cartons for shooting heads is "ST." For example, a 9-weight floating shooting head would be indicated on the carton as ST9F.

The first anglers to regularly employ shooting heads were steelhead fly fishermen on the big rivers of the Northwest, where the premium holding pockets for these fish were often far out in the stream beyond stretches of water that were too deep for wading The shooting head allowed the anglers to reach these pockets with extremely long casts. We have since learned that the shooting head is essential for many types of presentations in both fresh and salt water. Anytime you want to present a fly at a long distance through the water, the shooting head is a superior tool. In those situations when you want to sink your fly down deep in the water column, no line matches the effectiveness of a fast-sinking shooting head (or lead-core line made into a shooting head). Any serious fly fisherman is missing a great fly-fishing experience, and missing out on a lot of big fish, if he does not learn to construct, work with, and cast shooting heads.

A shooting head is identical to the forward portion of a conventional, level, weight-forward or double-taper fly line, and it can be purchased commercially as an individual item or constructed by cutting one out of a conventional line—although those made from double-taper lines seem to cast a little better. When it is rigged, the forward part of the line—the shooting head—will be attached to an extra-thin rear segment, called the shooting line.

When you are fishing, the shooting head is held outside the rod tip while false-casting. On the last forward cast, as the rod stops, the thinner (shooting) line to the rear is released. Because the skinny shooting line offers almost no resistance, the heavier, fast-traveling shooting head easily pulls a lot of the shooting line toward the target. One of the great attributes of this line is that it allows you to work and search a fly through considerably more water than you could with another type of line. And no fly line permits you to make longer casts than the shooting head.

When shooting heads were first sold, the manufacturers made them thirty feet long, because this was the length they had always agreed upon as being standard for measuring the weight designation of conventional fly lines. Thus the first thirty feet of a line that is designated as 6-weight weighs about 160 grains, while the first thirty feet of a line that is designated as 10-weight weighs about 280 grains. Manufacturers continue to use these designations for conventional fly lines today, so that when they began manufacturing shooting heads, it seemed reasonable also to make shooting heads thirty feet long so their weight could easily be measured and designated in the same manner.

But there's a problem with this approach. One of the most important facts about distance casting is that as soon as the line unrolls (or straightens), it will begin falling. Only so long as the line is unrolling in the air does it travel toward the target. If a commercial shooting head is thirty feet long, then no matter what the skill of the caster, as soon as that thirty feet unrolls, it will begin falling to the water. Make the head longer and you will increase the roll time—and the distance that you can cast the fly.

So instead of purchasing commercial shooting heads, I suggest that you make your own. They will probably provide you with greater distance on your cast than those sold commercially. And they are very easy to make. Buy a double-taper fly line one size larger than you need for the rod. For example, if you are casting with an 8-weight rod, then buy a 9-weight double-taper line. A double-taper line has a long level section in the middle of the line with identical tapers at each end. Thus from a single double-taper line you can make two shooting heads. If you purchase a weight-forward line for this purpose, you are wasting your money, because you can only get one shooting taper from it, since the rear portion of this line is not weighted and tapered, but is very long and thin.

The length of the shooting head you construct will be determined by your casting skill. A very good caster can effortlessly handle a shooting head from about thirty-eight to forty feet long. Anglers who can cast easily to about sixty feet seem to be able to handle a shooting head of thirty-four or thirty-five feet in length. The best way to determine what is right for you is to construct a head to the maximum length that you believe you can handle and try it out. If you find that it's a little too long for you, simply cut it back and make it shorter. Your testing guideline should be that the correct length of shooting head for you is the length you can hold outside the rod tip and false-cast comfortably. Another solution is to buy a head one or two sizes heavier than the rod calls for.

A number of materials can be used for the shooting line. The most common is monofilament. It allows you the greatest distance on the shoot, since it is so thin, light, and slick. When fishing the lighter fly lines, such as 5- through 7-weights, a twenty-pound monofilament shooting line seems to be the best choice. It does blow around and it will sometimes tangle, but its ability to glide so easily through the guides makes it the first choice when light lines are being thrown any distance.

For heavier lines and when fishing for strong fish—salmon, steelhead, striped bass, tarpon, and other saltwater species—thirty-pound shooting line is the universal choice of most experienced anglers. Monofilament shooting line is best, too, if you are really trying to get down deep. It offers the least resistance against the water of any of the materials that are commonly used for shooting lines.

Some anglers prefer a shooting line made from braided leader material (a line with a hollow core and a braided exterior). This kind of shooting line has two outstanding advantages. First, when it is stripped from the spool it falls loosely, with no coiling. The braiding prevents coiling, a problem with most types of shooting line. (Other kinds can have their coils removed, of course, by stretching them before you start fishing.) And second, the braided line shoots extremely well through the guides. The disadvantage of braided shooting line is that the material is very rough, and after lengthy periods of fishing, the rough texture of the line can cut right through the skin of your fingers as you grip the line when retrieving.

Convenience is another good reason for using shooting heads, because they allow for quick and easy loop-to-loop line changes to accommodate any change in the tactical fishing situation that you may encounter at streamside. Simply construct a loop at the rear of each of your various types of shooting heads—floating, slow sinking, fast sinking, what have you—and similarly construct a loop at the forward end of your shooting line. This gives you a convenient loop-to-loop system for quick line connects and disconnects. In this manner you can adjust to any changes in the fishing situation throughout the day by carrying only one reel on your rod, plus spare spools loaded with other types of shooting heads in your fishing vest.

A simple method of making a loop for both the shooting head and shooting line is to use a fly-tying bobbin and size A tying thread. Follow the directions in the following illustrations. And when making the loop-to-loop connection, always do so in a square-knot configuration (also shown), never in the bowline configuration that will weaken the connection and form a large bump that may become jammed on the rod guides.

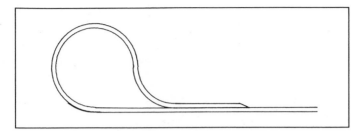

1. Use a fly-tying bobbin with size A thread (Nymo, flat waxed, Kevlar, or any other quality thread). Insert the thread through the tube of the bobbin as you normally would. Then remove the spool and wrap the thread around one of the bobbin legs four times before reseating the spool. The four turns will give you the tension necessary to swing the bobbin with force. If you need more thread, you will have to rotate the spool with your hands to feed the additional amount. To start, fold the fly line back on itself for about two inches to form the loop.

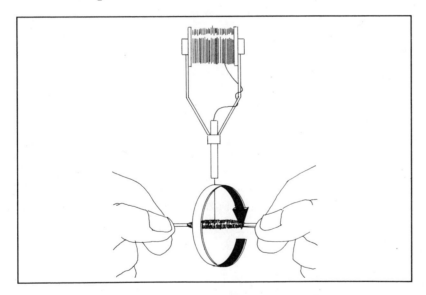

2. Lay the tag end of the thread parallel to the tag end of the fly line and make a few turns by hand to secure the loop. Grip the loop in your right hand and the fly line (both the standing part and the tag end) in your left hand. Rotate your hands away from your body to swing the bobbin. The faster you spin, the deeper the thread will bury itself in the outer coating of the fly line. With practice, you can lay each wrap against the preceding one.

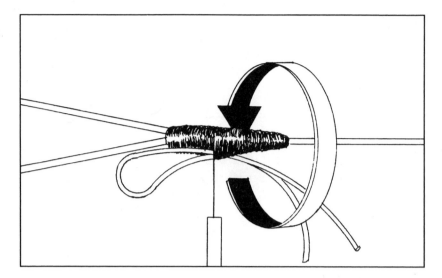

3. A wrap of half an inch is adequate, but you might want to stretch it to five-eighths or three-quarters of an inch. Stop before you reach that distance, and taper the tag end of the fly line with a sharp knife or razor. This will help make a smooth transition as you wrap it down to the single strand of fly line. To secure the wraps so they don't unravel, use a whip-finish. Many anglers prefer to lay a ten-inch piece of double mono with the loop in the direction the wraps are going. Mono that tests four to ten pounds is adequate. Make eight or ten wraps by swinging the bobbin gently. If you swing it too hard, you won't be able to pull the mono back out.

4. Cut the thread coming from the bobbin and slip the tag end through the loop of monofilament. Hold the fly line and pull

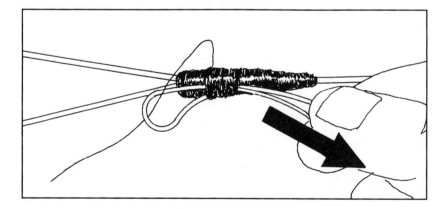

both the tag ends of the monofilament at the same time. This will draw the thread under the wraps and secure it.

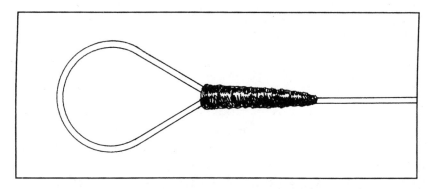

5. Trim the thread at the point where it exits the wraps. Then coat the wraps with a glue or rubber-based cement such as Pliobond. Take a moment to test the loop. Place a smooth object in the loop and pull on it with one hand while holding the fly line in the other. If the thread has not buried itself deeply enough, the loop will come out.

What type of shooting line is best? For most fly-fishing situations I recommend the commercial shooting line. It shoots well, handles nicely, and is relatively inexpensive.

With the shooting head in hand, where is the best place to use one? They are great if you are a bass fisherman, fishing smallmouths on a wide river such as the Susquehanna. Perhaps you enjoy fishing for trout that are feeding on the surface of a calm lake. You might be casting to seatrout in a saltwater basin, or fishing a farm pond and trying to get the fly well out from the bank. If you are an average (or below) fly caster in any of these situations, and you need to cast a longer distance than you could normally achieve with a weight-forward line, the shooting head can be very helpful.

For offshore fishing, many anglers like to use a conventional fast-sinking line. However, I prefer the shooting head. I never seem to be able to cast far enough offshore, unless the fish have been teased to the boat. Shooting heads are by far the best choice for offshore long-distance casting. And to drive the fly deep into the saltwater column, my favorite shooting head is an extra-fast-sinking (or lead-core) shooting head attached to twenty-five- or thirty-pound monofilament. No line goes down faster and has less resistance against the current flow than this type of shooting head–shooting line combination.

If you are not a particularly good caster and need a little extra distance—to drop the fly to forty-five to sixty feet away, for instance—you can make a modified shooting head that works well. (I often use this type of line when I take someone fishing who has only tried trout on small streams, or is simply very small or weak—children from twelve to sixteen who are not large or strong for their age or elderly people, for example.) To construct this line, build a shooting head of only twenty-five feet instead of the commercial thirty-foot length. But remember, make it one size heavier than the rod calls for. And use thirty-pound monofilament for the shooting line.

You will be amazed at how well even weak or very inexperienced anglers can fish with this outfit. I assure you that everyone who can handle a fly rod at all can easily lift a twenty-five-foot shooting head from the water. With this outfit they can raise the twenty-five feet of shooting head, make a backcast, come forward, and at the end of the forward cast simply let the shooting line go. This allows them to cast the fly easily to a distance of forty-five to sixty feet.

Where accuracy of presentation is important, a brightly colored line is preferable. If you are a fairly good or advanced caster, you will have learned to control your cast well, and bright color in the line allows you to see it unrolling in the air toward the target. That's a real plus, in my view. I feel that being able to watch the line travel toward the target aids considerably in getting an accurate cast, mainly because if you can see the line, you can slow or stop it when you feel it is the correct moment.

It is also an advantage to be able to see brightly colored lines in certain fishing situations. For example, when bass fishing a shoreline early or later in the day when visibility is low, a brightly colored line can help you stay in contact with your fly or popping bug. Or when bonefishing or seeking permit, a brightly colored line is preferred simply because it is important to know where the line and fly are located in relation to these skittish fish.

But there are some rare occasions when a brightly colored line can be detrimental to your presentation technique. If you work a bright line through or close to a school of fish, they will probably flare from it. Generally this occurs in clear water in situations in which the line must be dragged in front of the fish. Fly fishing for tarpon is an example of where a brightly colored line is often detrimental. This is why so many good tarpon fishermen use a line constructed with the front section composed of clear, or almost clear, monofilament.

But as general rule, when using a floating fly line in shallow water (less than five feet deep), a brightly colored line is still the best choice.

Leader Selection

Leaders are the next item to check, and they are such a critical part of fishing that I've given them their own chapter. Turn to chapter 6 for everything you need to know about leaders, tippets, and knots.

Reels

The two basic reel designs commonly used today in salt water are the slip clutch (sometimes referred to as anti-reverse) and the direct drive. With either model, the spool will make one compete revolution when the spool handle makes one full turn. From a design standpoint, generally a direct-drive reel has stronger gears and is better suited to fighting very large fish. A slip-clutch reel means that even if the fish is pulling line from the reel in an attempt to escape, you can continue to turn the handle, although no line will be recovered. The flaws in this design are that you often lose some control, and you waste energy turning the reel while recovering no line.

The direct-drive reel is considered by many experts to be the best choice for fighting larger fish, especially in salt water. With a direct drive you know exactly when you are recovering or losing line. If you are turning the handle, you are putting line on the spool. Many accomplished anglers feel that this is an important point. They don't waste any energy, and they know exactly how much line they are getting back from the fish. The disadvantage to a direct drive is that if you hold on to the crank when the fish is running, you can easily break the leader.

A sampling of saltwater reels. Top row, left to right: Scientific Anglers Mastery Series, Abel Model 3, Penn International, and Billy Pate. Bottom, left to right: Lamson LP-3.5, Islander, and Tibor Riptide.

There is another important consideration for those who work with their hands, such as musicians and surgeons. With a direct-drive reel, anytime the fish pulls line from the spool, the reel handle is going to revolve. Failure to let go of the handle means the leader will break. If you do let go, and that whirling handle strikes your fingers, they can be badly bruised or even broken. Just about everyone who has used a direct-drive reel and fought a fast-running fish has been rapped on the knuckles when the fish fled. I feel that all direct-drive reels should have only one handle. It is easy to locate during the battle, and it cuts in half the number of times your fingers will get banged if you fail to let go in time.

The shape of the reel handle is also important. I believe that a direct-drive handle should differ from a slip-clutch handle. With a direct-drive reel, you must release the handle instantly if a fish surges away, taking the line. The quicker you release the handle, the less chance there is of breaking the leader or having the whirling handle strike your fingers. And the smaller the handle, the less likely you are to be struck with it. For this reason, I feel that direct-drive handles should be smaller than most current designs, and they should be tapered so that the smaller end is away from the reel. This allows you to get rid of it easily. The handle should be no longer than one inch. Admittedly, this makes it a little more difficult to grasp the handle when cranking in line—but I think the benefits outweigh this disadvantage.

Slip-clutch reels are popular because they are more forgiving and easier to use with little experience. If you continue to crank on the handle

Modern heavy-duty saltwater fly reels are usually made from a solid piece of aluminum, which is then plated to resist corrosion. Shown here are the steps in making a Billy Pate fly reel.

while a fish is pulling line from the spool, the only harm done is that you are working for nothing. Second, there is no worry about cranking against the surging fish and breaking the leader or bruising the fingers. For slip-clutch reels, I favor handles that are slightly larger and easier to grip. The best handles are perhaps those that are slightly flattened and scored or roughed, allowing you to grip them firmly.

Anyone skilled with both kinds of tackle can fish as well with a direct drive as with a slip clutch. Proper fish-fighting technique requires that you pump large fish by raising the rod and reeling in only as you drop the rod tip toward the fish. The best fish fighters control the line not only with the drag, but also with the fingers of the hand holding the rod. The fingers trap the line against the rod blank during the upward pump with the rod. Then the fingers relax as the rod is lowered and the released line is spooled onto the reel. It makes little difference whether you use a direct drive or slip clutch if you know how to control the finger that traps the line.

Another misconception began with trout fishermen. It's about which hand you should reel with when fighting a fish. Many trout fishermen will cast with their right hand and reel with their left. They do this so they don't have to change hands when fighting a fish. That's fine for trout, where reeling in line is generally a small effort. But when a steelhead runs off 150 feet of line, or a bonefish or offshore saltwater species takes twice that amount or line or more, the situation drastically changes. First, during the heated run, you have plenty of time to switch the rod to the other hand—this is not the problem. Your "reel" problem is that you are going to have to recover all that line—and often very quickly.

While a few anglers who have for many years used their off hand to crank a fly reel may do well, the average person will perform a great

Narrow-spooled trout reels, like the one on the left, are inefficient. It's better to use a reel that has a much larger diameter, like the one on the right.

deal more efficiently if he does this with the stronger hand. That means that a right-hander will do best to reel with the right hand. Part of the problem is that a fly-reel handle revolves in a very small, tight circle, and this makes it difficult to retrieve at high speed. The average right-hander who uses his right hand to recover line with a spinning reel is turning the handle over a large diameter; for each turn of the handle, the spool revolves four to five times. Not so with a fly reel. The main reason for reeling with your dominant hand is that you can reel for longer, more sustained periods.

The drag on a fly reel is certainly important. No satisfactory reel used in fresh water should have such a light drag (or click tension) that it over-spins and backlashes when line is pulled quickly from the spool. The drags that have certainly stood the test of time in salt water on hard-fighting fish are those with a cork ring (often impregnated with some other material) that is pressed against the inner face of the spool during the battle.

Reels that have a series of washers contained in the small inner cavity tend to build up heat in the cavity, and the smaller washers often erode faster in the heat of battle. This is not to say that other types of washers are poor performers. But experience certainly has proven that the cork washer works extremely well over long periods of time. What is important, regardless of the type of drag used, is the rate of adjustment. Any

The author demonstrates his favorite method for setting the drag on fast-running fish. Adjust the tension until you can no longer pull off line through your compressed lips.

drag that goes from off to full force in a short motion (by either turning a small adjustment knob or flipping a lever) is liable to get you in trouble. When distracted by a fighting fish, you can easily establish too much drag and break your leader. Good drag-adjustment nuts or levers allow you to move through a relatively long span from off to full drag. Another important factor to consider on any fly reel is that the drag works only when the fish is taking line. There are a few fly reels where the drag resistance is on all the time. This means you must overcome this force when you are reeling in line.

Nearly all fly reels have a drag composed of one or more soft and hard washers. Such a drag works well only so long as the soft washers remain soft. Should they harden, the drag will be erratic and the leader will probably break during a fight. It is extremely important to release any drag tension at the end of each day's fighting. Leaving the drag's nut screwed down for long periods of time slowly squeezes the life out of a soft washer. In time it will harden, and the drag will be ruined. Actually, any reel—from a delicate fly reel through spinning, plug-casting, and offshore trolling models—should be stored with the drag relaxed to protect its soft washers.

If your reel has no drag washer (only a clicker), you may be able to modify it slightly to get a really good drag. With reels such as the rather inexpensive Pflueger Medalist, for example, you can do some work on

There are many fine reels available to saltwater fly fishermen today. Shown here are just some of the popular models:
Top Row—Tibor.
Middle Row (left to right)—Ross, Orvis DXR, Islander, and Billy Pate.
Bottom Row (left to right)—Lamson, Catino, Sage, and Scientific Anglers.

the reel to give you an excellent drag. Remove the spool and cut a section from the backplate that you can easily slip the end of your finger through. Smooth the edges and paint the plate before you reinstall the spool. When a fish wants to run, you can restrain it by simply applying pressure against the inner face of the spool through the hole you have cut. In fact, you can put on so much pressure that the leader can snap, so be careful with this maneuver. The spool, as on the Pflueger Medalist, may have a series of holes in it, and you would think this would hurt your fingertip when using it for drag pressure, but it really doesn't.

Here's another neat trick that results in a fine drag with a rim-control reel. Cut from an old belt (styled for men) a piece of leather that resembles a paddle. It should be about the size of a penny and no larger. The handle for the paddle should be about half an inch. Lash the handle to one of the braces between the two reel side plates in such a manner that the paddle itself sits over the rim portion that you would normally push your fingers against to restrain a fish. Now, instead of using fingertip pressure, you can press against this small leather paddle. If you use your fingertips or palm on a rim-control reel that is revolving as line peels off the spool, your skin, which is damp at the start of the run, will

A small leather tab on a rim-control reel makes a fine drag.

dry under friction. This can change the drag ratio. But the leather allows a constant, smooth drag.

Spool width on fly reels should be considered, too. The wider the spool, the more troubles that can accumulate, especially if a large fish is hooked. As line is recovered, it must be wound in a level manner. Too often during the heat of battle this is forgotten. Line piles up on one side of the spool, and then it begins slipping to the other side. This often results in the line jamming in the spool and the leader parting. Narrow spools eliminate this problem.

Trout fishermen who fish small streams and move from pool to pool to cast their offerings do a lot of reeling, although they may not realize it. Each time they leave one pool to walk to another, they wind in the line. Yet many trout fishermen prefer very tiny reels, with spool diameters of less than two and a half inches. Such small spools demand that you turn many revolutions to recover any line. Fly lines tend to take the position in which they are stored. Thus line pulled from a reel with a small spool comes off in tight coils that interfere with your casting unless they are removed. I prefer trout reels with a spool diameter of at least three and a half inches. If the spool is narrow, it can have a large diameter and still be as light as a tiny, wide-spool model.

Reel Care

Fly reels need very little care, but this small amount means the difference between one that will give years of service and one that fails—often during a fight. If your reels have a spring click that acts as a drag, then you need only place a small amount of grease on the spring to ensure that it will last a long time. But if there are any soft drag washers, you need to back off the drag at day's end. If the drag is a cork-type washer, almost all reel manufacturers have their own special lubricant, which they will supply upon request. Place a small amount of the lubricant on your fingertip and rub it well across the surface of the soft washer. Remove any excess with a dry fingertip. You don't want to add too much of the lubricant—just a smooth, thin film. Treated in this way once a year, such a drag will remain in good condition for years, even under hard fishing.

The shaft of any reel should be lubricated with a thin film of grease. Oil is still okay on freshwater models, but under a series of hazards the oil will disappear. Thin grease holds up better. The reel handle may also get dirt or grit inside the shaft and not spin. Remove the handle, grease the shaft lightly, and reinstall it.

The greatest concern about how to care for reels is among saltwater anglers. Almost all manufacturers tell you to use a warmwater spray or warm water on a sponge to wipe off the reels. Cold water does not take all the salt away; use warm water mixed with a bit of liquid soap. Try an old toothbrush to clean any areas that you can't easily wash with a cloth. The two places where salt will collect are the reel foot and wherever there are screws—which usually includes the handle.

Many freshwater reels, if cared for after every trip as described earlier, will usually last a long time in fresh water. I have several Hardy reels that have been in service in salt water for more than twenty years. The finish is a bit marred, but the reels still work perfectly.

Rods

Selecting the proper rod for your kind of fishing will mean the difference between endless days of enjoyment and endless frustration—and often broken tackle. Buying a more expensive rod will not make you a better caster. Only learning and practicing to cast will do that. But there are good reasons why the top manufacturers' products cost more. Simply put, some rods will outperform others designed for the same purpose—if you are skilled enough to utilize the better rods.

There are basically three categories of fly rods: those used for trout fishing; those used to cast flies a longer distance or buck the wind; and those that are mostly fish-fighting tools. The majority of rods fall into the first two categories.

Most fly rods that trout fishermen use will range from seven feet, six inches to nine feet in length. A few people advocate very short rods, those from five to six and a half feet in length. However, very few rods this short are manufactured today, simply because anglers have found them to be largely inefficient. They certainly are not more sporting, because the shorter the rod, the more leverage can be applied against the fish during the fight.

Boat rods for tough-fighting billfish and tuna are always short, and no experienced angler would consider fighting a powerful tuna or marlin

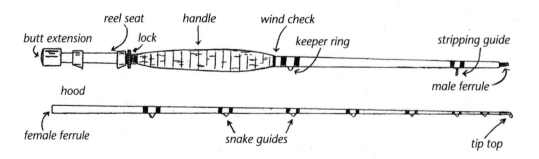

Rod nomenclature.

with a long rod. Short rods do work well in fresh water where fishing is done in what I call tunnels—very small streams with overhanging brush that severely restrict your casting. However, if on a small stream you occasionally run into such a situation, you can reduce the rod's length by simply sliding your hand up near the butt guide and placing the butt section behind your back. As soon as the cast is finished, slip your hand back on the rod handle to fish out the retrieve.

If you fish dry flies on small streams that are fairly open, a seven-and-a-half- to eight-foot rod is a great tool—although a nine-footer serves well, too. The shorter rods will allow you to tuck a cast more easily back under an overhanging branch. But if you are going to use dry flies, streamers, and nymphs, a nine-foot rod will be much more efficient. The longer lever allows you to roll-cast easier and to manipulate the line and fly much better than a shorter one. Indeed, there are very few cases in which a rod longer than nine feet will be a better tool for the trout fisherman who uses dry flies or fishes small streams.

The trout rod should be delicate, but a little on the soft side (not too stiff and powerful), and should throw lines ranging from 1-weight to 6-weight. Too many people, when selecting a trout rod, take it out and test it by trying to throw seventy-five feet of line. This tool will be used to make average casts from twelve to forty feet, and you want the fly landing gently on the surface. Some of the modern fast-action-tip rods can handle the entire fly line on the cast—but they are so quick that I feel they do not make ideal trout rods.

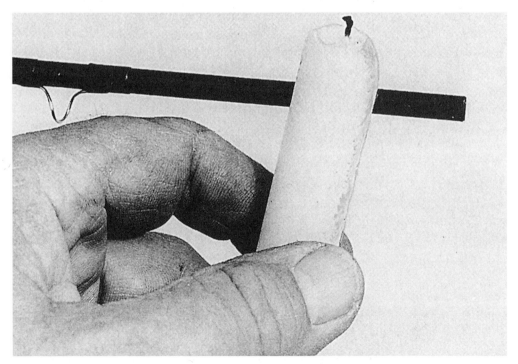

The male portion of a modern fly rod occasionally requires lubrication to keep it from coming apart. Just a few strokes with a candle will do the job.

The second category of rods is designed mainly to transport flies over long distances. Such fishing situations include driving bonefish flies into a breeze, throwing a wind-resistant popping bug across a lake, propelling a steelhead fly well away from you, fishing the shallows in salt water, or fishing for Atlantic salmon. This rod will handle a line from a 7- through an 11-weight. Such lines have the weight to drag a heavy or bulky fly a long distance. Frequently you will want to cast forty to seventy-five feet—or farther.

Fish-fighting rods are designed primarily for fighting big fish such as tarpon, amberjack, sailfish, tuna, and other husky adversaries. Near the end of the battle these fish must be physically hauled to the surface, and a rod with the backbone to do the job is needed. For many years we had rods that would do this, but they were so stiff and powerful that they were very poor casting tools. Today a number of manufacturers make graphite fly rods that are strong enough to defeat literally any fish we would likely take on a fly, and yet the tips are supple enough that they cast very well.

These fighting rods usually handle lines from 11- through 15-weight. Such rods often have a fighting grip made of cork between the rod handle and the butt or stripper guide. However, I don't recommend this design. While it certainly is a comfort to hold on to this cork grip when fighting a fish for an hour or more, it is not needed in order to use the full power of the rod when battling the fish. The entire rod below this grip is unbending. Thus, the most powerful portion of the rod is not being utilized. Instead, gripping the rod as close to the conventional handle as possible allows full use of the entire rod and will defeat the fish faster.

Handles on fly rods are important, too. The correct shape can make the difference between having fun and being uncomfortable, or maybe even getting blisters. Most trout fishermen prefer the cigar shape. It is also the most popular with most manufacturers. The half-wells is a handle that swells at the upper end, while a full-wells swells the same at each end. Half- and full-wells grips are almost always preferred by experienced anglers who use rods that throw line weights 7 through 13.

The half-wells with the swelling at the upper end of the handle is really all you need. The swelling at the forward end of the handle gives the thumb something to push against at the end of the forward cast— which many people find desirable. The cigar-shaped handle gives no support to the thumb during the cast and even tends to drift away from it at the end of the forward cast. Most trout fishermen don't really need the thumb support, since the casting is usually short range. The major reason that manufacturers make the cigar shape is that on the rack in the store, the tapering cigar handle is thought to have a more pleasing design. It therefore (supposedly) sells better. If you would like to replace a cigar shape with a half- or full-wells handle, any competent local rod builder can do it for you. Cork is still the best material anyone has come up with for handles.

Rod guides have a lot to do with how well you cast, how far you cast, and often whether you land a fish or not. It's a good basic rule to know that for every foot of fly rod, there should be one guide (not counting the tip-top), although there can be one more guide per foot. For example, an eight-foot rod should have eight guides and a tip-top, and a nine-footer should

Three basic handle shapes (from left to right): the cigar; a half wells, which swells at the top; and a full wells, with swelling at the top and bottom.

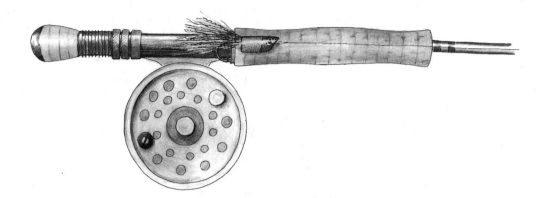

The full- or half-wells grip will help you cast longer distances with greater accuracy and reduce fatigue.

carry nine guides. If there are more than that, the guides will sometimes tend to overweight the rod tip, and with fewer than that the line is not well supported between the guides and tends to sag.

The largest guide, the one closest to the handle, is called a butt or stripping guide. This is the most critical one on the rod when you shoot line on the cast. Line, on the shoot, does not flow smoothly through the butt guide. Instead, it comes toward the guide in undulating waves. On a high-speed shoot the line tends to overlap the guide and then fold back before flowing through. Small guides act like a funnel, with a little hole that throttles the line and restricts the casting distance. I am convinced that the smallest butt guide on a light trout rod (throwing lines

Large butt guides let line flow through easily. Small ones, like the lower guide, create undue friction and restrict shooting line on the cast.

from weights 1 through 6) should be a 12mm; a 16mm would be even better.

It is also important to know that once the line has entered the butt guide, it is traveling almost dead straight through all the other guides. So only the butt guide needs to be larger than normal. When trout fishing, you often shoot a small amount of line. But you are forced to do this with only a small amount of fly line and the leader outside the rod tip. This makes it difficult to shoot much line, since the small amount outside the tip is being asked to pull the heavier tapered line through the guides and off the rod. For this reason, a larger-than-normal butt guide is always a good idea.

When using line weights from 7 through 13, the angler often wants to throw a long distance. This means considerable line must be shot through the butt guide to reach the target. As a result, I feel that the absolute minimum butt guide size is 16mm. A 20mm or 24mm is even better. The problem is that these guides look too large in relation to the rest of the rod—so anglers are slow to accept this idea. But if you try it, you will probably be able to shoot longer distances.

The butt or stripping guide is usually a ceramic ring, as is the next guide on the lower portion of the rod. In contrast, the rod tip generally is stainless or chrome plated, as are the light wire snake guides. Again,

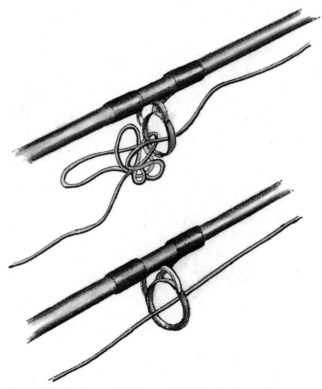

Even a slightly larger stripping guide will reduce tangles.

if the snake guides are too small, they will choke the line, restricting the ability to shoot line. While it is pleasing to see a rod whose guides taper in size as they near the tip, in actual practice, all snake guides should be as large as possible, so long as they don't overweight the tip.

Another advantage of having large guides—and the largest possible opening in the tip-top as well—is that if a knot appears in the line or backing when a fish makes a run, there is a better chance of the knot passing through. Some fly fishermen install single-foot ceramic guides on their rod tips, believing that they will increase distance when shooting line. My tests show that you actually get less distance when using these guides. Supporting this evidence is the fact that tournament fly casters, who actually measure all casts, tried and rejected them. These guides have much more surface and create more friction than snake guides. And because they weigh so much more, they tend to overload many light rod tips, creating undulating waves in the line during the cast, which effectively reduces the distance.

Clothing and Accessories

Most anglers are aware that using polarizing sunglasses to eliminate glare is an essential part of seeing fish (particularly trout and bonefish) before making the cast. I believe that amber- or brown-tinted polarizing sunglasses are preferable for most situations. But other colors have their uses, too. A blue-gray tint can be very effective on bright sunlit days on a snow-white bonefish flat. And medium yellow tints can work well on smaller trout streams where the water is shaded and often difficult to see through.

The color of your clothing is equally important, especially when fishing for trout. They live in clear waters and must be approached at close quarters before you make a presentation. I am a firm believer in having clothing that blends with the surroundings. For example, most of the vegetation and woodlands of the eastern United States and Canada are green during the warmer months when we fish for trout. Yet anglers insist on wearing khaki-colored fishing vests that present a strong contrast to the local vegetation and foliage. When fishing in these regions, I use Rit or common household dye to change my khaki vest to a forest green. And I return it to the normal color when I am fishing in the West.

When fishing meadow streams or angling for tarpon and bonefish on saltwater flats—where from the fish's perspective you are generally silhouetted against a bright sky—a pale blue or green color will blend in well. Even a white shirt is not bad, since the fish are frequently looking up at white clouds. Curiously, some brightly colored hats, even those with fluorescent colors, are in vogue among young anglers. But wearing these colors is the equivalent of flashing a mirror to tell the fish you have arrived.

In fly-fishing situations where you need to see the fish before casting, it is important to have the underside of your hat brim in the right color. Sunlight, reflecting from the water's surface, bounces off a light-colored brim and detracts from your ability to see what is below the surface. A dark underbrim reduces the surface glare and increases your ability to see. Any hat will reduce glare and help your vision (although the darker, the better). I prefer to use one with an underside of solid black, so I adjust mine by applying liquid shoe polish to the fabric. Just make sure you air it out before you put it on for a whole day of fishing.

4

SALTWATER FLIES

Many newcomers to saltwater fly fishing ask if there is a basic list of effective flies they can use in most waters, under most conditions, most of the time. The simple answer is yes. There are a number of flies that work, and they will be described in this chapter. Some readers may feel that the list is incomplete because their favorite fly is not mentioned, but I am confident this basic selection will do the job most of the time in the majority of places you will fish. I would add only one caution: You may have to alter the dressing, the color combinations, or the size to be most effective under your local conditions.

There are certain criteria that govern whether a fly will be productive. One of these factors, of course, is the presentation—which I will review in more detail in a later chapter. You need to know that with the exception of bonefish, most species will rise for a fly rather than dip down for one. (Bonefish are used to feeding on the bottom and therefore are concentrating on the zone below them.) Tarpon prefer a slow retrieve, while bonefish merely need to see some semblance of life in a fly. In fact, a fly can almost be "ticked" in place and a bonefish will pounce on it. Jacks and barracudas respond best to a fast-moving fly. And when it comes to permit, the situation gets even more complicated.

In the meantime, it helps to look at the design features of certain flies in order to understand why they are successful in salt water.

Silhouette

Whether you are fishing a nymph, streamer, or a squid pattern, the overall shape of the fly—when viewed by the fish—is extremely important. Bonito and tuna, for example, roam the open seas, where their favorite prey are small baitfish. Even though these predators may be hefty specimens, they will more likely be lured to the fly if the pattern is a sleek, small one that looks like their food.

Overall shape is critical to success. The silhouette should duplicate the general shape of what the pattern is trying to simulate. If striped bass are feeding on a baitfish with a deep body, such as an alewife, it's best to have a fly pattern that to some degree has this deep profile. In salt water you can often identify the shape of baitfish in the area by looking for dead ones that have been swept by the tide to the beach or into eddies.

Take a minute to check the shoreline for clues before you tie on your first fly.

Balance and Size

A skilled fly tier will construct a fly with proper balance, meaning that the fly is tied on a hook size that is designed for the pattern. Flies constructed on hooks that are too large, for example, will not swim properly. Hooks that are too heavy will also kill the action, and hooks that are too small will cause the fly to swim unnaturally or roll over on the retrieve. Proper balance and proportion also assure that water flows nicely over the pattern, creating the right action. With correct balance, the fly also moves smoothly through the air on the cast.

There are times when an outlandishly sized fly will draw strikes, but in most instances you want to offer a fly that is roughly the same size as the predominant bait. For example, if you use a teaser of ten inches to lure a billfish to your boat, removing the teaser and offering a five-inch fly would not be as effective in drawing a strike as would a fly closer to the size of the teaser. Similarly, a ten-pound bonefish has a very small mouth. To use a large fly to entice this fish would be ridiculous. That's why most bonefish flies range from half an inch to less than three inches in length.

Length

The length of a fly is important, too. For example, striped bass will sometimes feed on baitfish of a specific size. If the flies you are casting do not exactly match the color, but closely match the length, you can still draw many strikes. This is especially true when predators have pushed the baitfish to the surface and are gorging on them. Consider, too, that bonefish and redfish have relatively small mouths. Therefore, a five-inch fly might occasionally catch fish with small mouths, but shorter flies are a more attractive offering.

Structure

If you fish in fresh water, you know the value of being able to retrieve your fly through weeds and around boat docks and rock piles without having it snag. Vegetation can also be a problem in salt water. Floating grass, aquatic grasses growing on the bottom, and a shoreline full of mangroves and other line-catching structures will require special tackle. The trouble is that weedless flies are often fishless flies. The hooks on some of these flies are bent so they won't snag unwanted matter, but they are often very difficult to set when a fish strikes.

A number of products have been used to make weedless flies, but the most common material is hard or extra-stiff monofilament. This works well for a while, but after a few fish chew on it, the monofilament becomes so battered and misshapen that it is useless, and you have to clip it from the pattern. Solid trolling wire is sometimes better, because its stiffness offers excellent resistance to weeds. However, the wire bends out of shape easily. If you try to reshape it, the wire will probably break—and even if it doesn't, it is usually impossible to re-form to the original weed guard. I worried about these problems for a number of years before I came up with my own solution.

I now use a thirty- or forty-pound-test, plastic-coated, stainless-steel braided wire. If you buy a package of commercial steel leaders, they will probably be made from this material. This wire is generally composed

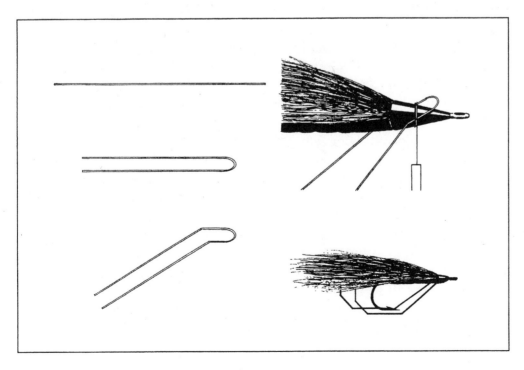

Lefty's special weed guard.

of seven or more very fine strands. The braided wire is then coated with a tough, supple plastic. (Do not use the uncoated wire—the end will untwist and make a useless weed guard.) This is usually placed in front of a fly for barracudas or bluefish and other toothy critters.

Each manufacturer has different colors of plastic coating on the wire. I have tried light tan, dark brown, and black, and I can see no difference in the strike ratio. However, I have not used the very black wire for a guard on streamer flies made of pale synthetics, such as a sand launce pattern. I think that nickel-plated or stainless hooks on many flies are appropriate if the pattern imitates a silver-colored minnow, and for this reason I do not use black wire. It simply stands out too much.

(Note that I am using the conventional plastic-coated braided wire, not the superthin material that appeared on the market a few years ago. This newer wire is not stiff enough for weed guards. The approximate diameter of the older wire I use is 0.03 inch.)

Hooks

Let's consider some of the requirements for saltwater fly-fishing hooks. First, bronze versions are not recommended because they sometimes rust quickly. Instead, use plated hooks or stainless-steel hooks. The regular-length Mustad 34007 and the longer-shank Mustad 34011 have been the most popular stainless hooks for many years. These stainless hooks are not as sharp as other hooks, nor do they possess the same strength, but flies tied on these hooks have landed fish successfully for years.

Size is also important. Many saltwater fly fishermen use hooks that are far too large. Freshwater anglers can catch large trout on a No. 22 hook, but the same anglers will use a No. 2/0 for a saltwater fish that is hardly much bigger. Many experienced fishermen now use a 2/0—or possibly even a 3/0—for giant tarpon of more than 140 pounds. In fact, there are few big saltwater fish that cannot be landed on a 3/0 hook.

Nevertheless, many striped bass anglers favor 3/0 to 5/0 hooks. The major disadvantage to using these larger hooks is that they are much more difficult to cast. Large hooks also have thicker wire diameter, so they will be tougher to set on strikes. The difference between casting a pattern dressed on a No. 1/0 and one dressed on a No. 4/0 is astounding. If a fish has a large mouth, like a striped bass, large hooks are not necessary, because the fish does not bite the fly. Instead, it opens its cavernous mouth and inhales the fly. I have landed a number of stripers between twenty and thirty pounds on a size 2/0 fly, which is the largest that I recommend.

Flies tied on very small hooks, such as a No. 8, will certainly interest bonefish. But a big bone is a hard-running fish, and such a small hook often dislodges because it does not hold enough flesh. I like to use a No. 4 or 2 hook for most of my bonefish flies.

Points and Barbs

Modern hooks have very small barbs, which I personally recommend. Unfortunately I have been hooked accidentally by a number of people, and a little bit of barb holds a lot of meat. Many anglers fear that they will lose fish if they use a barbless hook, but you need almost no barb at all to hold a fish during a fight. In fact, I have been using barbless hooks since 1956 and I cannot detect any difference in hooking and landing fish. I strongly urge everyone to use barbless hooks.

When selecting saltwater hooks, look at the points. If they are long and narrow, avoid them. Many saltwater fish have tough mouths, and a long, thin point will often curl when you set if in a fish, even if it is well sharpened.

Bulk

The amount of bulkiness, or slenderness, constructed into the fly will also determine how effective it is. Sand eels are sleek creatures that stripers, bluefish, and many other species feed upon voraciously. To be effective, a sand eel pattern should be tied so sleekly that in the water it looks as though the tier did not finish the job. The same can be said for needlefish imitations. They should be long, trim, and tied very sparsely.

Bulk is sometimes a good idea in special situations. If you fish at night, whether for snook or tarpon, you will need a fly that has considerable bulk and will push through the water. It will then create vibrations that the fish can pick up. A sparsely tied fly simply won't create the same effect. Remember that roiled or dirty waters almost always demand that the fly be tied with a lot of bulk.

Color

The color of the fly is often critical, particularly if you are trying to match what the fish are eating. On the open ocean and in many inshore waters, for example, almost all baitfish have either a blue or a green back and a white belly. (This corresponds to what other fish above or below them will see.) And when you tie flies that incorporate red and white, you can do it either very right or very wrong. If you tie the fly with the red on its back, or along the length of the fly, and the white in front, it won't be effective. But when the fly is mostly white in color with a small amount of red at its front, it will produce much better. I think the reason might be that as a predatory fish approaches this fly from the rear, it sees a long white belly and short, red gills.

Certainly when you are fishing for bottom-feeding species such as bonefish or redfish, it pays to start the day with fly patterns that are approximately the same color as the bottom. If the bottom is of light sand or marl, then a light-colored fly will generally be best. Much of the Bahamas and Christmas Island, for example, have this coloration. Start with a light pink, white, cream, or light tan fly. If the bottom is carpeted with rich, dark green turtle grass, then flies of this olive hue will often do better.

Attractor patterns that contrast radically with the environment where you are fishing are often so different that fish find them enticing. And when you can see a bright fly well, you'll find that it sometimes outproduces one that cannot be easily detected. Fluorescent chartreuse flies can be seen from a great distance, and I believe this is one reason why this color is so effective.

Flash

Almost all swimming fish give off some sort of flash as they travel through the water. The coloration may differ with different species, but the effect is the same. Generally those in stained water, such as snook and redfish, will give off a subtler tone—a sort of gold or copper flash. Those in clearer water tend to give off a brighter or more silvery flash. These factors should be considered when tying patterns to entice fish.

When Mylar first came onto the fishing scene (I noticed it in the mid-1960s), fishermen immediately realized that the flashes it emitted could be attractive to fish. After briefly experimenting with Mylar, I figured that if a little of it was good, a whole lot would be much better. So I constructed flies solely from Mylar—and they were a dismal failure. While there are a few species and situations where a fly constructed entirely of this material are effective, most of the time that's not true.

Much of the flash used in flies comes from a Mylar source, including familiar trade names such as Krystal Flash, Flashabou, and Cactus Chenille. The first two are strips of Mylar ranging from ultrathin to as wide as an eighth of an inch. Some strip Mylar has a holographic feature built in that increases its reflectiveness. It's manufactured in flat strips (Flashabou) or twisted (Krystal Flash). Cactus Chenille (which is also called by other names) is made by twisting extremely short strands of

Mylar into a fuzzy chenille that is highly reflective. It is mainly used for building fly bodies.

Strip Mylar can be bought not only in different widths but also in a multitude of colors. I find that I often get more strikes if I blend several colors. I can further enhance the pattern's attractiveness by using a combination of flat strips and twisted strips—for example, by combining Flashabou and Krystal Flash. Many flies, especially those that imitate baitfish, are generally more effective if a small amount of flash is added during the tying procedure. Krystal Flash, Flashabou, and similar reflective materials often induce strikes that will not come if the fly is devoid of flash.

Swimming baitfish resemble blinking mirrors as they move through the water. You see only an occasional flash. Bear this in mind when tying or selecting flies with reflective material in them. The best ones have just a moderate amount of flash. It is not a good idea, either, to attach material such as Krystal Flash or Flashabou, and then trim all the strand ends at one spot. This leaves most of the reflection at a single location—where the strands were severed. Instead, clip off the strands at different lengths along the entire body—this way you will see little sparkles of light throughout the pattern. Since few things in nature are one color, it also pays to mix several colors of flash material in a pattern.

Other fishermen have been using the technique, but famed outdoor writer Dan Blanton has popularized the trick of letting a number of strands of Mylar extend beyond the wing or tail of a streamer. He coined the term *flashtail,* and there is no doubt that at times this extra flash at the end of the pattern will draw even more strikes.

Sound

Building sound into a fly through its special construction can be another important element in its success. But let me first address the issue of rattlers or sound chambers, which some fishermen commonly use. I have experimented with every rattler I could find—glass, metal, and plastic—and I cannot see any difference in the number of strikes. I have even tried them with smaller and larger balls inside. Nothing has changed for me. Nevertheless, having confidence in your flies is half the formula for success. If you feel these devices are helpful and get you more hookups, keep on using them.

When I think about the sound of flies, I think more about their specific design. Most fly fishermen are aware that fish locate the creatures they feed on with two different sound sensors. One is located in the head; the other is the lateral line—a sound-sensing organ that runs along each side of the fish. Using these two sensors, fish are able to locate their food even in muddy water or at night. (Most saltwater fly fishermen know, for example, that snook feed more at night than during the day.)

There are times when having a fly that produces vibrations or sound waves underwater during the retrieve is essential. A good example is when you are fishing for tarpon in silty rivers such as those in northeastern Costa Rica. The tarpon here have grown up feeding in muddy water, and a sleek tarpon fly will draw virtually no strikes. But one with large eyes of either bead chain or lead that has a heavily dressed wing will certainly produce good results. When you need to make more vibrations or noise to attract predatory fish, the body and wing of your fly must "push" water on the retrieve. Sleek flies just won't cut it.

Translucence

This is not an essential element, but it's one worth thinking about when you are fishing in clear water where the baitfish are translucent. An opaque imitation of such baitfish will often serve you poorly. Fish such as albacore and tuna have incredibly good eyesight, and when they are feeding on bay anchovies, silversides, and similar baitfish, they prefer a fly dressed with translucent materials.

How do you get translucent flies? Mainly through the wing material. For years we used polar bear hair. Its hair is so translucent that it is similar to a fiber optic: It actually allows light to travel through it. However, this animal is now on the protected species list. Fortunately, plastic has come of age and we have many types of materials that can be used to construct fly patterns. You can make beautiful, translucent wings with Ocean Hair, Super Hair, and my personal favorite, Unique Hair, which is superb for streamer wings.

These materials resemble ultrathin strands of monofilament (although many are not nylon) and are usually crimped throughout their length—which improves their effectiveness as wings. They come in a huge array of colors, from black to fluorescent. Don't overlook the value of dressing some of your streamer flies with these translucent materials. It can make a difference in the stories you tell after your fishing trips.

Sink Rate

The sink rate of an underwater fly is critical to fishing success, yet it's often one of the most disregarded factors in getting a fish to take your offering. You may have used the correct pattern, cast the right distance, and retrieved at the proper speed, but if your fly is at the wrong depth in the water column, all your efforts will be in vain. For saltwater fishing you will need flies that work on the surface, ones that work just under the surface, some that fish a little deeper, and a few that dive well down in the water column.

A fly that won't sink quickly enough, or one that dives too fast, is often useless. Several examples come immediately to mind. A tarpon fly, such as a Whistler, is usually designed with heavy bead-chain or lead eyes and sinks quickly. Since it is heavy and bulky and lands with a bit of a splash, a weighted Whistler is rarely used when seeking tarpon in the Florida Keys. In such clear waters the wary fish would spook from the heavy impact. If the fly is thrown far enough in front to prevent the cautious fish from becoming alarmed, it then sinks too fast and will have descended by the time the fish arrives. However, the same pattern tied unweighted can be very effective.

When considering the sink rate, it's important to understand how fish catch their prey. Species that feed on the bottom are said to have "inferior" mouths—located near the bottom of the head. While they will occasionally take food in the water column, their mouths are designed to catch prey on or very close to the bottom. Examples of species with inferior mouths are redfish (channel bass) and bonefish. The opposite is true of tarpon and striped bass, which have mouths located in the middle of the head. These fish are better adapted to catching their food either in the water column or on the surface. Bottom feeders rarely take anything from the surface. When you are seeking these fish, weight your fly so that on the retrieve it will descend quickly to or near the bottom. And remember that fish that are not bottom feeders will rarely descend in the water column to take your fly. They will rise to it but almost never drop down to get it. This, of course, means that the sink rate is critical: The fly should ride in the water column either at the cruise level of the fish or higher.

Many factors go into selecting a fly with the correct sink rate. Obviously you can add weight to a fly to make it sink. However, the type of weight, how much is secured to the fly, the shape of the added weight, and its location on the hook are all important in determining how the fly sinks. For years the most common method of sinking a fly has been the use of lead fuse wire wrapped on the hook shank. Lead wire can be obtained in four sizes—½, 1, 2, and 3—from many fly shops. While the wires vary a little, size ½ has an approximate diameter of 0.008 inch, while the larger size 3 fuse has an approximate diameter of 0.03 inch. By wrapping the same fly pattern with different sizes of lead wire or varying the turns of the fuse wire on the hook shank, you can alter the sink rate.

Many fly tiers do not realize that a hook rides with its point down because of the weight of the bend. If the lead wire you wrap around the hook shank weighs more than the portion of the hook that is its bend, then the point will ride up because the shank is now heavier than the bend. This permits you to tie fly patterns on a straight hook that you can crawl on the bottom to reduce snagging.

Eyes

Many underwater fly patterns are tied without any type of eye. But for certain situations, eyes can make the difference between having fish strike your offering and seeing them ignore it. There are some baitfish in the sea, for example, that have developed a false eye pattern on the rear of their bodies. This is just coloration, but it appears to be a huge eye. If such a baitfish is facing south and a predator moves in for the capture, it will think the baitfish is going to flee northward because of this false eye. Instead, the baitfish flees south. This is just one instance where you'll need to duplicate an eye pattern.

There is no doubt that just before striking a smaller species, gamefish often concentrate on the eye of their prey. It is like a target or bull's-eye to the predator. Repeated experiments have convinced me that in clear water it is often not only those fly patterns with eyes, but those with *enlarged* eyes, that will draw more interest and strikes from predatory fish. For instance, I have tied two similar flies—but with different-sized eyes—and fished them during the same tidal phase. Almost always the fly with the larger eyes drew more strikes.

There are many kinds of eyes. One that has gained much popularity in the past few years is the lead eye, which looks like a dumbbell. Lead eyes come in six sizes, as shown in the table below.

Lead Eyes

Weight	Diameter
$\frac{1}{100}$ oz.	$\frac{4}{32}$"
$\frac{1}{50}$ oz.	$\frac{5}{32}$"
$\frac{1}{36}$ oz.	$\frac{3}{16}$"
$\frac{1}{24}$ oz.	$\frac{7}{32}$"
$\frac{1}{18}$ oz.	$\frac{1}{4}$"
$\frac{1}{10}$ oz.	$\frac{9}{32}$"

For bonefish, I generally prefer the one-fiftieth- or one-thirty-sixth-ounce lead eyes. For permit, and when I am bonefishing in water more than two feet deep, I use the one-twenty-fourth-ounce lead eyes. For most inshore fishing, such as for barramundi, striped bass, snook, seatrout, or threadfin salmon along a mangrove-lined shoreline, I suggest the one-thirty-sixth- or one-twenty-fourth-ounce lead eyes. The eighteenth- and tenth-ounce are heavy and require the use of a 9-weight or heavier rod to cast easily. These two eyes, the heaviest manufactured, are superb when you want to drive a fly deep in the water column, such as in channels or when fishing a reef. They are also effective when you are offshore and need to get your fly down quickly, before the fish leave the area.

Some fishermen are now using metallic eyes instead of lead. Brass and most of the similar metals weigh about 65 percent as much as the same-sized lead eye. While they will not sink as quickly for the same size, this is not necessarily a liability. Brass eyes are larger in diameter than lead eyes for the same weight, so you can place larger eyes on your fly and still not have too much weight. In shallow water, brass eyes can often be a better choice than lead of the same diameter.

Bead-chain eyes were the first weighted eyes used on flies and remain popular. They will not sink as quickly as lead or brass, so they allow you to attach rather large eyes that really are not very heavy. Bead chain is manufactured in four sizes:

Bead-Chain Eyes

Size	Diameter
3	$\frac{3}{32}$"
6	$\frac{1}{8}$"
10	$\frac{3}{16}$"
13	$\frac{1}{4}$"

Bead chain can be purchased in a brass or silver finish, and a few fly shops offer it in stainless steel.

One of the advantages of eyes is that they enable the fly to create more sound waves in the water. When waters are dirty from mud or silt, or the light level is low such as near or after dark, eyes may draw more strikes. Larger protruding eyes will, when the fly is retrieved, create sound waves that radiate out from the head, alerting nearby fish to the fly's movement. This is a particular advantage of bead-chain eyes. A very large chain will create considerable sound waves yet not sink too rapidly in the water column.

It is a simple matter to attach eyes to your flies, even if you do not know how to tie. Today most fly shops sell packets of Mylar eyes in different sizes and color combinations. These eyes have a sticky glue on the back; you just press them onto your fly pattern. They come in sizes ranging from one-eighth to one-twelfth of an inch in diameter. Because the eyes are printed on brilliant Mylar and often in highly contrasting colors, they really stand out on a pattern. If you want to position them on flies you already own, press them in place, then coat them with either several applications of head cement or a thin layer of five-minute epoxy.

Of course, the main reason for using lead, brass, or bead-chain eyes is to make the fly sink faster. And the faster the fly needs to sink, the heavier the eyes you need, with lead eyes being the best choice. The major reason that Crazy Charlies work so well is that they dive fast, permitting you to fish deeper in the water column. Another reason why weighted flies are often productive is their ability to affect the action of a fly. If the eyes are located near the head of the pattern, each time you stop your retrieve they will cause the fly to dip downward. This gives an up-and-down motion to the fly, much like that of the leadhead jig used on spinning tackle.

Fly Selection and Variations

You can fish successfully in most salt water with just six basic flies: a popping bug, Surf Candy, crab fly, Clouser Minnow, Bend-Back, and Lefty's Deceiver. If you are new to saltwater fly fishing, you may know some of these patterns by a host of other names, because many people have slightly altered an original and renamed it. But most fishermen are familiar with the original patterns, and you should have no problem finding out where to buy these flies or how to tie them.

The popping bug is an essential fly if you want to attract larger fish, such as cobia and amberjacks. These fish rarely take a streamer; they want something big. The popper is designed to create a disturbance on the surface of the water and suggest something much larger than the actual fly. It resembles an ocean creature that is helpless and unable to escape—a feature that few predators can ignore.

Popping bugs can be made from a host of materials, but cork, balsa wood, and closed-cell foam are the most popular. Several design factors can make this device easier to cast and more effective as a fly. The hook should be located at the base of the bug so that it does not dive on a backcast. This allows it to pop better, too. Many popping bugs have a cupped face, but I believe that if a hook is positioned at the base of the body and the face is slanted forward, the bug will make plenty of noise, and it will lift from the water more easily. Fluffy tails with protruding material drastically increase air resistance, which makes casting difficult. The best bugs have sleek tails so they don't foul when you cast them.

You will need at least two sizes of poppers. The smaller one should have a face diameter of about half an inch. The body can be from three-quarters of an inch to an inch and a quarter in length. A long shank also aids in hookups on any popping bug. And the tail should be attached so it does not tangle on a cast. This is a workhorse bug that you will use for snook, barramundi, bluefish, dolphin, striped bass, or almost any saltwater species that will take a fly. You will need the large popping bug only occasionally, when you want to interest fish that look for a big offering. A bug with a face about three-quarters of an inch in diameter is sufficient to make all the noise required. I do not believe color is important to the fish; I prefer bright-colored bugs simply because I can see them better.

The basic popping bug that for decades has been used successfully in salt water is generally referred to as the Gallasch Popper. It is named in honor of Bill Gallasch, who popularized it. This bug, usually dressed on a long-shank hook in sizes from 1 to 3/0, is effective all over the world. It casts well, fish like it, and it hooks well, too.

Bob's Banger is another great bug in salt water, and many other people have put their names on variations of this bug. The Banger makes a lot of noise—although in most saltwater conditions an increase in noise usually does not frighten fish. It is also sometimes a little difficult to lift from the water, because the hook is centered in the body. The Banger is constructed a bit differently from most other popping bugs. Long bucktail is usually attached to the hook, then the remainder of the shank is wrapped with Cactus Chenille or plain chenille. A hole is made in a closed-cell foam rod by heating a wire and searing through the center. While not necessary, the outer part of the foam body can be wrapped with colored reflective tape. The hook is inserted through the body and the fly is tied on. Through different body diameters, body colors, and tail colors, you can vary the noise and appearance of this bug.

The Offshore Popper is a very large bug. Including the feathers or hair, it may be as long as seven inches, with a face diameter of an inch or more. It is generally made from Ethafoam, so it is rather easy to cast on a 10-weight or heavier rod. The size, bulk, and noise of this bug cause it to attract large striped bass, cobia, dolphin, and a host of other saltwater species that want "groceries," not a sample.

The Billfish Popper is a specialty fly designed to catch billfish, although it will interest many offshore species. Construct a large streamer fly, usually a big Lefty's Deceiver (see below) type. Then make a soft foam head about three-quarters of an inch in diameter the way you would the body of a Bob's Banger. Force the foam head over the streamer fly. Experience in billfishing has taught me that you must secure the foam head to the streamer. When a fish grabs the fly and runs, a foam head that is not tied in will slide up the leader during the fish fight. Twice I have had smaller, sharp-toothed fish bite the foam head and leader—losing me a catch.

Bob Popovics, perhaps the most innovative fly tier in the world today, developed the Surf Candy—a durable fly that performs best when used as an imitation of a small sleek baitfish. It is one of the best ways to approximate a small meal for a predatory fish. The original Surf Candy's

TYING INSTRUCTIONS FOR ALBRIGHT SPECIAL

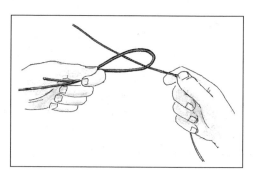

Bend a loop in the tag end of the heavier line or mono. Insert ten inches of the tag end of the lighter line through the loop and grip it with your left thumb and forefinger.

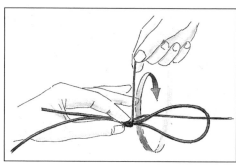

Wrap the tag end of the lighter line from left to right ten to twelve times over the two strands of the loop and the standing line of the lighter line. Wrap each loop closely to the last, carefully covering the wraps with your thumb and forefinger.

Insert the tag end through the loop so that it exists the loop through the same side that it entered. Hold the wraps with the left thumb and forefinger and pull the standing line.

Push the wraps toward the loop as you pull on the standing line. Be careful not to push the wraps over the end of the loop. You can use a pair of pliers to pull the standing line of the smaller line.

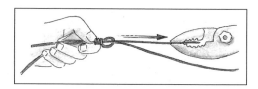

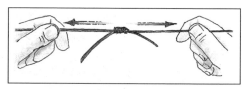

Pull on the standing lines of both the heavier and the lighter lines until the knot tightens.

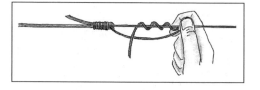

Loop the tag end of the smaller line over its standing line, then make three wraps as shown.

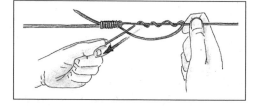

Pull on the tag end

Trim the tag ends of both lines.

forward body was coated in epoxy, but Bob found that flexible silicone, such as bathroom tub sealer, gave the fly more action. It is also softer, so when a fish strikes, it is more likely to hang on.

This terrific fly is generally tied in small sizes, most not exceeding four inches. The variations on this pattern are almost limitless, and many imitators have their name on this fly. For example, you can build the wing with either bucktail or translucent synthetic material. By matching the color of the local baitfish, you can create one of the finest flies known for salt water.

I have found crabs in salt water virtually everywhere in the world. They represent a lot of food to predators, and for species such as permit, tarpon, and striped bass there is no better bait. I recall once fishing with

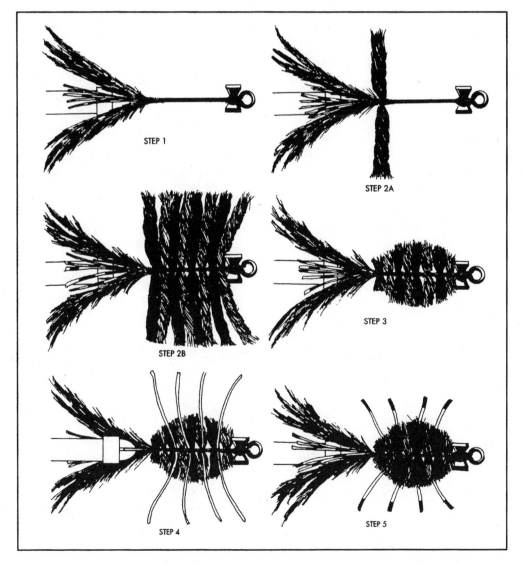

Tying Instructions for Del Brown's Permit Fly.

Del Brown, who has caught more than five hundred permit on crab flies. We found permit sitting just under the surface, obviously rising and taking something close to the top. Del drifted several crab patterns past feeding permit, and they ignored them. But the fifty-pound tarpon lying below and behind the permit rose eagerly to the flies. Because there was no shock tippet on his line, it quickly broke the leader. But the lesson was valuable.

You will find that most predatory fish will take crabs large and small, so fish with patterns you can cast easily. Crab imitations should range from half an inch to as large as an inch and a half wide. Bring along a selection of crabs that float, some that barely sink, and others that are heavily weighted to sink fast. In New England tiny crabs often hatch in prodigious numbers during late spring on a high tide. A floating crab fly the size of a dime, fished drag-fee in a current like a dry fly, will often be rewarding. For permit, tarpon, and even large stripers, a crab the size of a quarter is really the biggest you'll need.

One of the important factors for a crab pattern is that the weight must be concentrated at one end of the fly, usually near the eye. The reason becomes apparent when you realize how a crab flees from a predator: It dives at an angle, and so should your pattern. As for the crab's legs, rubber bands are generally used to imitate them. They work fine, but I prefer to use the strands of a skirt found on a largemouth bass spinnerbait. These inexpensive skirts can be purchased in many shops and through mail-order catalogs.

To float a crab imitation well, add a dry-fly paste floatant to an unweighted pattern. Since a crab fly is rarely retrieved any distance, I don't

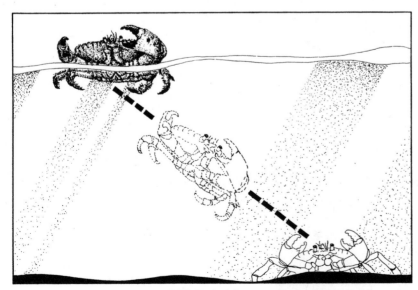
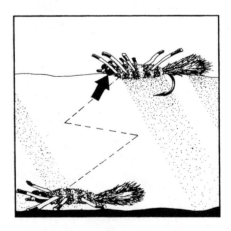

LEFT: Typical descent of crab. RIGHT: Del Brown's permit fly descending to bottom at steep angle.

use weed guards on mine. If you are forced to fish where they are a lot of weeds or hook-snagging coral, then a monofilament guard is helpful. Most of the time the best presentation is to let the crab simply dead-drift with the tide. Few fly rodders realize how effective this fly is in all salt waters.

The Bend-Back was developed in the latter part of the nineteenth century for bass fishing in the vegetation-cluttered lakes of the South. It is virtually weedless if tied correctly and fished properly, and it has produced better for me than any other weedless fly. I prefer Bend-Backs that have no body material on the hook shank, because they swim better, they are easier to cast, and body material often erodes if it is snagged on the bottom. You'll get more hookups if you tie the Bend-Back on 2X or 3X hooks; regular-length shanks often miss on the strike.

If I want to fish this fly deep, such as over an oyster bar, I wrap lead wire around the shank just in front of the bend and coat it with epoxy to prevent the wire from detaching. When properly constructed, the wing hides all or most of the hook, and the fly swims with the point up. If you throw the fly into the trees along water or up on a shoreline, you can gently tease the fly until it travels down the branches or along the shore and drops into the water. It can be fished in the densest weeds without snagging. It is my favorite fly for night fishing at pilings and boat docks, which have many ropes, wires, nails, and other snags. By placing a cone-head at the front, this fly can be fished deep with little fear of snagging.

Some of the best Bend-Backs are tied to represent baitfish. But attractor patterns can also work well. One of the best is a bright yellow or white underwing, with a little flash, and a chartreuse top wing.

The Clouser Minnow is the single most effective underwater fly developed in the last thirty years, and the best one I have ever fished. In fact, the Clouser is a favorite of fly fishermen throughout the world for both freshwater and saltwater fishing. I have caught almost ninety species of fish with this fly, from a five-ounce brook trout to a six-foot shark. In salt water the Clouser has consistently been one of the best flies for redfish; it is also good for albacore, striped bass, bonito, snook, ladyfish, barramundi, threadfin salmon, dolphin, bluefish, jack crevalle, and many others.

In 1989 I walked into Bob Clouser's Fly Shop in Middletown, Pennsylvania, less than two miles from Three Mile Island. Though Bob services trout fishermen in the region, the huge Susquehanna River less than a mile from his shop is also one of the best places in the country to try fishing for the coveted smallmouth bass. While we talked, Bob handed me several crude-looking flies that at first glance I thought were unfinished. "Lefty, I fished these yesterday and they really knocked the bass," he said. "Give 'em a try while you're out there today." I did, and the rest is fishing history.

One of the important qualities of this unique pattern is that it does a superb job of representing a baitfish. When you look at this kind of creature in the water, you do not see the gills, all the side markings, or any great detail. Instead, you see a *suggestion* of a baitfish, and often you see the eye. That is exactly what the Clouser Deep Minnow (or simply "Clouser") shows you if you tie it properly. It is important not to overdress the pattern. What you want is a fly that actually looks a bit unfinished, so that when it is brought back underwater it will offer that suggestion of baitfish, and also accentuate the lead eyes. The minimal dressing helps the fly get down deeper, too.

The Clouser can be tied sparsely, dressed with bulk, made to sink fast or slow depending on the weighted eyes used, and tied in lengths from one inch to twelve inches. Perhaps more than a third of the species I have taken were hooked on a fly with a white or yellow underwing and a chartreuse upper wing. In fact, some professional guides say, "If it ain't chartreuse, it ain't no use." If you use Clousers, be sure to carry a few of this color. In clear water, Clousers tied with translucent synthetics seem to outperform those tied with less translucent materials, such as bucktail. Clousers are often more effective if several different colors of flash material are integrated into the wing.

The Clouser Minnow and Lefty's Deceiver are the two most frequently used saltwater flies around the world. The Lefty's Deceiver has been used for decades to catch everything from billfish to small estuary species. As with the Woolly Bugger and other flies I have described, you can change the size and color combinations, add or delete weight, make it long or short, and use flash material in the wing or use no flash material at all. A host of imitators have placed their name on this fly, but the basic pattern remains the same.

I developed this fly in the late 1950s to catch striped bass in the Chesapeake Bay. I knew that a good underwater fly needs several characteristics to score well. It should be easy to cast long distances into the wind. It should have a baitfish shape and appeal to predatory fish. And its materials should not foul during the cast. According to most fishermen, the Lefty's Deceiver meets all of these criteria, and that's why it has become so popular.

Tied sparsely, a Lefty's Deceiver imitates a sleek baitfish such as a sand eel, or it can have lead wire on the shank and be tied bulky, such as the well-known Grocery Fly in New England. One of the best variations over the years is all-black with a red throat of Mylar and some purple Mylar flash on the sides.

Unfortunately, many people tie this fly incorrectly. Like the Clouser, it really isn't a precise pattern; it's more a style or a method of tying a fly. Unless you follow the proper procedure when you tie it, the fly loses some of its fish-catching appeal. Here are four of the most common mistakes that tiers make when they attempt to create the Lefty's Deceiver:

1. Don't use saddle hackles that are too thin when a wide profile is required. Wide hackles or neck hackles will generally work better.

2. Make sure you are using enough saddle hackles. A minimum of six (three pairs per side) is usually required, unless a very thin pattern is needed. With larger flies (Nos. 1/0 and bigger), four or even five pairs of saddles should be used—for a total of eight or ten saddles.

3. Many people tie the fly so that the saddles flare out from the hook shank. The original Deceiver was supposed to represent a baitfish, not a swimming frog. The neck feathers or saddles on each side are intended to flare inward. This more accurately represents the motion of a swimming baitfish. If the feathers are tied so that they flare outward, however, the fly does have a frog's kicking, swimming motion, which fish often find irresistible. I tie it both ways, depending on what I want the fly to do. Whichever way you choose, a correctly tied Lefty's Deceiver lifted from the water for the backcast will travel through the air like a sleek knife blade.

4. The collar of bucktail (or whatever substitute is used) should extend behind the hook bend. Too many tiers make this collar too short, which gives the fly the outline of a squid and can allow the wing to foul on the hook during a cast. If the collar is carried well in back of the bend, however, then the fly has the shape of a baitfish. The collar also forms little currents as the fly is retrieved. These "mini eddies" roll off the collar and move back along the saddles, giving the fly a swimming motion. Finally, the collar prevents the wing from underwrapping the hook on your cast.

A great fly called a Whistler, originated by Dan Blanton, is another superior pattern for a host of saltwater species. It is certainly one of the best flies for fishing deep or in dirty water. The bulky head and large bead-chain eyes push water, sending out sound vibrations that help fish locate the fly. The original pattern was tied very bulky with some weight, usually lead wire, added to the hook shank. But Dan also ties it unweighted so that it swims high in the water column. It has produced well for me in both fresh- and saltwater fishing.

The Seaducer is a very old pattern, dating back to the nineteenth century, and was first developed as a bass fly. It has one characteristic that few other patterns possess: It can sink so slowly in the water column that it seems to be suspended. The long, fluffy hackles that form the tail or wing, and the palmered hackles at the front, act like outriggers so the fly can be fished slowly in inches of water without snagging bottom. Because the fly is essentially nothing more than a hook with some feathers on it, it falls to the surface like a thistle. It can be dropped close to wary fish without frightening them. Like the Clouser Minnow and Lefty's Deceiver, this fly can be made short, long, and in a variety of color combinations.

The Sar-Mul-Mac is a superb baitfish imitation, also developed by Dan Blanton. Its name stands for "Sardine, Mullet, Mackerel." Like the Clouser Minnow and Lefty's Deceiver, it can be tied in various lengths and color combinations to match the local baitfish. The yellow and the pearl patterns seem to produce well. Some of the versions are tied with heavily weighted lead eyes; others are done in the conventional way with large glass eyes. It is a great fly all over the world.

Bonefish

The one fish species that is an exception to the patterns outlined above is the bonefish. Scientists have proven that bonefish will eat almost anything they can catch and get down their throats. This means a host of flies are effective, but you only need a very few patterns to successfully fish for bones. (Still, if you carry a lot of others, they will probably work, too.)

As I noted before, most of the time you should match the color of the bottom with your fly. On dark turtle grass, a darker fly is advisable. Conversely, on a lighter bottom, choose a lighter fly. When you are going for small bonefish, from half a pound to three pounds, I suggest using a No. 4 fly, with a few No. 6s for very calm conditions. For bonefish larger than three pounds, I rarely use a fly smaller than No. 4. If the bonefish are averaging four pounds or larger, my best success has been with No. 2 hooks.

There are five bonefish patterns that will serve you well in most of the world. (Many of them have been described above, but the additional details here are specific to the bonefish.) If I had to fish with only a handful of bonefish flies, I would choose at least two variations on the Clouser Minnow. Both are tied the same way, with a white bucktail underwing and pearl flash material in the middle. The upper wing of one version should use chartreuse bucktail, and the other could use light tan bucktail, about the color of khaki pants. If you are fishing for very large bonefish, the fly should be about two and a half to three inches long.

Next to the two Clousers, the Gotcha is the hottest fly I have ever used on light-colored bonefish flats. It is essentially a Crazy Charlie with an extended pink nose, which seems to be a trigger for bonefish. I am never without a few of these in my tackle box.

The Tailing Bend-Back fly is essential because bonefish will frequently go into water so shallow that their backs may actually poke above the surface. The two requirements for fishing a Tailing Bend-Back in these conditions are that the fly must land with a minimum of noise, and it must be fished over a rocky bottom. I recommend a fly that has no body material and a rather full wing. This results in a silent splashdown and causes the fly to ride just below the surface.

The Snapping Shrimp pattern is reliable when fished where the bottom is dark. I often tie the pattern as a Bend-Back style if I will be fishing turtle grass so it can slither through the vegetation. It resembles a brownish snapping shrimp with an orange claw. It is my favorite for water with a dark bottom.

My bonefish box always has a few crab flies in it. They can be made from a host of materials. The most effective patterns are usually created from a soft material, such as rug yarn, trimmed sheep's wool, or Furry Foam. The crab fly is also a superior pattern for permit, often found on the same flats as bones. If the bottom is very light in color, a cream-colored crab often produces well. For most situations, a crab that is dark—usually a greenish color—is preferred. The bonefish crab fly should be lightly weighted; metallic eyes will often be used for this purpose. I have had the best results if the weight is concentrated on one end.

Saltwater anglers have been using rabbit-fur strips in recent years on their flies for tarpon and bonefish. These are often referred to as Tarpon Bunnies or Bonefish Bunnies. The wing of a Tarpon Bunny is often a combination of a strip of rabbit fur and saddle or neck feathers. Usually the extended wing behind the fly is made of rabbit. For tarpon, a fly that does not sink too fast but rather suspends or slowly sinks in the water column is often the best. The Tarpon Bunny can be thrown on a floating or slow-sinking fly line well in front of an oncoming tarpon, and because of the fly's slow sink rate you can delay your retrieve until the fish is near your offering. This is a very effective technique.

The wing of a Bonefish Bunny is almost always made entirely of rabbit fur. Generally a little weight has to be added for the fly to sink quickly. Some anglers will wrap the shank with size 1 (0.013 inch) lead fuse wire to sink it. Others use one-fiftieth-ounce lead eyes to drive the fly quickly to the bottom. Since rabbit-fur flies undulate very well at slow speeds, it is important not to hurry your retrieve. In almost all situations, if you want to get the most action from rabbit-fur flies, a slow retrieve is best.

5

FRESHWATER FLIES

Regardless of the other tackle we use, we must offer a fly that will be acceptable to the fish we are pursuing. This fly must be tailored to the particular species, and frequently it must be matched to its habitat as well. Generally flies are designed to imitate food that predatory fish feed upon—although not always. Those not designed to imitate a food source exactly are called attractor flies. Attractor patterns do not resemble anything living in the water, but experience shows that fish really strike such flies. Just about any predatory fish is at some time susceptible to them. Attractor flies may be tied with vivid fluorescent colors and may be of radical shapes. Another very different fly type has no special name or designation, so I call it a creature imitation. Such a fly does not fall into any of the categories mentioned later, but it may imitate a food source such as crayfish in fresh water.

For most species we use either a surface fly or one that swims underwater. But for trout we have developed a number of specialty flies that range from those used on top to those that creep and crawl along the bottom. These special flies have names to designate their unique design and purpose. Dry flies fall into two categories: imitators and attractor or exciter types. It is worth noting that truly exact imitations are often not effective. In fact, the more closely the pattern resembles the insect, generally the less effective it is. The best patterns seem to be those that more or less imitate the insect fairly well—but do not look exactly like it. There are some accomplished tiers who can now create flies in their vises that look as if they could crawl, fly, mate, and eat. Such flies are certainly to be admired as works of art, but they generally do not fish well.

There are more than a dozen special designs for dry flies used in trout fishing. Among the most popular are the conventional dry, terrestrial,

An assortment of dry flies.

thorax, Paradun, parachute, Griffith's Gnat style, No-Hackle, spinner, Renegade or Fore-and-Aft style, skater, Variant, caddis, and stonefly.

Conventional Dry Flies

These are the common patterns that most of us use, such as the standard Adams and Light Cahill. The tail is usually of hackle tips, although I really like Microfibetts, which are more durable and stronger than hackle tips. They come in different colors to match the patterns being tied. One important factor when tying flies is not to clump the hackle tips together for the tail. This will cause the rear of the fly to drown. Capillary action sucks water up along the bunched strands, much as a teenager would draw a milk shake through a straw. By spreading the

Some methods of improving the fisherman's ability to see the fly on the water (left to right): a Krystal Flash wing, a brightly dyed feather, orange paint, and a bright tuft of yarn.

fiber tips, you eliminate this problem, and the spread fibers also give the fly better stability as it floats on the surface.

On conventional dry flies the body is constructed of either synthetic or natural furs. The wings are spread at about a thirty-degree angle on top of the fly, and they are usually made from either feathers or hair. Many anglers are also discovering that fluorescent polypropylene yarns

Small dry flies are hard to see; the smaller they are, and the older the angler, the more difficult this becomes. If you tie your own, you can make flies much easier to see by forming the wing from a strand or two of Krystal Flash. This material of twisted Mylar reflects light at all angles.

make fine wings—and are much easier to see. On overcast days or when I am fishing where there is a lot of glare on the water, I have great success with pure black poly wings. An even more visible wing can be made from pearl Krystal Flash. Even in my late years I can see a parachute dry fly with such a wing at least thirty feet away.

On the conventional dry fly, two or three quality hackles are wound around the shank to support the fly above the surface. The fly is then tied in two styles. One is very sparse and with a minimum of body materials. This is called a Catskill tie, since it originated in that area. The other is generally referred to as a western tie of the conventional dry fly. Such flies are usually tied with nearly twice the dressings. They float much better and are more durable. But on calm waters, where wary fish can take a long look at the fly, the sparsely dressed Catskill pattern may have advantages. The western tie is better on heavy or turbulent waters, where the more lightly dressed pattern would probably soon sink. The conventional dry is used more than any other type of dry fly. It has served generations of anglers and belongs in everyone's tackle box.

Parachute

The parachute dry fly is rapidly becoming popular. In waters that are hard fished, where the trout are wary, a parachute fly that sits on the water in a more realistic manner than a conventional dry fly will almost always catch more fish. If you are experiencing refusals on a conventional dry fly, switch to a parachute style. One of the most important tips for tiers is that when you wind the parachute hackle, each turn should be made beneath the previous one. Spiraling each turn on top of the last makes for a poorly dressed fly.

The parachute fly is exactly like a conventional dry fly, except that the hackle is wound horizontally around the base of the wing, rather than being wound vertically around the hook shank in the wing area. It

On the left side is a conventional Catskill-style dry fly, which rides up well off the water on its hackle tips. In rough water this is okay, but a natural mayfly is normally flat, with its body in contact with the surface. In calm water, trout take a longer, better look at your offering and will often refuse a conventional dry that sits up unnaturally high. But the parachute-style fly (middle) and the Paradun (right) present a more realistic appearance. Under tough conditions there latter two styles usually outfish conventional drys.

has several advantages. First, you don't need the highest-grade hackle to construct the fly. A Grade #3 dry-fly neck will do about as well as a Grade #1, which will cost much more. The fact that the hackles radiate outward from the hook means they will better support the fly on the surface. I personally feel that parachute flies give a more realistic impression of an insect to the fish that views the fly, since the hackles are in the same position as the insect's legs. And when tied with brightly colored hackles, these flies are easier to see on the float. A final advantage is that in rough water, a parachute-hackled dry fly will float longer and better than a conventional one.

The upside-down dry fly is a variation on the parachute fly. John Goddard, the English writer, whom I regard as one of the best trout fishermen I have ever accompanied, gave me some of these to try. Under very difficult conditions, I firmly believe that an upside-down fly will outfish either a conventional or parachute dry fly. The upside-down fly is tied with the hook point reversed, so it rides upright and out of the water. Standard dries often have the hook protruding below the surface and are easily visible to the trout. Upside-down flies have the hook well above the surface and pretty much hidden by the fly body. Upside-down flies are also tied in the parachute style. If you encounter some difficult fish, especially on calm water, you may do better with an upside-down fly. It is a little difficult for me to tie, and I find that I need a gallows tool for my vise to tie this one. But the results are worth the effort.

Thorax

Thorax-tied dry flies are now becoming popular. They were first developed in the 1930s by Dr. Edgar Burke, and more recently by Vince Marinaro. Thorax dry flies are also more effective in instances where the fishing is difficult. In all my years as a trout fisherman, I have seen only a very few mayflies floating with their wings spread apart, as is so common on most imitation dry flies we tie. Instead, the wings on a natural mayfly as it floats along are clumped together as a single unit. Thorax ties are the same—a single wing protrudes above the surface. The hackle supporting the body can be attached in several ways, although I prefer the parachute style. A parachute tie on a thorax dry fly is one of my favorites when fishing difficult waters.

Paradun

The Paradun is a variation on the Haystack, a favorite dry-fly variation of the northeastern United States. The Haystack has a tail spread

The drawing shows the three major types of fly patterns that imitate mayflies and caddisflies.

Top row, left to right: Paradun, Renegade or Fore-And-Aft, Variant, conventional Catskill-style dry fly, parachute tie, and thorax.

Bottom row, left to right: Elkhair Caddis, Goddard Caddis, spider, Griffith's Gnat, and spinner imitation.

wide to help support the fly, while the wing consists of a bunch of deer hair that is raised in a fan shape at the front of the body. The Comparadun is an offshoot of this fly, developed by Al Caucci. The Comparadun has two tails of two strands that are spread in a wide **V** to give the fly support. The body is made of material (often natural, but sometimes synthetic) that floats well. The wing is usually of deer hair and is positioned just forward of the center of the body, much in the same style as a thorax tie.

Griffith's Gnat

The Griffith's Gnat is a unique fly—and it belongs in every serious fisherman's box. There are times when trout will be sipping on minuscule flies, often difficult even to see. While minute imitations that exactly match these emerging insects will certainly do well, the Griffith's Gnat is usually just as effective. Best of all, almost anyone can tie this pattern.

I use a No. 16 though 24 light-wire dry-fly hook. Attach one of the smallest hackles to the rear of the hook shank (the favorite color is a grizzly hackle, from a good dry-fly neck), and then simply spiral the feather forward, palmer fashion. Tie it off and that's it! To the tier it resembles a minute caterpillar. But to the trout it must appear as one of the small emerging insects. It simply looks buggy. I can't tell you how many times this fly has saved the day for me when trout were sipping on extremely small stuff. Another method of tying the Griffith's Gnat is to first tie an ultrasmall tip from a peacock herl on the hook shank, wrap it forward to the eye, then palmer a grizzly hackle down the shank. I urge you to carry at least a dozen of these in various sizes, ranging from No. 16 to No. 24. If you clip the hackles from the bottom of this fly, it makes a great imitation of a midge or an emerger.

Palmered Fly

Similar to the Griffith's Gnat is the palmered fly, which used to be fished a great deal but is disregarded by modern fly anglers. In fact, it may have been the design of the very first of all dry flies. Nothing in dry-fly construction could be simpler. A good dry-fly hackle is attached at the rear of the hook and spiraled forward to resemble a caterpillar without a body. With only a hook to support, this fly floats extremely well. Some people use two feathers. The first is spiraled forward to within about an eighth of an inch of the hook eye. Then a much brighter feather, usually white, is wrapped around the pattern at the front. This is sometimes called a Bivisible; the white front collar certainly aids the

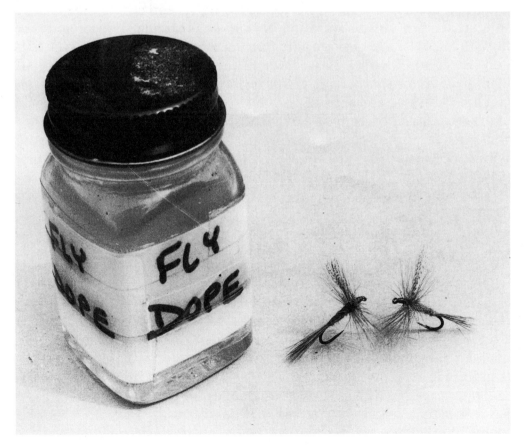

Dress your flies well before the season so you don't have to do it on the stream.

angler in seeing the fly during the drift. The palmered concept can be added to a number of dry flies to aid in the float, and the many radiating hackle points also give the impression of an insect moving its legs.

Fore-and-Aft

This is an old pattern, quite similar to the palmered fly. Instead of one feather being palmered the full length of the hook shank, the Fore-and-Aft is made with two feathers. One is wound around the hook at the back, then a body material is wrapped around the center portion, followed by another feather spiraled forward to the hook eye. The Renegade, which Dennis Bitten, an avid Idaho Falls angler, has proven many times to me to be a deadly trout fly, is a good example of the Fore-and-Aft. It looks like a beginner's tying effort, but for some uncanny reason this fly really works.

No-Hackle

Doug Swisher and Carl Richards have made famous this rather old pattern. It is a fly with a body and splayed wings and stiff tail feathers to support the fly, but no spiraling hackle, as is standard on most other flies. If you carefully observe a floating mayfly, you will see that the natural insect sits with its body on or in the surface film. It does not sit high above the surface, as is characteristic of so many dry flies. When you are fishing to smart trout, especially in slow water, the No-Hackle offers a much better imitation of a drifting insect. At times it will score when few other patterns are successful. I would only add one caution: I have found that these flies are especially difficult to tie (at least for me) if you want them to float properly. This is one of the few flies that I consistently buy at a tackle shop.

Spiders and Skaters

These are also flies that many anglers don't use often, but I find them at times to be the most exciting of all dry flies to fish. I always carry a few in my fly vest. Spiders and skaters are simple flies, usually on a short-shank hook, with large, stiff dry-fly hackles wrapped around the hook a short distance. The way to fish them to draw the most excitement is to skate them over the surface. I suppose that they imitate an insect trying to lift off the water. Dress the leader and the fly with a good paste floatant. Cast slightly across and downstream. Then hold the rod high and allow the water to push the fly line, leader, and fly sideways

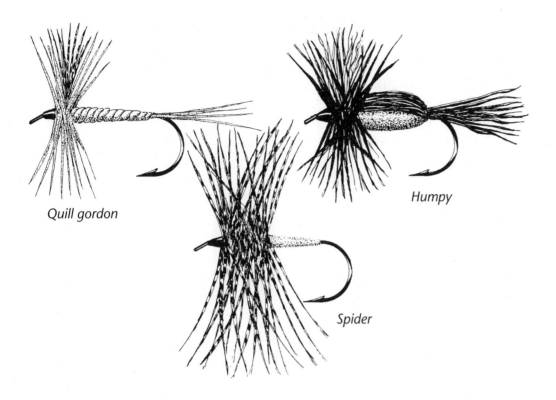

Quill gordon

Humpy

Spider

and downcurrent. This causes the fly to skitter on its hackle tips across the surface. By waving the rod tip back and forth while the fly is skating across the surface, you can add extra action to the fly and also manipulate it in front of a hungry trout.

Variant

This dry fly is different from a conventional dry fly in that the hackle supporting it is two or three times larger. And rarely are wings attached to a Variant dry fly. There seems to be no logical reason why this fly is so effective. The fact that it is a very old pattern may explain why it is rarely used anymore. Even so, it is a fly that deserves to be in anyone's box for those situations when other dry flies are not doing the job. Years ago we all had one problem in tying this fly: finding large enough hackle that was properly stiff. Today superior dry-fly necks are commonplace, and this problem no longer exists.

Spinner

There are many other specialty dry flies, including the spinner. After mayflies have mated and the eggs have been deposited on or below the surface, the insects die and fall to the water with their wings out-stretched. In fact, some people refer to the insects at this stage of the hatch as spentwings. The surface at times can be covered with their bodies, and trout (often big ones) will go on a feeding binge—on which anglers can capitalize.

Many fishermen tie the outstretched wings with hackle tips. But careful observation will show that such wings mat the fibers against the quill and usually don't give any representation of a spentwing. Hair-wings will do a better job, but they are also very bulky, and individual "spines" of hair don't do as good a job of representing the outstretched wings of the spinner.

George Harvey, an extremely accomplished American trout fisherman, is also a superb and innovative fly tier. George has developed a spinner that has highly realistic wings. Best of all, when dressed this way the fly can be seen for a long distance. Visibility can be a problem when fishing smaller flies that sit flush on the surface. George uses Krystal Flash, the ultrathin strands of twisted Mylar I mentioned earlier. He specifically uses the pearlescent variety, which exactly imitates the coloration of most spinner wings. About six strands are used during the tying procedure. Because the strands are spiraled, no matter the viewing angle you will see the light reflected in the wing. I have been able to make a cast of fifty feet and clearly see a No. 20 spinner floating along

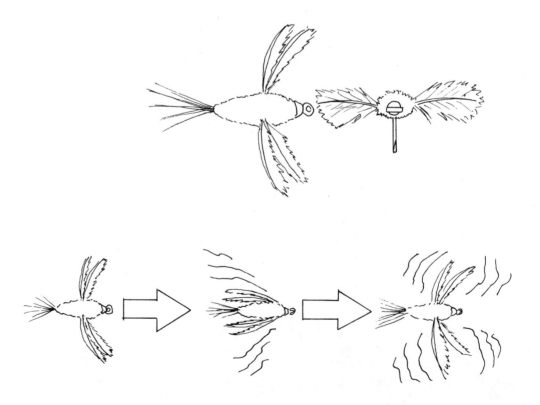

George Harvey night fly.

the water. This is a terrific asset when fish are barely sipping such small insects from the surface and it's hard to detect a take.

Using George's idea, I have for several years been tying all my para-chute-type flies with the Mylar wing instead of conventional materials. It is amazing how much farther and easier you can see even the smallest parachute on the surface.

Terrestrials

Terrestrials are land-based insects that fall into the stream. They offer a unique opportunity for the fly fisherman to attract hungry trout. This family includes leafhoppers, grasshoppers, ants, beetles, and many other kinds of insects that either drop off a bush or tree into the water or are blown or washed onto the surface when they venture too close to the river's edge. The major difference between conventional dry flies and terrestrials is that dry flies sit above the surface, while terrestrials float awash in the surface film. As a result, the terrestrial—and the corresponding fly—presents an entirely different profile to the fish.

When especially large numbers of a particular insect are falling on the surface, the fishing can be frantic. A prime example of this is in late August, especially in the West, when grasshoppers are tossed by strong winds into streams. They represent a real chunk of protein food, and all the trout in a stream eagerly take them.

A head-on view of a standard dry fly (left) and a terrestrial. The standard dry sits high up off the surface, while the terrestrial sits right in the surface film.

Grasshoppers

If I had to choose only seven dry flies for all of my fishing, two of them would be terrestrials: grasshopper and ant imitations. Of all the terrestrials, perhaps the most popular—and certainly one of the most exciting—is the grasshopper. But remember that big grasshoppers do not appear early in the year. So if you are going to fish hoppers when they first emerge, use small ones. I have never found hoppers to be very effective when tied on hooks smaller than No. 10—nor any larger than No. 4. My own experience has taught me that grasshoppers are most effective late in the season. I suppose that is because enough of them have blown or hopped into a river by then that the trout are beginning to recognize them.

Dirt banks that overhang a stream and usually have a lot of grass growing on them are generally called cutbanks. These often lean out over the water, furnishing a "roof" that allows trout to hide underneath and watch for food as it passes by. Such cutbanks bordering grassy fields can deliver some of the best hopper fishing. But I believe most people fish these cutbanks incorrectly. They cast a hopper tight against the bank. This is okay if the fish is holding where there is no overhanging bank. But if the fish is holding underneath such a bank, often it will not see the hopper. The hopper should be fished about a foot off the bank.

Let me explain the logistics. Imagine you are standing at the entrance to a garage beside your home and an airplane flies nearly directly overhead. From the doorway you can look up and clearly see the airplane. Now step back well inside the garage: You will not be able to see that airplane, which is hidden by the roof. The same thing happens to a trout. Should the fish be holding along the edge of a cutbank, it will clearly see a hopper drifting directly overhead. But if the fish is lying well back under the bank, the hopper will be like the plane—and remain unseen. However, if the imitation is cast so that it drifts a foot or so off the bank, or even underneath the overhanging bank, the trout will see it. Because a grasshopper offers a lot of protein, trout will move a considerable distance to take one, where they might ignore a small mayfly following the same path.

I have actually spent some time holding my breath and lying on the bottom of a trout stream while a friend tossed hoppers on the water. Watching them as they drifted overhead, I was struck by one thing. Every hopper I saw always had its legs protruding through the surface. While I have taken many fish on imitations of grasshoppers that had no legs, I now use patterns with legs. I simply feel more confident about the presentation.

There are several methods recommended for fishing a hopper. Some say that you should twitch it occasionally as it drifts along. Others maintain that a typical dry-fly dead drift is best. Yet other experienced anglers say that you should deliberately retrieve the line until the leader tippet is taut, and the current will then draw the hopper across the surface, leaving a tiny V. My personal best results have come from making a cast so that the hopper actually contacts the surface with a good *plop.* I twitch the fly two or three times within the first four feet of the drift, then allow it to dead-drift. I figure that hoppers soon get exhausted and stop struggling. Grasshoppers offer a large portion of food to trout. When they are taking these terrestrials, you can fool even a trophy fish.

Ants

If there is one terrestrial that every angler should carry, it is the ant. Just about anyplace you find trout, you will find ants. And trout seem to go out of their way to take them. In September in many parts of eastern North America, ants will fly in great migrations. If the water's surface is wide, or the wind gets up, millions of these ants will fall to the surface. It creates one of the best trout feeding binges you will ever see. Usually during September in the mid-Atlantic area, the big limestone rivers—

Three flies to carry on days when trout are refusing your offers, or when you can't get a big trout to take your fly, are the Turck's Tarantula (top), the Chernobyl Ant (bottom left), and the Madame X.

the Susquehanna, Potomac, James, and similar waterways—often are subject to millions of migrating ants falling to the surface. Some of the finest surface action of the year occurs at this time—not only for trout but also for smallmouth bass.

Every aficionado of ants has a favorite pattern. Among the most popular is the McMurray Ant, which is composed of two small balsa-wood balls suspended on a superthin piece of monofilament. The balsa wood is colored, and then a few turns of hackle are added to make a very realistic ant. It comes in a variety of sizes and is very effective. It also floats well. Another top-choice ant is one made from closed-cell foam. It's easy and quick to make—and it does catch fish. Ants made from dubbed fur have been around for years. They work well, although they tend not to float as well as some others. My favorite ant pattern is made from deer hair, not clipped, but attached to the hook and pulled forward to make the additional two lumps that form the ant's body. I like this ant because it falls to the water with a detectable *plop* that I think imitates the sound ants make when they tumble from a tree branch to the surface. I fish it in rather large sizes, from No. 10 through 14, rarely smaller. The times when I have been able to convince a reluctant trout into striking have frequently occurred when I switched to an ant.

Most floating ant patterns sit low in the surface film, and they are often hard to see. This is especially true when fishing under trees that shade the water, or early and late in the day. Many years ago I started applying fluorescent paint to my ants so I could see them better when fishing Maryland's Big Hunting Creek, near where I began my fishing career. I felt pretty proud of myself for being what I thought was innovative. Decades later, fishing with George Harvey and Ralph Dougherty, I discovered that they had been painting their ant bodies probably years before it occurred to me. George has even improved on the painting trick by tying, on the top of the ant body, a cut-wing fluorescent-dyed hen saddle feather, which is really visible. If you plan to paint a deer-hair or dubbed-fur ant body, you will need first to coat the surface with head cement before you can establish the bright spot of paint.

There is a special period in dry-fly fishing when the floating ant will outfish every other dry fly. Usually this is in September, but it can vary depending on where you live. Ants take wing and migrate for incredible distances. You will see tiny rings appearing on the surface as fish subtly suck in the ants that have fallen to the water. During intensive migrations, the surface is literally covered with their bodies. Trout and smallmouth bass go wild. Use any floating ant imitation and you will have some of the highest success ratios of casts to hookups that you could imagine.

Even older than the floating ant is the sinking ant pattern. It was one of the early wet flies, recognized as a deadly weapon in the angler's arsenal. Simply wrap the body, usually with brown or black thread, and then coat the thread with clear cement. I prefer to fish it up and across stream, much as you would a nymph. It is particularly effective in slow pools, where the trout can take a prolonged look at the offering. Nos. 12, 14, and 16 do best for me.

Jassids

One of the most popularized of all the terrestrials is the small black jassid—a leafhopper. Charley Fox and Vince Marinaro, who introduced most North American anglers to terrestrial fishing, wrote extensively about this insect. Like the Griffith's Gnat, it often will fool finicky trout sipping on some small insects that I cannot see or identify. In fact, after carrying a few ants and hoppers in my terrestrial box, this would be my third choice.

The jassid is usually tied with a bright jungle cock feather dressed on a No. 18 or 20 hook. The bright feather makes it easy to see. Indeed, it was this feather that gave me the idea of painting the backs of my ants with a bright paint. Jungle cock is now difficult to obtain, but you can make jassids out of many small feathers. Select a pair of very short, small feathers. Coat them with head cement and glue them together. Add a minute bit of dubbed fur to the hook shank, plus two or three spirals of a good, tiny dry-fly hackle, and then lay the wing flat on top of the hook.

Caddisflies

Another dry fly, the caddis does not imitate mayflies. Rather, it imitates the large body of caddisflies that inhabit most trout rivers. As water quality declines in many rivers, mayflies (which need a very clean habitat) are declining. Caddisflies, which can tolerate less pure waters, are consequently on the increase. This means that anglers should become more alert to the possibility of using the caddis dry fly.

The basic difference between a mayfly and caddisfly is that mayflies hold their wings vertically above the water as they float along. Caddisflies fold their wings along the body in the shape of a pup tent, with the wing protruding well behind the body as the fly sits on the surface.

Caddisflies and mayflies do not stand on their legs with their bodies high above the surface—yet many of our imitations do just that. The Catskill-tied fly, for example, is one that is slenderized and appears delicate. But its very light construction causes the body and wing to ride high above the surface. This is an unnatural attitude, which the trout rarely sees. That's why parachutes, Paraduns, and thorax flies are much better weapons for the angler working slower water. These imitations have the body close to or sitting on the surface. In slow, slick water the fish can make a much more careful examination of its prey, and the trout does not have to be in a hurry to take it.

Two of the best imitations of the caddis when fishing in slower water, or when the surface is very slick, are the Goddard Caddis and La-Fontaine's Dancing Caddis. These flies float with the body resting on the surface film—and thus appear more natural.

Caddisflies can be found in many sizes, from those dressed on No. 8 hooks to some so small that a No. 18 or 20 hook is appropriate. Most effective caddisflies are dressed on No. 12 and 18 hooks. However, a mistake that many fairly skilled fly fishermen make is to use imitations that are not small enough. There is often a hatch of very small caddisflies, which some call microcaddis. Always carry a few patterns to match these tiny creatures. I like Gary Borger's imitation, for example. It is simply a little bit of polypropylene wound on a hook for a body, one hackle spiraled forward to help support the fly, and a wing of the same polypropylene laid back along the body.

While caddisflies hatch in many colors, I feel that all you need are dark and light brown, and a few in light gray. With these colors in various sizes you will find that you can handle most caddisfly action. Of all the caddis dry-fly patterns, the most popular (and deservedly so) is one developed by Al Troth called the Elkhair Caddis. It is not suitable for imitating the very tiny microcaddis, but for all other caddisfly hatches I find that this fly does the job very well. It is best fished in faster water. Other imitations produce better where the water is slower and the fish can have a longer, better look.

Stoneflies

These creatures usually crawl out on rocks when they change from nymphs to winged adults, and then fly away to mate. For this reason, few stonefly patterns have ever been developed. But sometimes local conditions can make stoneflies a very desirable pattern. Two examples come to mind. When the tremendous willow fly hatches occur on western rivers in late spring, the fish feed on these huge stoneflies and ignore virtually all other foods until the hatch is over. This is the time to match the hatch with a stonefly imitation. Another time when stoneflies can be effective—although many trout fishermen are unaware of this bonanza— is in the dead of winter. At this time a small (No. 18) black stonefly hatches in prodigious numbers. The trout are tuned into these emerging insects. I have had some great dry-fly fishing in Maryland, where I live, in mid-February, when these small black stoneflies emerge.

Underwater Trout Flies

Aside from streamers (which we will review separately), there are three major groups of underwater flies that attract trout: wet flies, nymphs, and soft-hackle flies.

Wet Flies

Wet flies are imitations of drowned insects and were probably the first artificial flies used for catching trout. Now they have fallen from popularity, even though some of the wet flies of old are still every bit as effective as they once were. One of the most popular methods of using wet flies is to fish what is called a "cast," or a series of two or three flies on the same leader. The fly on the bottom (usually the heaviest or largest) ensures a good turnover of the leader. The other patterns are attached with short sections of leader called droppers.

One of the real tricks to fishing a cast of wet flies is to make sure that the droppers are no longer than four inches—or about the width of the average man's palm. If they are longer, they will frequently entangle in the leader. A great advantage to using a cast of flies is that you can offer the trout several different colors, styles, or sizes of wet flies at the same time. However, it will often become evident that the trout definitely prefer a particular one. And it's not always easy to decide which one is getting the action.

Most wet flies are dressed on No. 12 through No. 1 hooks, but occasionally a No. 10 or 18 will turn the trick. Here are some of my favorite wet flies:

- Leadwing Coachman
- Royal Coachman
- March Brown
- Alder
- Black Gnat

Nymphs

Nymphs are often the single most effective flies for catching trout. These flies are imitations of the underwater stages of many aquatic insects. When you consider that nymphs make up perhaps 90 percent of the total diet of most trout, then it makes sense to fish these buglike creatures.

A sure sign that a trout has taken your drifting nymph is when you can see the white of the inside of the trout's mouth—then it's time to strike!

Nymphs are imitations mainly of mayflies, but also of stoneflies, caddisflies, and other aquatic insects. They range in size from those dressed on tiny No. 24 hooks to monster nymphs dressed on No. 2 hooks. Most nymphs are tied on hooks slightly longer than standard, since the bodies of the naturals are usually long and thin.

It is good to remember that trout will often refuse a dry fly that does not float properly. But trout understand the currents beneath the surface perhaps even better than they do those above, since this is where they do most of their feeding. For this reason, the better you can drift a nymph drag-free to the trout, the more strikes will be forthcoming.

Best of all, you do not need a huge array of nymphs to fish them successfully. If you have several nymphs in light, medium, and dark tan, but in assorted sizes, you can usually score well. As fish become smarter, we need to entice them with smaller nymphs. The standard a decade ago or more was to fish nymphs in sizes from No. 10 through 16. But today you will find that sizes No. 16 through 22 are often more effective, even on large trout.

There are a few nymphs that seem to work just about everywhere and most of the time, too. Obviously you may have to vary the size, and you might have to either weight them or get them down deeper in the water column. But the following nymphs should always be in a serious trout fisherman's fly box. A Gold-Ribbed Hare's Ear is in my judgment the best all-around pattern. In a new place, I always try it first. If the size and sink rate are okay, the fly generally produces. Dave's Red Squirrel Tail Nymph is another top choice. A Zug Bug has fish appeal that few nymphs possess. One of the oldest patterns is the Pheasant Tail Nymph, and the Gray Muskrat Nymph is another hot item. In many places a Yellow Stonefly Nymph (sometimes called a Golden Stonefly) will turn the trick. And Gary LaFontaine's Sparkle Caddis Pupa is a must. A personal favorite on waters from California to Maine is the Prince Nymph. I have also been using John Barr's Copper John. This dressed-up Brassie fly is, I believe, one of the finest nymph patterns I have seen.

Here is a list of my favorite nymphs. All have produced well for me across North America, as well as in New Zealand, Chile, and Europe.

- Gold-Ribbed Hare's Ear
- LaFontaine Sparkle Pupa
- Prince Nymph
- Pheasant Tail
- Zug Bug
- Whitlock's Squirrel Tail
- Muskrat Nymph
- Yellow Stonefly
- Copper John

I carry all of these patterns in Nos. 10 through 22. Usually I prefer to slightly weight each of them, too.

Soft-Hackle Flies

Soft-hackle flies are unique in that they do not imitate a specific insect. Instead they offer something that appeals to the trout in shape, color, and action. Some anglers insist that these are better imitations of a drowned insect. Others feel they are counterfeit nymphs. This is really an academic argument. What is important is that soft-hackle flies are deadly. They certainly are more effective in most cases than wet flies, and in many situations I can outfish my nymphs with them. As with nymphs, you only need a few soft-hackle flies to be effective. Try them in assorted sizes from No. 10 through 16. My favorite soft-hackle flies are:

- Partridge and Yellow
- Partridge and Green
- Partridge and Orange

Emergers

Another fly that trout fishermen are beginning to use more often, and one that has resulted in catching trout at times when anglers used to fail, is the emerger. These are patterns that represent the look of an aquatic insect as it emerges from the nymphal stage to become an airborne adult.

Emergers can be tied so that they can be fished in the water column, or as floating nymphs still held captive in their nymphal shucks as they struggle on the surface trying to free themselves. When you are tying this fly, selecting the proper hook and correctly dressing it are vital to success. The fly should not be tied so that it sinks like a nymph; nor should it float like a dry fly. It really represents either a fly that is swimming up through the water to emerge, or one that has already reached the surface and is trying to rid itself of the nymphal case and fly away.

Streamers

The dry fly is regarded as the ultimate way to take fish on a fly—especially trout—so it has captured the soul of most writers who address the sport of fly fishing. Nymphs and wet flies have received the next most attention, although many purists regard them as not-quite-ethical methods of catching trout. But strangely, streamers have been mostly ignored. I find this odd, because they are among the most versatile flies any fisherman can use. I have had success with them whether I'm fishing for little bluegills or giant blue marlin. I know that if I had to choose a single style of fly for *all* of my fishing, the streamer would be the winner.

These flies can be trolled (as they are in New England and other parts of the world), but they are more often cast. They range in size from less than an inch for trout, bluegills, and crappies, to enormous versions used to take ocean species. There are a number of different styles of streamers, all designed for specific fishing situations. The most conventional has the relatively long hook shank, usually dressed with chenille or a similar material, and a wing that lies along the top of the shank. A variation of this style is the well-known Matuka pattern, whose wing is secured to the shank, eliminating the possibility of the rear of the wing fouling around the hook. The Zonker represents another variation on the conventional streamer, in which a rabbit-fur wing is placed on top of the body.

The hackle streamer or Seaducer is another style, while the Clouser Minnow is yet another. The Lefty's Deceiver that I mentioned earlier has the wing secured at the rear to prevent underwrapping the hook. A collar that flows beyond the rear of the hook helps form a minnow shape in the water. This collar also creates small currents that increase the action of the wing. The fly is very sleek out of the water and easy to cast.

The Bend-Back, a very old bass fly that was developed to fish in the thick vegetation of the South, has become a very popular semi-weedless fly. The use of either monofilament or wire weed guards is still another method used to prevent a fly from snagging during the retrieve. The woolheads and the famous Muddler Minnow are streamer variations. Carrie Stevens, a famed New England fly tier, designed a fly that I have found extremely useful. It has been renamed the Thunder Creek Fly. Bucktail is tied in so that it faces forward, and then it is brought back and secured again on the hook shank. This fly is exceptionally easy to cast and never tangles in flight. It has been one of my favorite smallmouth flies since the late 1940s, when I first found a sample in Maine.

A good assortment of largemouth bass flies. Top row, left to right: Dahlberg Diver, pencil popper, and Marabou Gerbubble Bug. Second row, left to right: a Red & White Hackle Fly and a black Lefty's Deceiver. Third row, left to right: Half & Half and Clouser Minnow. Bottom row, left to right: Bend-Back and Dave's Hare Jig.

Like all flies, streamers come in two basic types: exact imitations and attractor patterns. Both are effective, often in the same place, at the same time, and on the same species.

The original streamers were simply imitations of baitfish that various predatory fish feed upon. Fly fishermen soon realized that fish often fed on juveniles and small swimming creatures. Tying undulating feathers or hair on a long-shank hook to represent a swimming baitfish was so successful that hundreds of patterns were developed to more closely imitate the local species of baitfish. The first streamers were probably tied with a chenille body and a wing of either feathers or hair. Two examples that over the decades have taken many fish are the Black Ghost (featherwing) and the Black-Nose Dace (bucktail wing). In recent years some incredibly good imitations have been developed, using older standard materials along with some modern ones such as Mylar and epoxy.

Attractor streamers, on the other hand, are often outlandish in color and shape, and even experienced anglers don't know why there are times when such a fly produces well. These flies range in color from all-black through some brilliant fluorescent combinations. Often, very flashy materials are used, too.

The shapes of streamers vary widely—and there are good reasons for this variety. If you are fishing at night, when waters are roiled and dirty, or anytime that the fish's vision may be impaired by local conditions, the shape of the fly becomes very important. The most effective flies for such fishing have large heads, which "push" the water. The head and forward portion are wide, and the wings are usually very bulky. All of this is an effort to create something that when retrieved through the water will create vibrations that the fish can sense and locate. Most streamers that are supposed to represent baitfish should have the general shape of a baitfish.

Hackle Flies (Seaducers)

Streamers that have stood the test of time have a unique design that is critical to their success. One example is the hackle fly, which was developed in the 1800s by bass fishermen. This fly is the one I referred to earlier as the Seaducer. It is popular for both freshwater and saltwater fishing, and it has particular characteristics.

The tail of this fly has six to eight saddle or neck hackles. They are tied splayed (like a pair of frog's legs), so that when the fly is moved through the water, these legs close, and they spring apart when the fly is stopped. They also continue to undulate for a brief time. This alone is attractive to many species. But this fly has the full length of the hook shank palmered densely with wound hackle.

This hackle accomplishes three purposes. First, it presents a bulky shape, which to a fish must make it look as if it's a relatively large morsel. Second, the many hackles extending out and around the hook shank act much like outriggers. They support the fly in the water and resist letting the fly sink. Finally, these hackles allow you to fish in very shallow water without fear of snagging the bottom. On the retrieve the fly can be brought to a stop, and it will sink so slowly that you can pause it in front of a fish. Then a short twitch to get the tail and collar moving will often trigger a strike. The hackle fly's wound collar creates mini eddies as the pattern is retrieved. Water tumbling through and over the many spines of wound hackle sweeps back, eddy fashion, over the tail feathers, giving them additional motion. This is a good example of how the design of a fly is so important.

Clouser Minnows

The best streamer I have ever used is the Clouser Minnow. As I mentioned earlier, it has been successful for me on lakes and rivers, and in larger formats in the ocean, too. (For a full description, see chapter 4 on saltwater flies.)

Four patterns have worked for the author for decades wherever he fished for northern pike. Top: Rabbit Leech; middle: Clouser Minnow; bottom: Lefty's Deceiver and Bend-Back.

Woolly Bugger

The leech patterns are imitations of a food that many fish desire, although they really are a form of streamer fly. Even the Woolly Bugger would be considered a streamer, since it is often fished like one. In truth, it is not really a streamer or even a nymph; it is a combination of both.

The Woolly Bugger is nothing more than the old Woolly Worm pattern with a flexible, soft tail, usually of marabou fibers. It can be dressed on hooks as small as No. 14, and as big as No. 2. Usually Woolly Buggers are dressed on hooks that are 2X or 3X long, rather than on standard-length hooks. The body is typically chenille, but I have determined that one of the best body materials is several strands of peacock herl twisted into a rope and wound on, with a dark, soft, webby hackle spiraled over this body. To prevent the herl from breaking, I usually wrap fine copper or gold wire with the twisted herl. For larger flies, marabou is used for the tail. But for smaller flies I find that using the fluff at the base of a neck or saddle hackle lets me tie a better full tail that is exactly the same as marabou. Woolly Buggers can be dressed so that they are unweighted, or weighted with beadheads, coneheads, or lead wire, depending on the fishing conditions.

While Woolly Buggers are tied in colors that range from fluorescent salmon pink (great for Alaskan salmon) to subtle, dark hues, two colors

A good selection of smallmouth flies. Top row: Lefty's Bug. Second row, left to right: Woolly Bugger, Cactus Minnow, and Red & White Hackle Fly. Third row, left to right: Baby Bass Clouser and Clouser Crayfish. Bottom row, left to right: Clouser Minnow and Half & Half.

are by far the most popular with trout fishermen. All-black Woolly Buggers are fished more than all other color combinations, and the next choice is an olive hue.

The fly can be fished in several ways. In lakes and deeper water it is often tied with various weights, then cast out and allowed to sink slowly. Watch the line as the fly descends, since fish will often take the Woolly Bugger as it falls. If not, retrieve the fly slowly at the desired depth. In shallow streams it is sometimes allowed to fall right to the bottom, and then brought back so that it crawls along the streambed. It can also be cast across current and allowed to sweep along with the flow; you can allow it to dead-drift or give it slight movement with the rod tip. The Woolly Bugger can also be fished as a streamer—cast out and brought back slowly or rapidly. It is certainly one of the most versatile flies for catching trout and other freshwater species.

Sculpin

The sculpin is another pattern that I would class as a creature imitation. It is not really a streamer, but it does represent a small minnow that lives on the bottom: the sculpin, which has no air bladder and will rest on the streambed when not swimming. It also feeds mostly during the very early and very late hours of the day. Thus sculpin imitations are not as effective at midday as they are early and late. Almost all sculpins are tan, brown, or olive. I prefer to tie my sculpins weighted, and I much favor the patterns dressed with materials that tend to sink. While many sculpin flies have been dressed with deer hair, I personally favor those tied with a material that tends to sink better, such as wool. Since sculpin flies are fished close to the bottom, it helps to have the fly tied in reverse, with the hook riding up. If not dressed reversed, then they should carry a weed guard to prevent snagging on the retrieve.

Guilty Pleasures

There are three flies that most experienced trout fishermen carry—two of which they are often ashamed to use—but they are deadly in many areas. The more popular of these "ashamed-to-use" flies is the Glo Bug or Egg Fly. This is a round fly, tied on a very short-shank hook to resemble a drifting fish egg. It is most commonly tied with gift yarn, but materials that are translucent are often more effective. For example, an Egg Fly tied with Antron will often outfish the same pattern made from yarn. There are also "Egg Balls," which have tiny sticks of Mylar protruding. These certainly work. Some fly fishermen use a Double Egg: two round egg imitations on the same hook shank. Regardless, almost all species of trout and salmon fall for the Egg Fly.

Another fly that many people don't like to admit using—but generally carry anyway—is the San Juan Worm. This is simply a sticklike piece of yarn, usually tied on an English-style bait hook. The fly represents many of the worms that trout feed on and it comes in several colors. Bright red or orange is the most popular choice. When all else fails, desperate anglers will reach for a San Juan Worm or an Egg Fly.

While it is not as effective in the rivers of the West, another fly you should always carry is the Green Weenie. This is simply an inchworm imitation. In the mid-Atlantic area in late spring or early summer, millions of these green fluorescent worms lower themselves from branches on silken strands. They fall into streams in uncounted numbers, where trout gorge on them. Perhaps because they are so brightly colored, they imprint strongly in a trout's brain. Whatever the reason, however, you can catch trout from early spring through late fall on this exceptionally effective fly. It is usually tied on a 2X-long, No. 10 or 12 hook. There are some variations, but the basic tie involves winding chenille or another body material the length of the shank, then tying off. Like the Egg Fly, it is extremely simple to tie. If you live in the eastern half of North America, I urge you to carry a few of these for those days when trout refuse your other offerings.

6
KNOTS AND LEADERS

Knots and leaders are the connecting elements between the rod in your hand and the fly on the water. If each element has been properly assembled, you won't have to worry about making drag-free presentations to a fish—or having a trophy trout or a bonefish run off with your favorite hand-tied fly.

There are hundreds of knots: Some of them are good, some are better, and some are very bad. Fortunately, you only need to know a few basic ones for saltwater fishing, and only a few more for your freshwater tackle. If you follow the instructions in this chapter and master these knots, you can go anywhere in the world and make connections for your tackle that will serve you well between your backing, line, leader, and fly.

Leaders

Leaders are the essential connections between the end of your line and the fly itself. There are four basic types, each with a specific purpose. Those used to catch trout are perhaps the most complex. These leaders have to control drag and allow the fly to float naturally with the currents. They must also allow a very quiet entry of the fly onto the water. For most general fishing, however, we have a basic tapered leader, which is used for salt water, salmon, bass, and a host of other species. This leader can be composed of either several strands of different diameters of monofilament knotted together, or a single strand tapered from a large to a small diameter. Such leaders must turn over the fly easily at the end of the cast. They also allow you to manipulate the fly.

Level leaders are made of a single strand of monofilament of the same diameter, and they have special applications. The fourth kind of leader is one with a bite tippet on the end, which can be of wire or heavy monofilament. This connection is built so that sharp-toothed fish—such as pike, muskies, barracudas, wahoo, and similar species—cannot sever the connection to the fly.

Fly fishermen have developed some terminology to describe leaders. Here are a few of the common terms:

• **Butt section**: This is the thickest part of a leader and is connected to the end of the fly line.

• **Midsection**: The part of the leader between the butt section and the tippet.

• **Tippet**: The thinnest and weakest section in a tapered leader.

• **Bite tippet**: Sometimes called a shock tippet, this is a piece of wire or heavy monofilament attached to the front of the tippet connected to the fly.

• **Class tippet**: The International Game Fish Association has established special requirements in order for an angler to be awarded a world record. It has divided the tippet strength into various classes. A *class tippet* is usually defined as a specific strength tippet that would qualify for a world-record catch.

• **X**: This letter helps to designate the strength of the tippet. For example, a leader may be referred to as a "twelve-foot 6X." If you subtract the number in front of the X from nine, you get the approximate strength of the tippet. For example, a seven-and-a-half-foot 5X is approximately four pounds in strength. Because many companies make monofilament with slightly different processes, the pound test can very slightly, but it's rarely more than a pound off this formula.

• **Diameter**: For many years if you wanted to know the diameter of a leader, you simply subtracted the X factor in thousandths of an inch from 0.011. For example, with a tippet of 5X, subtract 0.005 from 0.011. A 5X leader would then be 0.006 inch in diameter. A 6X leader would be 0.005 inch, or one one-thousandth of an inch thinner. The newer monofilaments throw this arithmetic off a little, but the rule is still valid enough to be useful.

Leader Materials

You can purchase leaders made from a variety of materials, depending on the type of fishing you are doing. There is common monofilament, which can vary in its degree of limpness. Some leaders (mainly the butt section) are made from very thin strands of monofilament that are braided. A rather new product is fluorocarbon, which resembles nylon monofilament. This material is slightly larger in diameter than the same-

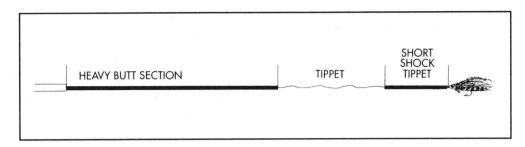

HEAVY BUTT SECTION   TIPPET   SHORT SHOCK TIPPET

Typical shock tippet leader.

strength monofilament. The advantage of fluorocarbon, however, is that it possesses the same light-reflective index as water—which means that the fish are less likely to see it. It also has a specific density approximately 1.8 times that of water, which means it will sink slowly.

For extra-clear waters and for exceptionally sharp-eyed fish (such as the tuna family), fluorocarbon tippets may offer some real advantages. However, I do not believe that using a tapered leader made entirely from the more expensive fluorocarbon offers much of an advantage. I suggest using it only in the tippet connected to the fly.

Leaders also come in various colors, from clear to brilliant orange and yellow. Some tapered leaders have a metallic core; these are designed to sink quickly when you are fishing for trout with nymphs and streamers. There is also a special material that you can add to your leaders to give them some shock absorbency. This material is often called Power Gum or Shock Gum; one manufacturer calls it Bunjeebutt.

I find it surprising that perhaps the most important function of a leader is not always appreciated. If you fish calmer water for trout or bonefish, for example, you know that you need a longer leader. But most people don't know why the leader needs to be lengthened. The main reason is to get the impact of the fly line farther away from the fish. It is the crashing of a fly line to the water that alerts the fish. This is why the most popular trout lines are 3- to 5-weight—especially for dry-fly fishing and delicate work. The calmer the water and the more difficult or wary the fish, the longer the leader must be. This applies to fly fishing worldwide.

Trout fishermen must have leaders that will cast flies properly. These may be as short as six feet, or as long as eighteen, but the most useful are those that are seven and a half, nine and a half, or twelve feet in length. Many commercial leaders don't have a butt section that's large enough in diameter and also long enough. Other hand-tied commercial leaders have a butt section made of stiff or hard monofilament. Every leader needs flexible weight in its butt section.

On a spring creek where wise fish reside, a sixteen-foot leader is not usual. And in late spring or early summer when giant tarpon have been cast to many times, they move to the white sand flats on the ocean side of the Keys. If you use a short leader here, you will only spook the fish. It is not unusual under such conditions for experienced tarpon fishermen to employ a leader of sixteen feet as well. When I bonefish I find that most of the time a twelve-foot leader is the shortest I want—unless the wind is really puffing. But on a calm day I quickly lengthen my leader to sixteen feet. Such long leaders—if properly tapered and matched to the rod and fly—will turn over well.

Another important function of leaders is to present a near-invisible connection between the fly and the fly line. Obviously, if you were to tie your fly directly to the line, few fish would ever strike. A leader also has the function of either creating a drag-free drift or allowing you to manipulate the fly. The difference between these two leaders is substantial. It is important that the tippet not be too large in diameter, lest the fish see it and not strike. But larger-diameter leaders can spoil the action of the fly. The tippet must be supple enough to allow the fly a natural freedom of movement on the surface or beneath it.

Another factor in good leader design is the ability to unroll properly, but still allow the fly to come to the water rather quietly. This is where using the correct materials and building proper tapers is so important. Remember, too, that you can attach a bite tippet to the front of your leader to prevent cuts or fish with rough mouths from abrading through the connection to the fly.

Finally, a careless act by many fishermen has caused the deaths of many birds. If you clip off a piece of leader material and throw it away, birds may pick it up for use as a nesting material. Unfortunately, they often get tangled in it when they fly away. Instead, take the leader pieces home and discard or burn them. But never throw them away where you're fishing.

Tapered Leaders for Trout

Almost all trout leaders are tapered. These fish are sharp eyed and wary, and they live in a relatively small environment, even when you consider a fair-sized river. Otters eat them, cormorants gobble them down when they are small, raccoons harass them, ospreys and eagles pluck them from the water, and fishermen are always bothering them. In hard-fished waters, many trout have been deceived a number of times by what looked like a tasty fly, only to find they were hooked to an angler. No wonder they are so wary!

For this reason, the insect imitations that we offer trout must float or drift to them in a natural manner. While even the novice dry-fly fisherman knows that his fly must float without drag, many longtime trout anglers do not understand that nymphs fished in the water column should also come to the trout in a natural manner. Drag occurs under the water just as it does on the surface, and trout are very aware of this behavior. Correctly tapered leaders are essential whenever you are fishing for trout.

There are several schools of thought on the subject of building a tapered leader. For years we have been told, for example, that we should use stiff material in the butt section. I believe this is a mistake. When your rod sweeps forward and stops, the line behind you begins unrolling from the tip. Gradually it arrives at the leader—which must also unroll to deliver the fly. Common sense should tell us that if a supple fly line unrolls and arrives at the leader, a stiff butt section is going to resist unrolling. What you really need is enough supple weight in the butt section to cause the leader to continue to unroll. You need a flexible butt section, but one heavy enough to let the inertia from the line continue to unroll the remainder of the leader. You do not want a butt section that is stiff and unyielding. Instead, you want it heavy enough to carry the energy to the end of the cast yet also very flexible, so it will unroll easily.

I believe that the best tapered leaders (for any kind of fly fishing) should have a butt section that is limp, but heavy. For most trout dry-fly leaders, I like a butt section of at least 0.023 inch in diameter. This part of the leader should comprise nearly 50 percent of the total length. It should then taper rapidly from the butt section to the tippet.

In much of trout fishing, the leader is designed not to manipulate the fly, but to allow the fly to drift naturally along in the current. This is an important factor to understand when you are pursuing trout. If the leader pulls on the fly while it drifts, the fly will swim unnaturally, and most of the time the trout will ignore it. Instead you need a leader with a special taper. Leaders can be hand-tied, so you should learn how to make or modify your own. However, some manufacturers today make tapered dry-fly leaders that are really better than those you can build yourself. If you fish where there's a great deal of underwater vegetation, then a commercial, knotless, continuously tapered leader may prevent you from picking up this plant life and possibly losing a good fish.

Building a Dry-Fly Leader

To properly construct a basic dry-fly leader, I use a butt section that is heavier and longer than what's been recommended for years. (For anyone who disagrees with this approach, all I ask is that you read what I'm about to explain and then try it yourself.) When I build my own leaders I use limp monofilament, such as DuPont Stren Easy Cast, Berkley XL, or my favorite, Silver Thread. All of these monos are basic spinning

Drawings A, B, C: We already know that the key to success hinges on drag-free float. Even if it does drift drag-free, you must be able to cast the fly accurately to reach the fish. These two factors are determined primarily by the tippet's length and diameter. A 5X tippet generally performs effectively—though, obviously, tippet strength must be increased for bigger fish.

Any leader that falls straight on the water will almost surely be affected by drag. To benefit from a drag-free float, you must have a certain amount of slack in the tippet just before the fly. While formulas have been advanced for matching the tippet size to the hook size, we feel these are invalid. You can dress several different types of dry flies on one hook size (such as a Catskill tie, hair wing, and a spider), and each of the three will offer a different amount of air resistance. To determine the correct tippet and length, you must actually cast the fly when it is attached to the tippet. Then, after observing how the fly and leader fall to the water, you make the necessary adjustments.

In Drawing A, the tippet has fallen back on itself. Plenty of slack exists in

front of the fly, so a drag-free float should occur. In the trade-off, dry fly fishing, you only need a butt section, two intermediate segments, and the tippet. Start by determining how long you want the total leader to be. The butt section will be slightly less than one-half the leader length. With a little practice, you will be able to approximate it with reasonable accuracy. For most assignments, monofilament testing twenty-five pounds (no more) works well.

The second leader segment (B in the illustration) is one-half the length of the butt section; and the next segment (C) is one-half of Segment B. For more fishing situations, a two-foot length of monofilament works well as the tippet. The following example should help you put it all together.

Let's assume you want to build a 10½-foot leader for bonefish, bass, or any other fish. Make the butt section five feet of twenty-five-pound test. Drop to fifteen-pound test for Segment C and make it fifteen inches long (one-half of

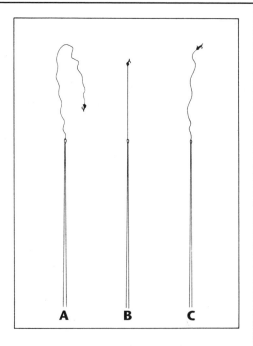

two and a half feet). Add two feet of tippet and you have a leader that measures ten feet nine inches.

Remember that to adjust the length of the leader, you simply change the length of the butt section, and all else will fall into place.

lines. My favorite tippet material is Scientific Anglers clear mono. It has the proper limpness and high knot strength, and it has worked extremely well for me.

I would like to mention that there is really no standard among manufacturers as to how a nylon's diameter relates to its strength. Lines of the same pound test can vary in diameter by several thousandths of an inch. For example, I have measured twenty-pound test that ranged from 0.017 to 0.024 inch. However, the average diameter of twenty-pound test monofilament line is about 0.019 inch.

One of the most highly touted formulas for a nine to ten-and-a-half-foot dry-fly leader has for decades called for a butt section of 0.017 inch—approximately fifteen- to seventeen-pound test. The butt section is about ten inches long. In my view this is entirely too thin, too short, and too lightweight. Remember, what you need in the butt section is enough flexible weight to cause the leader to continue to unroll toward the target.

This basic saltwater fly selection will catch fish nearly anywhere.

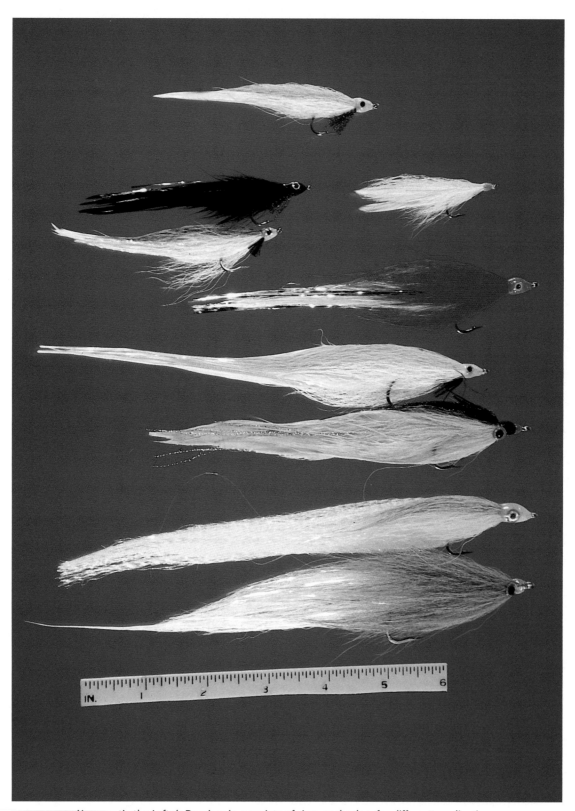

You can tie the Lefty's Deceiver in a variety of sizes and colors for different applications.

Clouser Minnows and Half & Halfs

Surf Candies

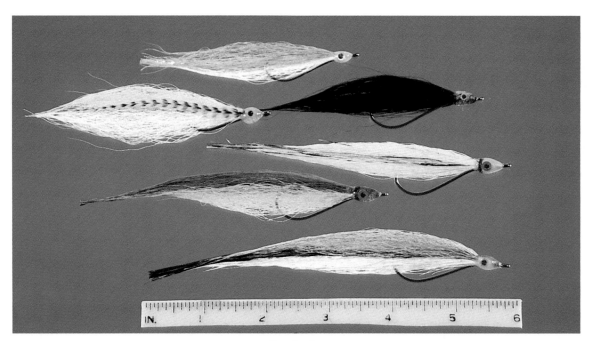

Bendbacks

Crab flies

A Collection of Popping Bugs of various colors and sizes

A basic bonefish fly selection

When gamefish chase a school of baitfish to the surface, the water becomes alive. Casting just off this "nervous water" is almost sure to catch fish.

Wherever large numbers of birds congregate on the water, there are sure to be gamefish. In this photo, a trawler is kicking up baitfish and other creatures, which will attract gamefish and seagulls.

When two bodies of water at different temperatures or speeds come together, they create a tide rip where gamefish will feed. Rips are usually easy to spot and occur consistently in certain areas, so be sure to fish in them.

You can see a bonefish's fin peeping up from the surface of the water in this photo. If you watch patiently, you'll be able to determine the general speed and direction of the bonefish as it feeds along the bottom.

Here is my suggestion for the best dry-fly leader, constructed in the popular ten-and-a-half-foot length. First, construct your leaders with monofilament that is all the same brand; high-quality spinning line is a good choice. The butt section should be from monofilament approximately 0.022 inch in diameter, or about twenty-five pound test. The butt section should be about half the length of the entire leader. Make the butt section for a ten-and-a-half-foot dry-fly leader about five feet long. (For a twelve-foot leader, I suggest a 6-foot butt section.) Connect to this butt section six inches of twenty-pound test (approximately 0.019 inch), and then add six inches of fifteen-pound test (approximately 0.017 inch). Add six more inches of twelve-pound test (approximately 0.014 inch) and to it tie another six inches of eight-pound test (approximately 0.009 inch). Connect about eighteen inches of 4X, 5X, or 6X tippet (approximately 0.007 to 0.005 inch).

Remember, if each segment is a few inches off, it won't matter. And if you would like a longer or shorter leader, use these lengths as basic guides and adjust each link accordingly. Let me emphasize that a continuously tapered commercial leader will work better than you trying to tie all these strands to the right lengths. In fact, I have stopped tying my own, since I can use a commercial leader over and over with the aid of a looping device.

Tippet

The most critical part of a trout leader is its tippet end, where the fly is attached. Remember, you need to cast accurately to where a fish is rising. If the tippet is too long or too thin, the fly will fall back on it. A too-long or too-thin tippet may give you a drag-free drift, but it can't give you accuracy. If the tippet is too thick or too short, it will fall straight on the water. Drag will occur, and the trout will usually refuse the fly.

The length of the tippet depends upon several factors: your casting skill, local fishing conditions, the line and rod you're using, the length of your leader, and—most important—the size and air resistance of your fly. A myth that has been floating around for years suggests that you can divide the size of the hook by four to determine which size tippet you need. For example, if you are using a No. 12 fly, you will need a 3X tippet. Nothing could be farther from the truth. Let's take two flies tied on identical No. 12 hooks. As an example, we will use a Catskill-tied Quill Gordon and a Humpy. The Quill Gordon is very sparsely tied and offers virtually no air resistance on the cast. The Humpy is a bulky, heavy fly for its size that offers considerably more resistance on the cast. There is no way that the tippets used for these two flies should be of the same diameter or length, despite their identical hook sizes.

Here is how you determine the right length and size of tippet for your casting skill and fly. Add a length of tippet material to your leader. Attach the fly and make several casts. If the fly falls back on itself in a crumpled mess, the tippet is either too thin or so long that it can't turn the fly over. While you'll get a drag-free drift, your accuracy will suffer. Clip off a section of tippet, reattach the fly, and cast again. If it still falls inaccurately and with many waves, repeat the process. When you get it right, the leader will fall straight toward the target area, creating soft waves a few inches across just in front of the fly. Later, if you switch to a smaller fly, you will find that this tippet will fall straight because it is too thick or too short for this less air-resistant fly. You will have to remove the tippet and repeat the process described above until the tippet again falls accurately with soft waves immediately in front of the fly.

Since commercial tapered leaders perform best when they are new, you don't want to destroy this taper. This is what you do when you repeatedly attach new tippets, which use up a portion of the leader with each knot you make. Instead, try this technique, which I have used successfully for years. Almost all continuously tapered leaders of less than ten and a half feet have less than twenty-four inches of tippet. (If the leader is much longer, the tippet may extend to twenty-four inches, but rarely will it be longer.) Measure back twenty-four inches from the end of the tippet, cut it off, and discard it. Construct a nonslip loop knot in the end of a tapered leader. Properly constructed, this knot is stronger than the leader you tie it in. Then take a length of tippet material from a spool and build a nonslip knot in it. Connect the two loops with a square-knot configuration. Now when you have to replace a tippet, all you need to do is unloop the current tippet and add a new one with a nonslip loop. With this method, one commercial leader will serve you for many fishing trips. As the knot wears, simply cut it off the tapered section and install another one to get more service from the original tapered leader.

Much has been written about dry-fly leaders, and almost every experienced trout fisherman has strong opinions about which ones are best. The fact is, many leaders can be turned over well if you cast well. The leaders I have suggested here will work well for people who are not particularly good casters and also for those are experienced.

Line Weight

What many fishermen fail to consider about making a delicate presentation to trout, especially with dry flies, is the weight of the line. They don't understand why on rough water or fast water they can use a short leader, but on very calm water they need a much longer one. Experience has shown that when casting below a riffle, the agitated water allows them to use leaders as short as seven feet with dry flies. But when they fish a beaver pond, a limestone stream, or a similar slow-moving, quiet pool, it becomes necessary to switch to a much longer leader. Why is this?

Remember that it is the impact of the fly line on the surface that frightens the fish—not the dry fly, which usually descends softly. If you fish many waters where there are calm pools, quiet surfaces, or wary fish, you can up your score by switching to lighter lines. I believe that a 1- or 2-weight line is impractical. If you want to use one, that's fine, but for most delicate dry-fly fishing I feel that a 3-weight fly line is the lightest (and the best) tool to use. You can also get by with a 4-weight. Anything heavier, in my opinion, will only reduce your chance of success. A 3-weight line weighs 120 grains, while a 6-weight weighs 160 grains. That's considerably more weight, and I believe it can affect your fishing.

Some anglers question whether they can adequately cast dry flies with such a small line. Unless there is excessive wind blowing (so much that even a 6-weight line might give you trouble), you will be able to cast well with a 3-weight. Consider what a dry fly weighs and you will realize that a 130-grain line can easily deliver your offering. Incidentally, I have helped many novice dry-fly fishermen score better by selecting a line one size lighter than what their rod suggests. This lighter line will not generate the same amount of force or speed as a perfectly matched one—hence you get a gentler presentation.

In no other area of fly fishing is the leader more critical to success than in trout fishing. You can catch bass, snook, and a host of other fish on a dozen different leader designs. But when you are trout fishing, your leader is as important (or more so) as your selection of fly, the type of rod and line you use, and the cast you make.

Tapered Leaders for General Use

With the exception of trout fishing, tapered leaders generally fall into a single category, and the same principle applies here: You need a butt section that is flexible yet heavy enough to transfer the energy of the cast through the line and leader to properly deliver the fly. It is a little difficult to buy the exact tapered leader you need for every fishing situation, although companies are responding to this need. Still, I think it is best for fly fishermen to know how to build their own tapered leaders. And in some cases you may want to modify an existing leader for a changing situation.

To begin, you will have to construct your tapered leaders from various diameters of monofilament. It is helpful to know that you can join two sections of monofilament more easily if they are of the same apparent limpness. If you use monofilaments that are all the same brand, you will find that your knots form and close better. For example, you could use all Ande, or all DuPont Super Tough. Any of the premium-brand spinning lines will work well for fly fishing. Spinning and plug-casting lines are usually limp, but not too much, and they have a high knot strength.

Incidentally, when you are finishing a leader, after all the knots have been closed firmly be sure to trim them close. If not, they may cause you trouble when you start casting and fishing. Also, never use rubber or similar material to remove coils from a leader. This will cause small ruptures in the leader that will easily break. Instead, grasp a portion of the leader in your hands and then run it several times through your clenched fist. The friction heat that builds up will eliminate almost all coiling—and do the leader no damage.

You need only one knot to build tapered leaders—either a surgeon's knot or a blood (sometimes called a barrel) knot will do. The surgeon's knot usually doesn't tie well in lines testing more than forty pounds. I prefer using a blood knot down to a thirty-pound test. With lines testing less than thirty pounds, I generally use a surgeon's knot. It's quick and just as strong. If you use a surgeon's knot on a line that tests less than ten pounds, make it a triple surgeon's rather than a conventional double. If you use the blood knot, I recommend that on a line testing more than twenty-five pounds you should make only three turns with both tag ends to join the strands. On diameters smaller than this, make one more turn with the lighter test than with the stronger. For example, on twenty-pound test you will make four turns, but on fifteen-pound you will make five turns.

Because you will be casting different sizes of flies with medium to powerful rods—and you may be encountering wind—your tapered leaders will vary slightly in each situation, but the procedure for tying them is the same. When fishing with lines from 9-weight through 12-weight, and throwing flies that are difficult to turn over (crab patterns, large Lefty's Deceivers, Clouser Minnows, Whistlers, and similar patterns), I recommend that you use a butt section of sixty-pound test. If your rod is 7 through 9 in size and you are throwing smaller flies, I recommend using fifty- or no smaller than forty-pound test for the butt section. For 5 and 6 rods, try a thirty-pound butt section. One of the most important factors in building good tapered leaders is to begin with a heavy, flexible butt section.

Building a Basic Tapered Leader

Start with a butt section that is half the length of the total leader. If you begin with a ten-foot leader, make the next section one foot in length. The thirty- and twenty-pound sections will remain one foot in length for all tapered leaders. If you increase the leader to twelve feet, increase the length of the next section to two feet. If you make a fourteen-foot leader, increase the second section by another foot (up to three feet); for a sixteen-foot leader, increase the second section an additional foot (to four feet). Add approximately two feet of tippet (of fifteen-, twelve-, or ten-pound test) and you have a simple formula for making a great tapered leader for most fresh- and saltwater fishing situations. (As you saw earlier, however, this formula does not apply to trout fishing.) Do not worry about being too exact. Unlike some tapered leaders, you won't need a micrometer to build these examples. Finally, add your tippet.

If these directions sound difficult when you read them, take a look at the chart below and you will see how simple it is to build leaders. And while this advice may seem unusual to many fly fishermen, try casting one of these leaders and compare it to other versions. I think you will be convinced.

I remember telling Bob Clouser about this concept. Bob guides smallmouth bass fishermen for most of the summer on the Susquehanna River near his home and shop. Many of his clients are not good casters, and Bob, of course, likes to fish his leadhead Clouser Minnows. Soon after I showed him this formula, he called me. "I can't believe how well my clients are turning over their flies," he said. "This formula works on short or long casts and even into the wind."

Here are six formulas for making different lengths of leader, all with fifty-pound-test butt sections, if you are using a fly rod of 8-weight or larger.

Leaders

Length	50 lb.	40 lb.	30 lb.	20 lb.	15, 12, or 10 lb.
8'	4'	1'	6"	6"	1½–2'
9'	4½'	1'	1'	6"	1½–2'
10'	5'	1'	1'	1'	2'
12'	6'	1'	1'	1'	2'
14'	7'	1'	1'	1'	2'
16'	8'	1'	1'	1'	2'

Remember that all of the monofilament you use should be from the same manufacturer.

Level Leaders

Tapered leaders are not necessary in some fly-fishing situations. Indeed, in many cases they do not serve as well as level leaders. A level leader is one composed of a single, uniform strand of monofilament.

Generally you will need it wherever you can let your line and leader fall to the surface without fear of frightening the fish. A typical situation in which a level leader works best is in lily-pad-choked waters. The bass are not going to see your leader. Nor will it have any impact on the surface, which is covered by the pads. A tapered leader, with strands connected by knots, can create problems here. The knots will pick up grass, or snag in the lily pad leaves or stems. In this situation a level leader of fifteen- or twenty-pound test, connected to the fly line and the fly, is ideal. Such a leader usually needs to be only about six or seven feet long. It will turn over beautifully and eliminate the problems that a tapered leader would create.

A level leader also works where there is floating grass or the surface is choked with vegetation, such as in many largemouth bass and pike environments. The same applies in saltwater areas where grass has been distributed on the surface by the tide. Floating grass can snag on the knots used to build the tapers, spoiling your retrieve. Furthermore, this grass disguises the line and leader's impact on the water anyway, so that a tapered leader is neither desirable nor necessary.

When you are throwing a fly under low, overhanging brush, a short, level leader will do the job better than a tapered one. A tapered leader often slows the cast down at the end, opening the loop. A short, level leader, however, will let you throw a tight loop under the branches. For some species you may have to add a short shock leader. Snook fishing in such situations is best done with a five- to seven-foot leader of fifteen- to twenty-pound test. It should have a one-foot section of thirty- or forty-pound mono between it and the fly to avoid cutoffs.

Another situation in which I prefer a level leader is when I am using a sinking-tip line and have removed half (five feet) of the sinking tip's front portion. This gives me a floating line with a five-foot sinking tip—a great line to use with a popping bug or Dahlberg Diver for snook in the back country. A short level leader is attached, usually with four to six feet of fifteen-pound test. If I throw a bug or Diver into a hot spot and start an immediate retrieve, the fly will move noisily along the surface. If the retrieve is delayed, though, the short line will cause the fly to be dragged a few inches under the surface. Then, when I start my retrieve, the fly will swim back to the surface and begin gurgling; it'll keep making noise so long as I continue the retrieve. If I stop, the bug will sink below the surface again. A level leader is by far the best one to use with this technique.

For some years experienced fly fishermen have recognized that they do not want to use a long leader when fishing a sinking fly line. The line sinks quickly and the long leader goes down slowly. This forces the fly to ride high above the line in the water column. Short leaders—rarely longer than four feet, and often shorter—are the ticket. There is no need to taper very short leaders; simply attach a level length of monofilament to the end of the sinking line, tie on your fly, and start fishing.

Knots

Knots are the one common denominator that links our brand of fishing—from the deep sea to shallow spring creeks. They also lead to success or heart-stopping failure. We think of knots as links in a chain that connect us to the fish at the other end of the line. And we all know that the weakest link in the chain will fail first. Choosing the right combination and tying it correctly makes the entire line stronger. If one of your goals is to maximize your tackle and its performance, then your knots must be a vital part of the system.

Knot Basics

A knot is nothing more than a connection—in the line itself, between two lines, between the line and the leader and the tippet, or for attaching a fly. Each type of knot has a specific purpose, and no single one will suit more than a few situations. The key is to know which one to use and when to use it. If you can master the knots in this chapter, you can be confident that you'll have a reliable connection between your backing, line, leader, and fly.

Newcomers to fly fishing often feel overwhelmed by the choice of knots and what they perceive to be the complexities of building a leader. Yet with only nine or ten knots, you should be able to handle almost any fly-fishing assignment from trout to tarpon and bass to bonefish. These knots are the speedy nail knot, conventional nail knot, whipped loop, surgeon's knot, Huffnagle knot, Bimini twist, non-slip mono loop, Trilene knot, George Harvey dry-fly knot, and figure-8 knot.

But first let's look at some of the ways we talk about these connections. Here are a few of the basic technical terms that relate to knots:

• **Tag end**: The part of the line in which the knot is tied. Think of it as the short end of the line. *Tag end* will also be used to denote the short excess line that remains after a knot is tied. This would normally be the portion that is trimmed.

• **Standing part**: The main part of the line, as distinguished from the tag end. This would be the line that goes to the reel or the longer end if you are working with leader material.

• **Turns or Wraps**: One complete revolution of one line around another. It is usually achieved by passing the tag end around the standing part or a standing loop.

• **Loop**: Technically, a loop is a closed curve of line. It can be formed by bringing the tag end back and alongside the standing part or by tying a knot that creates a loop.

By itself, the overhand knot is the weakest and poorest knot you can tie. In several more sophisticated knots, it becomes one of the steps, and that's why we are including it. Fly fisherman know it as a wind knot (caused by improper casting).

__Step 1__ Hold the standing part of the line between the thumb and forefinger of the left hand about eight inches from the end. With the tag end between the thumb and forefinger of the right hand, rotate your right hand and bring it toward your left hand. A loop will form against the standing part of the line.

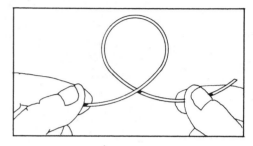

__Step 2__ Slide the loop formed in Step 1 under the thumb and forefinger of your left hand, holding it firmly. With your right hand, pass the tag end over the standing part and slip it through the loop.

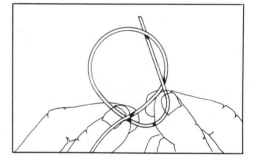

__Step 3__ Moisten the knot and pull both hands apart steadily to tighten.

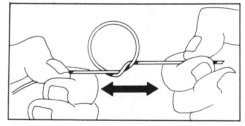

• **Double line**: A double line is similar to a loop—except instead of working with the loop that is formed, you use both strands of line together. If you were to pinch the round end of a loop shut with your fingers, you would create a double line. A double line is also created with certain knots, such as the Bimini twist.

• **Breaking strength**: Regardless of the material, any knot begins to slip just before it breaks. The tighter you can draw a knot when tying it, the more force it can withstand before slippage occurs. A knot's effectiveness is expressed as a percentage of the line's unknotted strength, with the maximum rating at 100 percent. Most well-designed knots exceed 90 percent of the line strength on a straight pull when tied properly and drawn down as tightly as possible.

Knot Facts

• Lubricating a knot by dipping it in water or moistening it with saliva prior to drawing it down will help seat it smoothly with a minimum of friction. With heavier lines, you must use a tool such as a pair of pliers for the final drawdown. Extensive tests show that it is virtually impossible to achieve maximum tightness with your bare hands when using mono that exceeds fifteen-pound test. Some people insist on adding silicone or another slippery lubricant to help seat a knot. Remember that the additive remains and often increases the risk of slippage when a load is applied.

• The finer the diameter of monofilament, the easier it is to seat the knot securely. Diameter may also be a limiting factor when selecting a knot. Some excellent knots work well with fine-diameter line, but prove useless in heavier mono because they cannot be drawn tight.

• Fly fishermen frequently join monofilament of different diameters in order to build tapered leaders and to secure shock tippets to a thinner tippet. These knots will close easier and better if you use monofilaments that are the same apparent limpness. If you use hard or stiff monofilament and try to tie in mono that is more limp, the knot is very difficult to close. When joining two lines of equal or unequal diameter, you will tie a better knot if both monofilaments are the same brand from the same manufacturer. Dissimilar monofilament differs in stiffness, making it more difficult to draw the knot tight.

• Another important factor is how well the coils within the knot are closed. Never overlap a coil. A knot will break under severe strain where a coil overlaps. If the coils lie perfectly together, a knot will remain strong. But if a coil crosses over another during closure, the knot will break there under stress. Too many fishermen make this basic mistake.

• If you want to compare different knots and don't have a line-testing machine, try this experiment. Tie each knot in a separate length of line or to two identical hooks. Have a friend hold both hooks or one end of each line with a pair of pliers. Use a pair of gloves to protect your hands (and safety goggles for your eyes) and pull evenly on the other end. You will quickly learn which knot is stronger! And while you are running this test, try jerking the lines. Some knots are very strong under a steady pull, but fail under impact. The spider hitch is a well-known example.

• When you select knots, recognize that some take longer to tie than others. The more time-consuming connections may be a little stronger and worth the effort when you are not trying to rejig your tackle while watching a school of fish on the surface. For the latter situation, you should know a few knots that can be tied very quickly and still do a satisfactory job.

Trimming a Knot

Once you seat a knot properly, it can be trimmed closely, because it won't slip. Use a pair of nail clippers, scissors, cutting pliers, or other tools made for the task. If you attempt to burn or heat the tag end of monofilament to create a burr, you could easily damage both the knot and the line. Tying an overhand knot in the tag end to stop slippage usually falls short and indicates that you are not seating the connection correctly. Trim the knot close to the tie so that the tag does not protrude or extend. If it does, it could catch on the guide or tip-top or it might pick up weeds. When a tag end should be left a little longer, I will indicate that in the instructions. Otherwise, trim the tag end at a forty-five-degree angle facing back toward the knot.

When a knot must pass back and forth through the guides while fighting a fish, coat the knot with a rubber-based cement that remains flexible. (Epoxy, for example, is much too rigid when it hardens.) There are now glues on the market that are specially designed to be used with nylon monofilament, and these adhesives will increase the knot's strength. However, remember that most of the cyanoacrylate glues are water soluble—something you don't want to discover while you are fighting a big fish. A proper coating will then protect the knot so that it does not nick or catch on a guide.

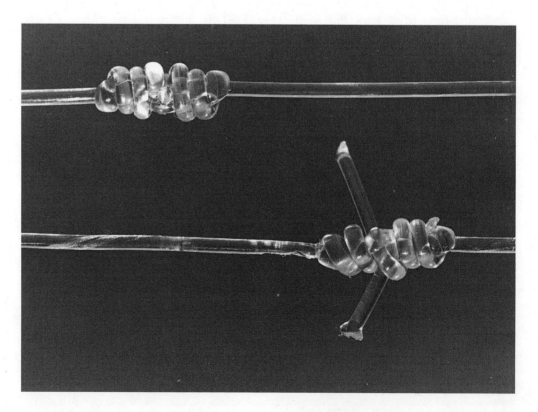

If knots are closed correctly, they won't slip. Therefore they should be closely trimmed, as shown above. Protruding stubs, like those below, catch the leader, grass, and other materials.

Clinch-Type Knots

After tying thousands of knots for testing on my machine, I finally realized that there is a better way to close clinch-type knots. First, let me emphasize that most fishing knots are really variations on either the clinch, nail, or overhand knot. Clinch-type knots include, for example, the blood knot, improved clinch knot, and uniknot. How many times have you tried tying a blood or clinch knot (or another variation on a clinch) and had it come down so far, but fail to close properly?

Here is my suggestion. Once you have formed the knot and it is ready to be closed, pull on the tag end (or ends, for the blood knot) until it lies flush against the spirals or twists around the main line. Once it lies flush, wet it and pull the knot closely. You should have no further trouble closing clinch knots easily and firmly.

Follow the Directions

Mastering anything takes time and practice. This is why I recommend that you tie a knot several times before you add it to your list. You have

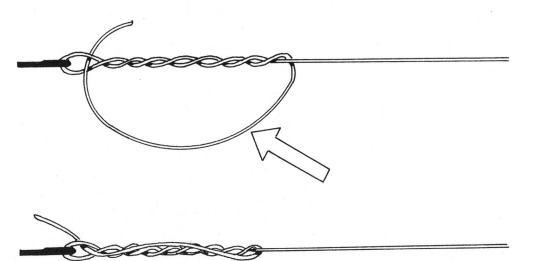

How to properly close and clinch a knot.

to be able to tie it quickly, accurately, and comfortably. But remember that the only place to learn to tie a specific knot is in a relaxed atmosphere off the water. Recognize that not everyone can tie all knots well. Most of us rely on two or three knots from each category to cover most situations. Once you develop a system that works for you, stick with it.

The directions for all of the knots in this chapter, along with the accompanying illustrations, are precise. If the instructions tell you to go over first and then under, follow them carefully. And pay particular attention to the recommended number of turns. For lines testing from 8X to six pounds, for example, the Trilene knot should have five turns around the standing part of the main line. Four turns are not enough to keep the knot from slipping, and six turns may prevent you from drawing up the knot securely.

Speedy Nail Knot

Along with the conventional nail knot, this is one of the preferred methods for most anglers to attach their tapered leader or the butt section of a leader to the fly line. The speedy nail knot can be made with practice in about ten seconds or less, but it is difficult to use when connecting the backing to the fly line. That is where you would use the more common conventional nail knot, although it does leave a blunt end where the fly line is connected to the backing. And this blunt end can catch on the retrieve.

Step 1 *Hold the fly line in your left hand with the standing part to the left and the tag end to the right. Place a small needle on the fly line with the point of the needle to the right. Then, lay the tag end of the leader on the needle so that the end extends about one inch beyond the point of the needle.*

Bring the other tag end of the leader (this is the tag end of the leader to which a fly will be attached or the remainder of the leader built) around to form a big loop under the needle. About two or three inches of this tag extends to the left after the loop is made. Hold everything together securely with the left hand.

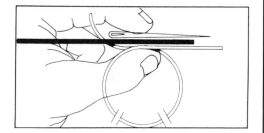

Speedy Nail Knot

Step 2 *Take the right leg of the loop in your right hand and start wrapping it around the fly line, leader, and needle. The wraps will move from right to left.*

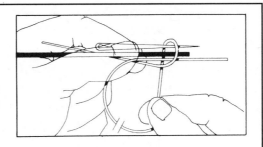

Step 3 *Continue the wraps in Step 2 until you have six to eight wraps. It is essential that you hold everything securely with your left hand and keep the leg of the loop in your right hand taut. Any slack will cause the wraps to unravel. Note that each wrap is laid tightly against the preceding one.*

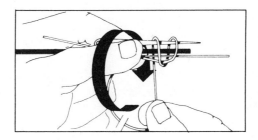

Step 4 *when you have completed the required number of wraps, use the fingers of your left hand to hold them in place. With your right hand, pull slowly and steadily on the tag end of the leader; you started with about one inch extending specifically for this purpose. Keep pulling until you have drawn the entire leader under the wraps.*

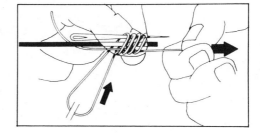

Step 5 *Pull on the tag end and the standing part of the leader simultaneously to semi-tighten the nail knot over the needle. Then carefully work the needle loose from under the wraps and remove it. Remember that the needle slides out from right to left.*

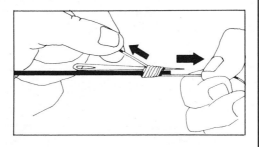

Step 6 *Position the nail knot on the fly line and tighten it completely by pulling on the tag end and standing part at the same time. Trim the tag end and the speedy nail knot is finished. With practice, you should be able to tie this in less than fifteen seconds.*

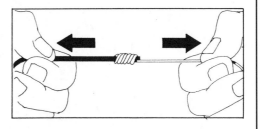

Speedy nail knot (continued).

Conventional Nail Knot

Also known as the tube nail knot, this popular method supposedly originated with Joe Brooks, a noted fly fisherman and outdoor writer of the 1950s and 1960s. He apparently learned the knot in Argentina using a horseshoe nail and then brought the technique to the United States and wrote about it in *Outdoor Life.* This is slower to construct than the

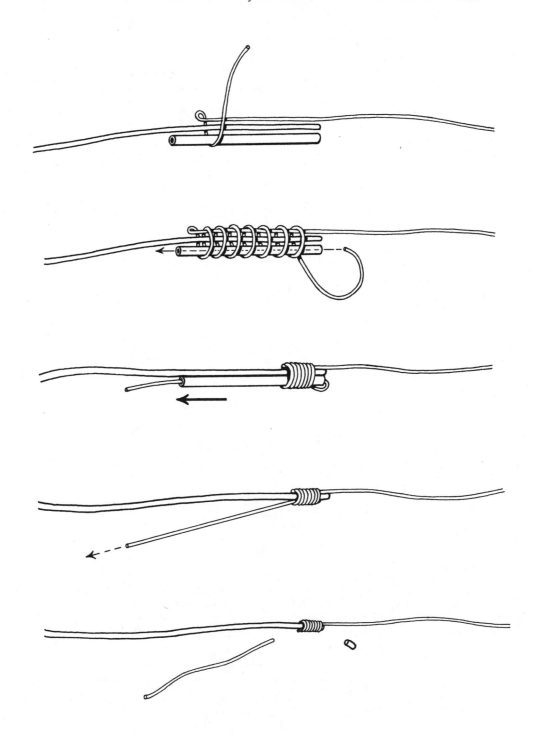

Conventional nail knot.

speedy nail knot, but there are some situations in which the faster version will simply not work. One example is when you install a nail knot somewhere along the fly line as an indicator. If you're night fishing, for instance, you may want to place a knot you can feel where you would normally make a pickup for a backcast. For clear lines, such as those made from monofilament, it's a good idea to place a nail knot where you can best lift the line from the water to backcast.

The conventional nail knot is easy to tie, and when made properly, it creates a strong connection. It also flows well through the guides if it is trimmed correctly and tapered smoothly with glue.

Whipped Loop

This connection has a number of uses. It can connect leaders to fly lines, backing to fly lines, and shooting heads to shooting line. This is my preferred way to attach backing to a fly line. A loop is made in both ends of the fly line by folding the line end back against the main line.

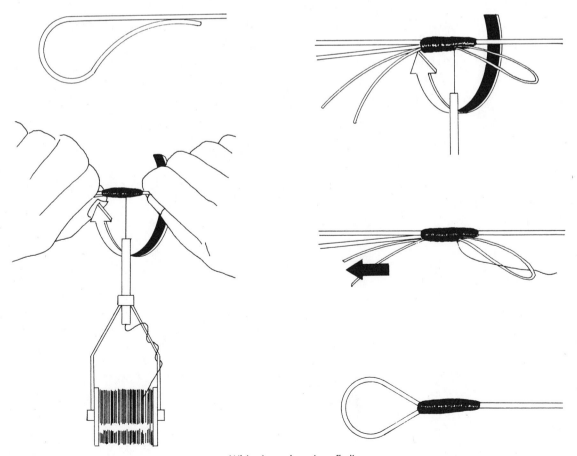

Whipping a loop in a fly line.

And some lines, such as those with Kevlar core and most monofilament lines, do not work well with a nail knot (the knot can slip off). The whipped loop works very well. Always test the loop for strength when completed by holding a nail or thin rod inside the loop and pulling on the main line. Properly tied, this loop is stronger than the main line.

These loops never hang up in the guides because of their round ends. Properly constructed, they never pull out during the battle. Loops offer the outstanding advantage of allowing you to interchange lines on the reel, or to quickly substitute another leader. The ability to interchange leaders is a vital factor in being able to cope with different fishing conditions. I consider the nail knot a disadvantage in this regard. However, with a little practice, you can build a strong whipped loop in less than thirty seconds.

Surgeon's Knot

There are many situations in which you must connect two different diameters of monofilament together, or in some cases connect braided wire to monofilament. The surgeon's knot will do this quite well in monofilament lines up to sixty pounds in strength—or in connecting monofilament to braided steel wire up to forty-pound test. With mono testing more than sixty pounds and braided wire stronger than forty pounds, other knots are recommended. The most important factor in constructing a good surgeon's knot is that once the knot has been tied, all four ends must be pulled very tightly, or a weak knot may result. For building tapered leaders, the surgeon's knot is almost always stronger

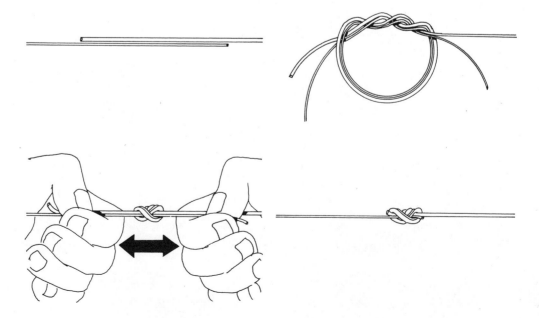

Surgeon's Knot.

than a blood knot, and it is much quicker to tie. You can quickly join six-pound-test leader material to forty-pound test.

You can also use this knot to connect two lines of the same diameter. Whichever method you choose, when tied correctly, this knot has a strength exceeding 90 percent of the weaker of the lines used in the connection. I consider this to be a knot that every fisherman should know. Incidentally, physicians tell me that they have never seen this knot used in a surgical procedure, so the origin of the name remains a mystery.

Huffnagle Knot

This knot has a number of names, but *Huffnagle* seems to be the most common. There are slight variations on it, although all forms are superb

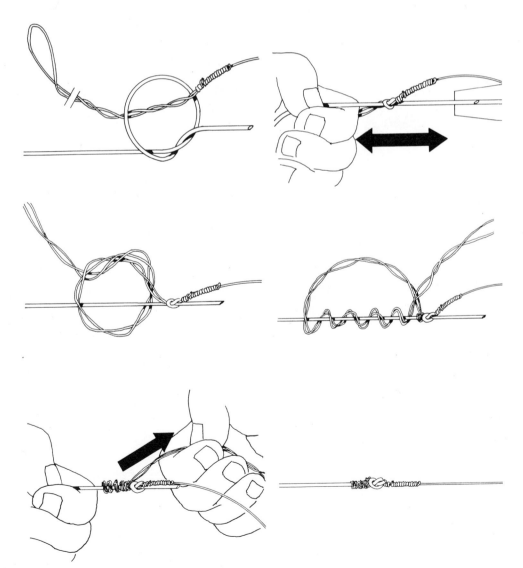

Huffnagle knot.

for joining very large-diameter monofilament (used for shock leaders in saltwater fly fishing) to a thin tippet, or to a tippet constructed with a Bimini twist. One of the advantages of this knot is that it forms one of the smallest connections when joining large (80- to 120-pound) monofilament to a small strand. And it lies straight once the knot is complete, giving the fly improved action on the retrieve.

Bimini Twist

This is the single most important knot a saltwater fly fisherman can learn. It has great importance to freshwater fishermen who want to tackle large, powerful fish on very light tippets. Whenever you want to

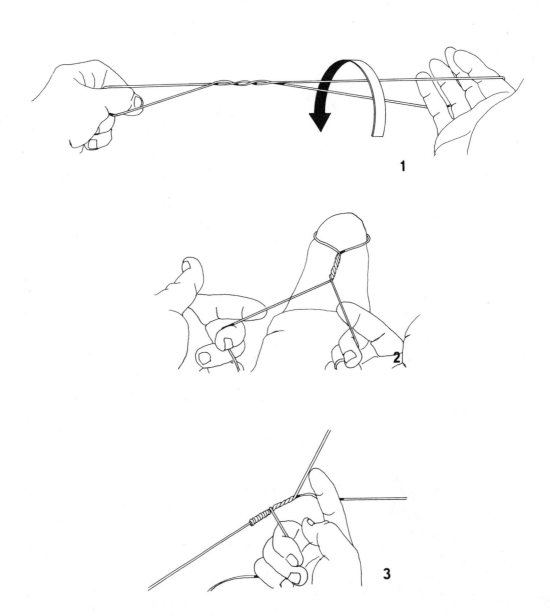

Bimini twist.

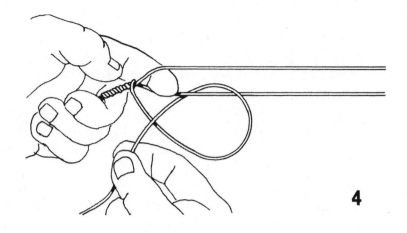

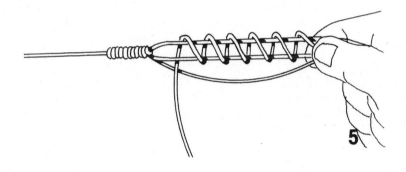

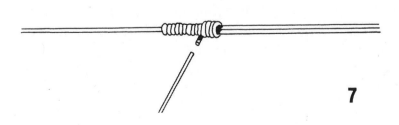

Bimini twist (continued).

connect a fragile line to another line and retain 100 percent of the strength of the fragile line, you must use this knot.

The Bimini twist is a wrapping in the line that is stronger than the line itself. Most important, it is a loop (or two strands) that is used to tie the knot. Because the Bimini twist is stronger than the line, and you are tying the knot with two strands of the line, almost any connection will be stronger than the main line. This is why the Bimini is used throughout the fishing world, from big-game trolling to fishing with a four-pound fly tippet.

Most knots result in a connection that is weaker than the line with which they are tied. The Bimini twist will never slip, so it never breaks. When you build a Bimini twist, you end up with a doubled line or loop extending from the Bimini. That is where the value of this knot lies. For example, if your tippet is twelve-pound test and you want to join it to a shock leader of one hundred pounds, almost all other connections would result in a knot of less than twelve pounds breaking strength. But when you make a Bimini (which is stronger than the line), beyond the knot you have two pieces of twelve-pound (or twenty-four pounds) with which to attach a hook or other line. Almost any knot you tie with this doubled strand will be stronger than one made with the single-strand twelve-pound. The Bimini is one knot that every serious saltwater fisherman should use, but more freshwater fishermen should use it, too. With a little practice, this knot can also be tied in less than thirty seconds.

Nonslip Mono Loop

The nonslip loop is an old knot that I worked with for months before finally improving it. It is the strongest loop knot possible, and I now use it more than any other to connect monofilament leaders to flies. It often tests close to 100 percent of the unknotted line strength.

There are many situations where a loop, rather than a tight connection, is best between the tippet and the fly. This permits the fly to move more freely. Anytime a heavy tippet is connected to a smaller fly, for example, the junction can impede the action of the fly. Popping bugs, for example, are much more effective when you attach them with a free-swinging loop. A fly such as a Clouser Minnow will also be much more alive on the retrieve, as will almost any underwater fly.

This is especially important when tying braided wire or heavy monofilament to the fly, but many nymph and streamer fishermen also prefer a free-swinging loop. The uniknot or Duncan loop has been used by fishermen for this purpose. Unfortunately, this is not the strongest loop knot. Actually it is a form of the clinch knot—one not known for great strength. Another drawback to the uniknot or Duncan loop is that dur-

Step 1 *Begin the knot before you pick up the fly or lure. Make an overhand knot in the line and then pass the tag end through the eye of the hook or lure. Allow about twelve inches of tag end until you are proficient. Insert the tag end back through the loop in the overhand knot, making certain it goes back through on the same side it came out originally (see illustration).*

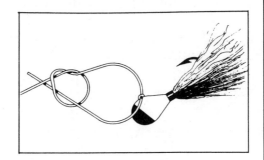

Step 2 *Wrap the tag end around the standing part the required number of times (see text).*

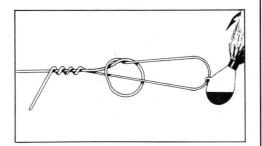

Step 3 *Insert the tag end back through the loop of the overhand knot. Again, make sure it reenters from the same side it exited (see illustration).*

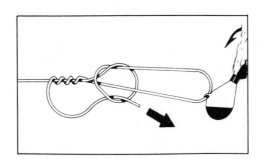

Step 4 *Moisten the knot and start to seat it by pulling slowly on the tag end. This pulls the wraps together. Before the wraps are totally tight, hold the standing part of the line in your left hand and the lure or hook in your right hand. Pull your hands apart to finish tightening the knot, and trim the tag end.*

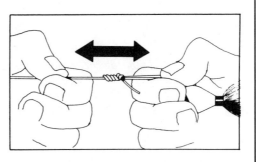

Nonslip mono loop.

ing a battle with a fish, the knot frequently will tighten on the hook eye, requiring you to either move it back to the former loop or retie it.

But the nonslip mono loop forms a loop that does not slip, and most of the time the knot does not break—the tippet does. In other words, tied correctly and closed securely, it will usually test as a 100 percent knot. The nonslip loop is vastly superior to the uniknot or Duncan loop, and every fly fisherman who prefers using loops should consider using it.

For maximum strength this knot has to have the correct number of turns around the standing line. When you are using tippets that test roughly from 8X to six-pound test, make seven turns around the standing line. When you are using line from 8- to 12-pound test, make five turns; four turns are used in line from 15 to 40 pounds; three turns in 50- to 60-pound test; and in 80- to 120-pound test, only two turns are needed. Remember that the line should enter and exit the overhand knot the same way for maximum strength.

Trilene Knot

While most people use the improved clinch knot to attach their tippet to the hook eye, a much stronger knot (one that usually breaks at or near 100 percent of line strength) is the Trilene knot. It is very easy to

Step 1 *Insert about six inches of the tag end through the eye of the hook and then pass it through a second time, forming a double loop about the size of a dime (one-half inch in diameter). The smaller these loops, the easier these knots will be to draw down. Hold the loops with the thumb and forefinger of your left hand after adjusting them to the proper size.*

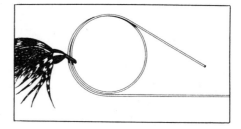

Step 2 *Holding the loops in your left hand, make five turns with the tag end around the standing part (four turns with lines ten pounds and over). Bring the tag end through both loops (created in Step 1). Do not go back through the new loop as you would in the improved clinch knot.*

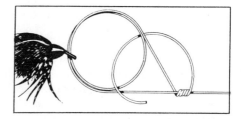

Step 3 *Moisten the knot. It will draw down better if you pull on the tag end as well as the standing part. You may have to use your teeth for the tag end, or alternate pulls. Be sure to seat this knot as tightly as possible before trimming the tag end.*

Trilene Knot

tie, and with practice is quicker and simpler than the improved clinch (of which it is a variation). What is very important is that you do not "improve" the Trilene as you do the clinch. This actually weakens the knot, since it can't be drawn tight enough to keep from slipping when the improvement is added. This knot can be weak if you don't firmly close it, too.

Maximum strength from a Trilene knot is obtained when lines testing from 8X to six pounds are made with five turns around the main line. With eight- to twelve-pound test, four turns are recommended, and with fifteen- or twenty-pound lines, three turns are best. The Trilene knot is not recommended for lines stronger than twenty pounds, and it is tough to draw it tight even in lines testing about twelve pounds. Remember, too, that this knot is difficult to tie with very small hooks (No. 18 and smaller) because the line has to be threaded through the eye twice.

George Harvey Dry-Fly Knot

This knot should never be tied in a ring-eye hook. Use only those hooks with down or up eyes. I have also been told that this is a very old knot. George Harvey showed it to me years ago, and I use it exclusively when connecting dry flies to tippets. It has several outstanding advantages. Properly tied, it has near 100 percent line strength. It looks complicated at first, but it merely involves two procedures performed twice.

The knot is tied on the thread wrappings of the head of the fly instead of to the thin metal of the hook eye—something I find comforting when fighting a very large trout on a fragile tippet. Maybe the most important advantage is that this knot never allows the fly to tilt to one side, because the tippet enters the hook eye and grabs the fly around the head. It always floats straight. Many other knots (such as the improved clinch) can slip to one side on the hook eye and give the pattern an improper float, while the George Harvey never does this.

Figure-8 Knot

This knot is good only for use with braided wire, either coated or uncoated. It is an excellent connection for wire but a very weak knot when tied with monofilament. It is also one of the easiest of all knots to tie. That said, one important factor must be considered: The final closure of the knot should always be performed absolutely correctly. Carefully

George Harvey dry-fly knot.

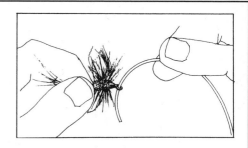

Step 1 *Insert about four to six inches of tippet through the front of the hook eye as shown. If you push the tippet through the back of the hook eye, the fly will ride unnaturally.*

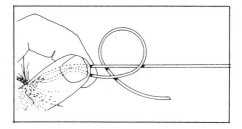

Step 2 *This is one of the few knots where you don't hold the fly or the hook at this stage. Instead, hold the tag end and standing part of the tippet together. Using the tag end, make a circle around the standing part about the size of a dime or smaller. A larger circle makes it difficult to finish the knot.*

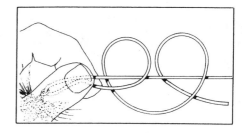

Step 3 *Make a second circle of the same size around the standing part.*

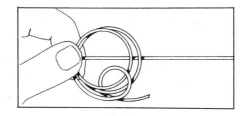

Step 4 *Hold the two circles together and pass the tag end of the tippet through both circles.*

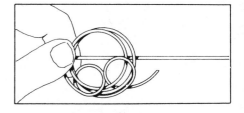

Step 5 *Make a second pass with the tag end through both circles. Be sure to continue holding the circles in your left hand.*

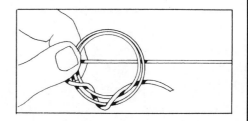

Step 6 *at this stage, the knot should look like the illustration.*

Figure-8 knot.

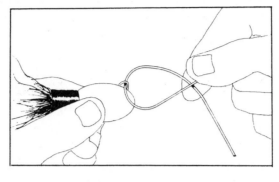

Step 1 *Insert three to five inches of the tag end through the hook eye and then pass it under the standing part to form the loop.*

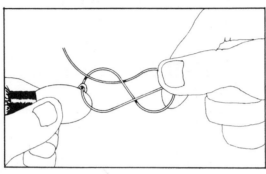

Step 2 *Pass the tag end over the standing part, forming a second loop of a figure-8. Slip the tag end back through the loop you created in Step 1, exactly as illustrated.*

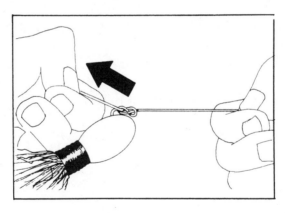

Step 3 *To tighten the knot, pull on the tag end with a pair of pliers. Never seat the knot by pulling on the standing part. If you do, kinks in the braided wire created during the building of the knot will be drawn into the leader and could affect the action. Trim the tag end once the knot is seated, leaving about one-quarter inch, so that you can untie it.*

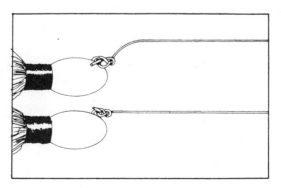

Step 4 *The top illustration shows how a kink forms in front of the hook if you pull on the standing part of the line to seat the figure-8. The bottom drawing reflects the straight leader that occurs when you use the tag end to tighten the knot.*

form the knot. Then, when closing it on the hook eye, pull all slack wire from the tag end. This ensures that any kinks formed while building the knot will be pulled outside so that they can be trimmed off. If you pull on both ends, or on the main line end, you will draw some of the kinked wire in front of the hook, and this will cause the fly to twist erratically and spin on the retrieve. When you trim the excess wire away, leave about three-sixteenths of an inch of wire outside the hook. Then if you decide you want to change the fly, you can carefully "tease" open the knot, remove the fly, and add another. Slowly close the knot, and the wire will return to its original shape. This knot is very strong in braided wire and never slips. However, as noted above, it is a very poor and weak knot when used with monofilament.

Final Thoughts on Knots

Learning to tie knots well and construct proper leaders focuses on a state of mind rather than pure physical ability or lack of it. For someone who has never seen it done, tying a shoelace stands out as a major challenge. Most of us could do it blindfolded without sacrificing any speed. Similarly, any of the knots and leaders described in this chapter can be mastered on a step-by-step basis once you have made up your mind you can do it.

The task is to determine those select knots that are essential for your kind of fly fishing, and then practice them and use them regularly until they become a matter of habit.

7

READING THE WATER AND SEEING THE FISH

Scientists have conducted many surveys to determine who catches fish. In a number of different angling situations, it has been determined that about 10 to 20 percent of the anglers catch most of the fish. That means that most of the fishermen catch only a few. One of the major factors in why some fly fishermen catch more fish than most is that they know what to look for, and how to locate the fish they seek.

Being able to see fish is an enormous asset in catching them, and when you are pursuing some species it is vital to success. This is true in both fresh water and salt. But three natural conditions conspire to keep you from seeing your quarry. One is the wind, which stirs up the surface of the water and disguises or hides activities that are going on at the surface and below. Another factor is rain and waves, which can muddy a stream or stir the bottom. Waters that have been roiled with sediment or stirred by the wind, and surfaces so distorted that you can't see beneath them, are challenges over which you have little control.

A third factor to remember is that most of the time, fish really don't look like themselves in the water. A smallmouth bass with its mottled coloring, for example, is very difficult to see. A brown trout—even a big one—lying on a gravel bar is nearly invisible until it moves. Most of the time you should not be looking for something that resembles a trout or a bass. When you are looking for trout that are nymphing, it will be an open mouth, a flash off the body, or a movement of the tail that will help you to locate the fish. In flowing water the surface is often ruffled, making it tough to see. But if you stare at a certain spot, the

A trout is so well camouflaged that it is very difficult to see until it moves.

surface often smooths briefly, allowing you a clear window to look through.

Many fish have silvery sides, such as tarpon, permit, and bonefish. Over the eons these fish developed their highly reflective scales for a very important reason: They act like a mirror. When you look at bonefish, tarpon, or permit, you aren't going to see the fish most of the time. Instead, the fish will reflect the environment over which it is swimming. This may sound impossible, until you first see a six-foot tarpon cruising along over dark green grass and then realize that you didn't notice it until it was within a few yards of the boat. Had that same tarpon been swimming over a white bottom, you would have noticed it a hundred yards away. While the silvery sides reflected the light-colored bottom, the dark back would be a giveaway. Unfortunately permit and bonefish have very little on them that is not silver—making them harder to see. Still, bonefish have a faintly blue tail, and permit have a dark edge along the back and tail that can give them away. Often bonefish or permit are easier to locate over a light-colored bottom if you look for the shadow of the fish. Many times the shadow will be darker and more visible than the fish.

Sun Glare Reduction

A constant source of irritation for fly fishermen can be too much or too little light on the water. Too much light produces glare, and too little light doesn't allow your vision to penetrate the water. Whenever possible, keep the sun behind you, or at least to one side. In this way the glare is reduced to a minimum. Light is polarizing at eighty-eight degrees from the sun. So if you can get the sun directly to your right or left, there is an area of water in front of you that will be devoid of glare. It is the same effect as looking through polarizing glasses—even if you aren't using any. When you are fishing shallow waters and poling directly toward a bright cloud on the horizon, it is almost wasted motion if you are trying to see under the water. The white cloud, reflecting on the surface, makes it nearly impossible to see anything underwater. The wise angler will always plan his approach so that he uses the light to his advantage. This may mean wading to the other bank or moving the boat in a different direction to get the best light conditions.

Peering into shadowed areas or looking against a dark background, such as a high bank or trees, will also reduce glare. When moving slowly along a lake shoreline, or prowling a trout stream on a bright day,

Eliminate glare by pointing toward the fish.

you may have noticed that where there is shade, you can clearly see the bottom and any fish in the water. Again, planning your approach to take advantage of this condition can often mean more hookups.

Many anglers, especially younger ones, wear no hat when fishing. You can conduct an interesting experiment that proves the value of using one. Stand on an elevated streambank or lakeshore while wearing no hat, and look into the water. You will see a certain amount of the bottom. Then put on a hat with a light-colored underbrim; you will immediately see more of the bottom. Now exchange this hat for one with a dark underbrim, and you may be surprised at how much more of the bottom you can see. The bright glare of the sun causes you to squint when you don't wear a hat. This reduces your vision. A light underbrim reflects back to the eyes some of the glare reflected off the water, and again your vision is reduced. The dark underbrim will enable you to see the bottom—and any fish—much better. A simple way to blacken a hat brim is to paint it with liquid shoe polish. Be sure to let it dry for twenty-four hours before wearing it!

Sunglasses

It doesn't take many trips for even a novice angler to realize that polarizing sunglasses are a necessary tool when searching for fish. They also protect your eyes while casting, because they greatly reduce glare and reduce the possibility of getting hit with a stray line or hook. There are endless varieties of sunglasses from which to choose. Fortunately, manufacturers are now aware that anglers need polarizing sunglasses, and these are easily available. The most commonly used and least expensive are those with soft plastic lenses. However, these soon scratch and become nearly useless. Over a period of years, the average angler who wears these will buy many pairs. Much more economical are those made of hardened plastic or glass. With minimal care, these will last for several seasons of hard use.

If you have good distance vision but have trouble seeing things close up, you can save money by purchasing polarizing glasses with a small magnifying glass in the lower portion of each lens. You can also buy an inexpensive pair of small magnifiers that you can stick on the inside bottom of the glasses. People who wear prescription glasses have two choices. They can always buy clip-ons, which are temporarily attached to their regular glasses. I have tried every type I can get my hands on, and none are really satisfactory to me. The best answer, and it is a bit expensive, is to buy a pair of prescription polarizing sunglasses. With any glasses you receive, if possible, buy the scratchproof type. They will re-

Experienced fly fishermen will use three different tints of polarized glasses for different light conditions: gray-blue, brown-yellow, and yellow.

main free of scratches so much longer, and the extra investment is relatively small.

Polarizing glasses come in several shades or tints, and there is no single tint that's best for all kinds of fishing. The most popular is a tan color. This seems to build contrast and makes fish easier to see under a variety of conditions. Some offshore skippers claim they can spot fish better with the blue-gray type, but I find the tan best for those conditions, too. If you fish trout streams, where you often are in shade or not-too-bright sunlight, a slightly yellow tan is good. This yellow really builds contrast, and on overcast days on saltwater flats, I find these invaluable. However, these yellow-tinted lenses are not recommended for bright sunny days on light-colored flats, where they cause too much eyestrain. In fact, on white sand flats, such as those on Christmas Island, I find that even the tan color is too bright, and my eyes tire quickly. On such brilliant flats I prefer the dark blue-gray lenses.

A clever manufacturer will construct polarizing lenses for the fisherman's most likely viewing angle. There are occasions when not enough glare has been removed. Sometimes you can avoid extra glare by tilting your head slightly to one side or the other. It's a good technique and worth knowing.

Keeping glasses clean is essential, and there are some tricks to doing so. Obviously you'll want to store soft plastic polarizing glasses in a protective case and use care when you put them down to avoid scratching. (Many glasses develop scratches because they are laid down with the front of the lens contacting a surface. Always place them down with the lenses vertical.) Glasses also need to be cleaned, especially if you are fishing in salt water, where the spray and salt crystals will quickly scratch and ruin the lenses. The best cleaner is a package of alcohol swabs or alcohol wipes. These are one-inch square pads saturated with alcohol. They cost less than three cents apiece, and I use them for a variety of purposes—but particularly for sunglasses when I am on salt water.

Another handy product can be used to keep water off your glasses in wet or windy conditions. It's called Rain-X, and it's simply an automo-

I always carry clean paper napkins in a plastic bag to clean my polarized sunglasses.

tive product that helps to keep windshields dry. Just rub a bit on your glasses. It often keeps the lenses dry for several days of hard fishing.

Just about every angler has found that glasses will fall off your face and sink quickly if they are not somehow attached around your head or neck. Usually a strap or other device that goes about the neck and is attached to the side frames prevents them from being lost. The problem I have found with most of these devices is that they allow the glasses to slide down on my nose when I sweat. You can purchase some glasses that have a built-in tensioner that keeps the frames tight against your

Water splashing on your glasses can inhibit your sight. Use a coating of Rain-X— available in auto parts stores—which causes water to immediately run off the glasses.

head. Many women object to them because they pull against their hair; I find that the constant tension sometimes gives me a headache. I came up with an inexpensive solution that allows you to adjust the glasses as tight or loose as you prefer—and they will never move, once you adjust them. Best of all, there is no tension. Use two pieces of Velcro and attach one to either side of the frame with a piece of string (I use an old fly line). Position the glasses where you want them, then mate the male and female Velcro and they'll stay there perfectly!

If you use polarizing glasses where the stream is shaded, you have little need for side shades. But if you fish open areas, such as many western rivers and certainly salt water, glare that comes in from the side reflects on the inside of the glasses. This can create problems when you try to see the fish. You can make your own side shades or buy them from a number of commercial firms.

Trout Tips

When you are reading the water and looking for fish, there are some tried-and-true methods that I have learned over the years. Here are few of my "secret" tips:

• Never get in the water if you don't have to—or at least before you need to. Water conducts sound approximately four and a half times faster than air.

• Take your time when you are reading the waters and looking for trout. Unlike many saltwater species, trout will usually continue to rise for some time. By carefully observing a fish, you can determine exactly where it is taking the flies and what kind of flies it is eating. Often you can time its rises, too, so you can drop your fly just as the fish is coming up.

• When the surface is broken as a fish rises, this does not mean the fish is at that spot. The trout will probably be forward of that ring. If you then cast at it, your fly will fall downstream of the trout and remain

The trout fisherman is doing it right here—keeping low so the fish doesn't see him while he casts to it. He also stays out of the water to reduce the chance of the trout hearing him.

unseen. What many anglers do not realize is how far forward the fish may be.

• The depth of the water has much to do with how far ahead you should cast. If the trout rises in less than two feet of water, a cast that falls two or three feet in front of the fish will generally be right. But as the water deepens—depending on where the trout is holding in the water column—you may need to cast much farther ahead. When in doubt, make it a rule to cast a little farther ahead than you think is necessary.

• Whenever possible, approach a trout stream from the sunny side. You can see the fish in the shaded areas better, and they are less likely to see you. But be careful about casting a shadow on the water!

Here John Zajano demonstrates excellent approach technique. He is free of bright objects such as dangling hemostats. Wearing a camouflage shirt and olive hat, and crouching behind a rock, he has a good chance of hooking a trout.

Inshore Fish

Learning to spot fish is an acquired skill. The ability to see what others do not often means the difference between success and failure. It really is like stalking; there are many "signs" that will help you determine where the fish are.

Watching the Surface

The surface of the water can often help you locate or see the fish. It isn't necessary, sometimes, to actually see the fish—so long as the surface dis-

To spot fish in water less than a foot deep, look at the surface. Here a distinct ripple reveals a school of bonefish cruising through the shallows. Anytime you see a wave or ripple that appears to be going against the current, it's likely caused by moving gamefish.

turbance reveals their location. For example, redfish, bonefish, trout, pike, or any good-sized fish swimming in water less than a foot deep will produce a perceptible wake. This can be seen under calm conditions from a long distance. But remember that the fish is moving, and the wake will be trailing along behind it. To successfully offer your fly, you must throw far enough in front.

There are many other surface indicators of fish. An offshore skipper will frequently see billfish either free-jumping or basking. No one seems to know why they do it, but sailfish especially will suddenly leap into the air once or even several times. A leaping sailfish can be seen from a long distance. Basking billfish often will appear to be sleeping just under the surface. Generally the dorsal fin, and often the tail fin, will be sticking out of the water. Other fish will do this, too. Cobia and tripletails, for example, love to hang around markers, and on slack tides (high or low) they will rise and lie just under the surface and be clearly visible.

If you enter a quiet basin early in the morning, you will often see tarpon that are laid up and resting. They lie motionless with a part of their dorsal or tail above the surface. I have seen permit do the same thing; I suspect there are many other fish that will, too. Twice I have spotted northern pike lying alongside a log with the tail and dorsal fin sticking several inches above the surface. Snook, seatrout, and barracudas on a grass-covered flat will often lie over a white sand hole. They will sit motionless, ambushing any hapless baitfish that wanders by. If you know the habits of the fish you are searching for, you can often see them from a long distance. Almost any fish that is located under calm conditions will be extremely easy to frighten. This means your approach and presentation must be done with the utmost care.

Tailing Fish

One of the most exciting of all surface indicators is a tailing fish. It will stand on its head, or at least tilt at an angle, so that while it is rooting out a morsel of food, the tail is above the surface, waving a *come-hither.* I think tailing fish offer some of the most exciting visual treats in fishing. In salt water bonefish, permit, and redfish are frequently seen tailing. Mutton snapper will sometimes come to the flats and tail. The boxfish, which no one pursues with a fly rod, also tails on the flats. (Many inexperienced bonefishermen have stalked a boxfish, thinking it was a bone. But it has a different appearance. The little vibrating tail sets up a peculiar spray of water much like a small pump. Once recognized, a boxfish will rarely fool you.)

But some freshwater fish will tail, too. I have frequently located a good trout because it was tailing. In lakes and in some streams that are rich in aquatic growth, trout will tilt downward and run their heads into the weeds, shaking them in an effort to dislodge nymphs, sow bugs, scuds, and freshwater shrimp. They ram headfirst into the weeds, wiggle their bodies back and forth to loosen the food, and then back downcurrent to eat whatever tumbles free of the vegetation. When they are dislodging the insects, they will frequently tip their tail or dorsal fin above the surface.

In both fresh and salt water, when being chased by a predator fish, be it a bass or a barracuda, minnows will leap above the surface in an attempt to escape. Any angler who sees baitfish leaping frantically above the water and can get a streamer fly in front of them is almost guaranteed a strike. The fish are in a feeding mood and will strike almost any properly presented offering. Small silver sprays of minnows are often seen on bonefish flats. These little showers are often tough to spot, but an experienced angler looks for them. I believe that bonefish feed on them. But they do give away the presence of a bonefish, so that you have a better chance of seeing it.

A sudden swirl on the water, no matter how little, was made by something below. That's a good excuse to investigate. Saltwater flats fishermen often refer to "nervous water"—though you can see nervous water offshore, too. What they are saying is that the surface has a different and minute rippling to it. Minnows, for example, or baitfish offshore, will

When bonefish swim in the shallows, their tails often come out of the water.

create myriad tiny ripples that are distinct from the area surrounding the nervous water. This same phenomenon happens on lakes, especially big ones like the Great Lakes. Anytime a wave pattern looks different from the other waves around it, you probably have either baitfish or predator fish in that area. It's always worth investigating.

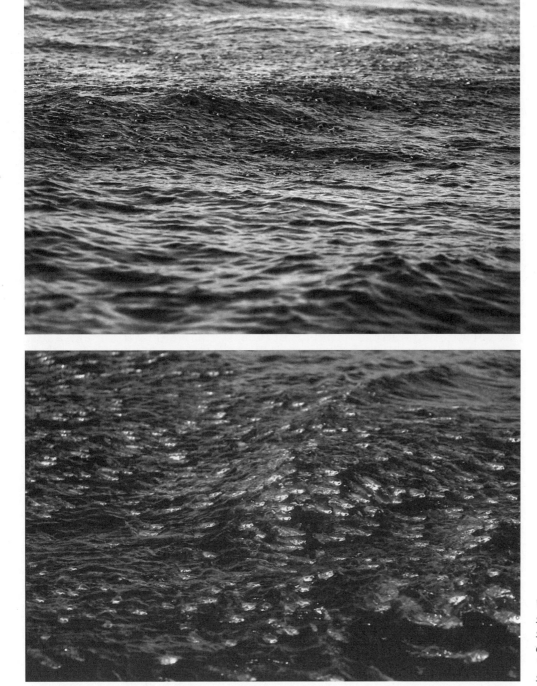

When gamefish chase a school of baitfish to the surface, the water becomes alive. Casting just off this "nervous water" is almost sure to catch a fish.

Another surface indicator of fish occurs where two masses of water with different temperatures collide. This causes an upwelling of the warmer water striking the cooler water. Such currents do two things: They often produce a temperature that results in productive fishing, and the upwelling can carry a lot of baitfish to the surface. This, of course, attracts predator species. Many times when the two bodies of water collide, there will be a difference in the colors of the water, such as where the Gulf Stream meets the inshore water. This is so markedly different that the water changes from the deep purple of the Gulf Stream to the pale green of inshore water in a matter of inches. But in many lakes (particularly the Great Lakes), the meeting of these two bodies of water of different temperatures is indicated by a single fine ripple or line. To the knowing angler, this is the hottest spot in the area to fish.

Rings on the Water

Of course the most recognizable surface disturbance made by a fish is the ring created when a trout rises to a dry fly. A trout, rising and sucking insects from the surface, is for many fly fishermen the greatest of all thrills. This ring is one of the quickest ways to locate a trout. However, take a closer look. Often what appears to be a rising trout is not one taking insects from the surface. A trout sucking in insects that are drifting on top will frequently leave an air bubble. If you watch a trout take half a dozen flies and there is never an air bubble, it's a good bet that the fish is not taking them off the top. Instead, the trout is following, up and through the water column, aquatic insects that are emerging.

These insects have lived for a long time on the streambed. Now they are drifting or swimming to the surface, where they will open their wings and fly away to mate and die. Trout feeding on these emergers often appear to be feeding on floating flies—but they aren't. They are hurrying after insects traveling upward in the water column. The trout then turns to descend to catch another one. During that downward turn, the body of the trout will often break the surface. The observant trout fisherman will note that if no bubbles ever appear, it is likely that the fish is taking nymphs or emergers below, and the angler will not try to tempt the fish with a dry fly.

Bubbles

Bubbles can also tip off the knowing angler. Tarpon breathe both underwater and above. One of the quickest ways to locate tarpon is to see them rolling. The head rises above the surface and moves forward slightly. Then the front of the body comes barely out as the fish breathes air, and it tips downward and disappears. When you are traveling in areas such as creeks and small bays where tarpon have been rolling, you may not see the fish. But you can often tell they are there by seeing a series of bubbles floating on the surface. Many times when a tarpon rolls and breathes, the expelled air (in the form of bubbles) will remain on the surface for several minutes—a tip-off for sure. Another place where bubbles can give you a lead on a fish is where a snook or other fish has crashed against the shoreline or under overhanging brush while chasing a baitfish. Such a foray will often leave considerable bubbles that are easily detected, if you know what to look for.

Vegetation and Mud

If vegetation grows right to the surface, the movements of fish can often be easily detected. This is especially true with northern pike and bass, which seem to enjoy cruising among concentrations of lily pads and similar waterweeds.

Another indicator used to locate fish in shallow water is mud. If the water is clear and fish begin feeding on the bottom, they will stir up a lot of mud in an effort to dislodge food that is hidden in the soft bottom. Bonefish create such muds with great frequency. In the Bahamas, for ex-

Small puffs of mud indicate that a bonefish has been rooting out food. Large mud streaks like this one show where a ray has been thrashing the bottom. Other species often follow working rays, so you should always try a cast at muds like this.

ample, as well as in the Yucatan area, I have seen muds as large as a football field. These were created by hundreds of bonefish nosing around in the bottom. The same thing occurs when seatrout or weakfish burrow in the bottom to get at shrimp, crabs, and other food morsels. Generally the tide will dissipate the mud. To be sure that you are offering your fly where the fish are actively rooting in the bottom, determine the tidal current's direction and move to the upstream end. Locate the brightest mud. This indicates the freshest and most recently disturbed bottom. Mud disturbed where fish have already moved on will be less intense and is not worth fishing.

Solitary bonefish will also create miniature muds, which can be invaluable in locating them. The larger fish can create a muddy spot as big as a dinner plate; once seen, this is easily detectable again. Usually the fish will tilt its head downward and close to the bottom, sensing a morsel buried just below. The bonefish will hover over the prey, then suck in both the prey and the small amount of bottom covering it. The silt and loose material pass through the gills, creating a puff of mud while the bonefish swallows its prey. An observant angler will see a tiny, thin cloud of indistinct mud. This says a bonefish has sucked a hole in the bottom, but some time ago. Looking around, you locate another dense mud cloud. Following this can often lead to a feeding fish as you chase from a thin mud cloud to one more recently made.

Rays in the Shallows

Another mud indicator is seen when a ray is working in the shallows. Stingrays, leopard rays, and other rays will swim along, then decide that prey is hidden below. To frighten the prey out of hiding, the ray will hover just above the bottom and flap its powerful wings violently up and down. Shrimp, crabs, small fish, and other prey species will panic and attempt to flee. The ray, although slow moving, will gather in many of these escaping victims. But because the ray is slow, many fish that are much quicker are keen to move in and capitalize on the situation. As the ray pounds the bottom, the faster fish will hover either above or tight against the ray, waiting for prey to attempt to escape. The swifter fish quickly grabs the escapees. Since these predator fish are in a feeding mood, you too can capitalize on the situation. If you see a streak of mud in the shallows, move in and be sure to carefully approach the streak where the mud is the brightest or densest—that is where the ray will be working. Cast a popping bug or streamer fly directly in front of the ray and retrieve it. If there is a predator fish in the area, you will probably get a hookup.

Always examine swimming rays. Gamefish often follow them around to steal the food that the rays flush from the bottom.

The arrow points to a ray that is "muddling" on the flats. Many fish hover over these rays and can be easily caught on flies.

Fish will follow rays even when they are not actively pounding the bottom. The fish will swim along very close to a ray for two reasons. First, they anticipate that the ray will soon be pounding the bottom. The other reason is that a bulky object like a ray is likely to frighten many prey species just by its approach, giving the swifter fish an opportunity to feed. This is quite similar to cattle egrets, which walk alongside cattle and feed on the insects that are frightened by the hooves.

Fish will follow rays in deep water, too. The largest cobia I ever saw (easily more than a hundred pounds) was following a huge manta ray at least ten feet wide in air-clear waters off the northeast coast of Australia. Cobia and tripletails are frequently seen swimming with a ray, even well offshore.

Water Debris

Another surface indicator that many people use to score with is floating debris. Dolphin (note that these are dolphinfish or mahimahi, not bottle-nosed porpoise) in offshore waters are famous for this, but many other species in the open sea are attracted to floating objects such as trees, logs, boards, and barrels. Weed lines are also great attractors. The line of weeds closest to the shoreline is usually not productive. This is often called bay grass and is composed mainly of stringy shallow-water grasses that have drifted seaward and clumped together. True seaweeds, such as sargasso weed, are a haven for many small fish. The baby fish of many species are born in the open sea and have few places to hide and grow up. These weeds offer that haven.

It's enlightening to dive just a few feet beneath the surface and peer upward under a bunch of floating sargasso weed. All sorts of tiny fish live there. On calm days you can slowly cruise in a boat alongside floating weed lines and locate all sorts of predator species that are also cruising and looking. Even schools of fish such as bar jacks and dolphin can frequently be seen investigating these weed lines.

Oil

This is another surface tip-off to some species of fish. Bluefish, for example, will often attack menhaden and other species of baitfish that are rich in oil content. If hungry blues are feeding well beneath the surface on such oily prey species, an actual oil slick will form. It is often faint, but easily detectable to the knowing angler. Even when you can't see the oil, the surface where the oil lies will often be calmer than the surrounding area.

Color

Discolored water, usually brownish or greenish, sometimes indicates fish. This is why good charter-boat skippers prefer to handle the boat from topside, rather than from the comfortable cabin below: They can see water discoloration or moving fish from this vantage spot. Many captains can actually tell you what kind of fish causes a specific discoloration. In Key West in wintertime, schools of jack crevalle sometimes roam the Gulf side, feasting on tiny sardines. These schools of jacks cover more than an acre, with individual fish ranging in size from eight to twelve pounds. They appear under the water as a yellow-amber color. Well below the surface, bluefish will chop so many menhaden that an oil slick of green can be seen on the surface. In New Guinea, when fingermark brim (baitfish) collect in feeding schools, the water turns to a dull pink—the color of their many bodies. Dark spots or intense small ripples on the surface often are indicators of densely packed baitfish.

Here is another way to locate fish. A pod of tarpon, even if they aren't rolling, when approaching over light-colored bottom will appear as a dark blue mass that is much different than the bottom color around them. This is also true of large schools of bluefish, tuna, and other species. Channel bass are reddish brown in color when they enter shallow bays, as they do each spring along the Outer Banks of North Carolina

Underwater bars appear as dark areas in the water. Baitfish will congregate there, as will gamefish.

or in the Mosquito Lagoon in Florida. A large school is easily seen as a big copper-colored area.

Water Depth

Here is another factor that must be considered when you are trying to locate fish. If the water is less than a foot deep, you should look in an entirely different manner than if the depth is greater. Fish worth catching that are moving in water less than twelve inches deep will produce visible wakes or ripples on the surface that indicate their presence and the direction in which they are swimming. Thus you should be looking carefully at the surface for indicators.

But when fish are deeper than one foot in the water column, you need to look for them very differently. Instead of staring at the surface, you must train yourself to look at the bottom only. At first this may sound foolish, but it is perhaps the most important factor in locating fish more than a foot below the surface. To demonstrate this technique, let me cite an example. If you were looking at a car being driven past you on the street, you would, of course, see the car clearly. What you might not see is someone standing on the pavement on the far side of the street, simply because you were concentrating on the car. But if you were looking

By concentrating on the sea floor, you can often spot well-concealed fish like this redfish.

at a person, and a car drove between you and that person, you would surely notice the car. The car interrupted your vision.

If you stare intently at the bottom and any fish swims over that bottom (between you and what you are looking at), the fish interrupts your vision and you notice it. I can't emphasize too strongly how important it is to learn to look at the bottom when the water is deeper than a foot.

Eddies

The angler who approaches an eddy in a stream often never sees fish that are there. There is a myth that all fish face upstream, but it's not true! What fish normally do is face into the current. There is a distinct difference between *upstream* and *into the current*. Most fish in a body of water will, in fact, be facing upstream. But if there is an eddy along the shoreline, the fish will be facing into the current. If you are going to locate fish, you need to be attentive. Approaching an eddy, fish may be facing downstream, if they are holding in close to shore. Others may be facing toward the near or far shore, depending on their location in the eddy.

Birds

Almost any fisherman knows that hovering birds indicate baitfish beneath. The incredible eyesight of gulls, terns, and other species means that they will quickly locate the feeding area. The *action* of the gulls will tell you if larger fish are disturbing the bait: When the bait is lying near the surface, unconcerned about predators, the gulls will often wheel in slow spirals, watching and waiting. But when the gulls drop down in quick, tight circles, or dart to the water and obviously pick up something as they tower upward—that's the time to head full bore for the birds. Field glasses are often a help. Some of the newer ones are made with a sealed plastic, or fiberglass housing and are completely waterproof, even if dropped overboard.

In the warmer seas of the world, frigate birds are a prized indicator, usually of a single or several large fish. With a seven-foot wingspan, and the lightest bones of any bird of their size, they go to sea and stay aloft for as much as a week. They have no oil feathers, so if they fall into the sea, they may drown. But they soar over the open waters searching for baitfish. With their long, hooked bills they can dive down and pluck small fish that are just under the surface. They earned their name from the fast-sailing frigate ships that were able to overtake slower sailing ships and steal their gold and other goods. The frigate, while airborne,

The frigate bird is one of the best indicators of big fish on the open ocean in the warmer seas of the world. If you see a frigate bird circling low, or diving at the surface, race to the scene—there's almost surely a large fish there.

will often harass another bird that has captured a small fish. It frequently forces the other bird to drop its catch, so the frigate can dive and steal it. If bait or predators are around, frigate birds will see them long before anglers will. And if a frigate bird dives suddenly for the surface, push the throttle to the wall and race to the spot—there will be either baitfish or predator fish at the scene. Frigates are one of the best ways to locate billfish and large dolphin.

If you can see baitfish showering above the surface, that's the best time of all. A cast into that spray can draw an immediate strike. Sometimes while running and looking, you'll come across a huge flock of gulls sitting on the surface. Unless you have an urgent destination, hang around for a few minutes, break out a sandwich, and wait. The gulls are there because, from aloft, they have located a large school of baitfish and they are simply resting until a school of larger fish finds the food.

Remember, too, that you will scatter a feeding school of fish by racing your boat through it. Work the boat from the outside edges—never run it through the school. You'll be aided immeasurably if the captain of the boat approaches the school from the *upwind* side, allowing you to toss your fly with the wind into the feeding fish. If you are the only boat—and if you stay on the edges of the school—you can often catch a number of fish before the school moves on or is frightened and dives. The best approach, if the fish are wary, is to come in on the school from the uptide or upwind side, cut the motor, and drift to them before making a cast.

Splashes

When running offshore—or even inshore, for that matter—many skippers are looking off in the distance in the hope of seeing their quarry. I

The circling birds and rippling water surface indicate that baitfish are desperately trying to avoid the predator fish below them.

Bright, big splashes like these, either inshore or offshore, are a sure sign that some predatory species is forcing baitfish to the surface. Always get to breaking fish like these as fast as possible.

can't tell you how many times I have been with an experienced guide or charter captain who was looking in front of and around the boat as it sped along. These captains frequently locate fish that I would never have noticed, often by splashes that showed fish were feeding on bait on the surface. Tuna and bonito, for example, often are located first by the little white splashes of water they make as they chase bait to the surface. Some fish make a specific type of splash, and with some experience you can even tell what kind of fish is feeding in the area. King mackerel and several other species will sweep up from down deep to take a baitfish at the surface. The swift upward chase often carries these fish many yards above the surface, where they resemble a launched rocket. I have seen large mackerel clear the water at least twenty feet in an arcing leap. Many small species, such as queenfish, will also leap a few feet above the surface as they chase bait.

Edges and Seams

Fish are creatures of the edges, just like many other animals. Deer, for example, feed mostly along the edges of the forest. Groundhogs nibble grass close to cover, and foxes hunt along the hedgerows. Shade makes another kind of edge. Fish will lie just inside the edge of the shade, in ambush, waiting for prey to come to them. The edge created by temperature changes in large lakes or the sea also congregates baitfish, thus drawing predators to the area. Two different water temperatures will form an edge that invites predators. It's also worth looking for a rip on the sea. This is simply two converging currents, and such an edge is a prime place to inspect with your fly. When fishing, look for any kind of edge and probe it with your fly.

If there are two currents of different speeds, the fish seem to gravitate toward the edge where they meet. Anglers often refer to places where two currents are joined as a seam. The fish will lie along the slower-moving current, only inches from the faster water. This allows them to rest, yet they can dart out and quickly grab any morsels that are transported by the swifter current. Many steelhead anglers make the mistake of walking to the base of a riffle to start casting across and downstream. But they often miss the best spot in the pool. The place where the water tumbles down through the rapids has a quieter edge where it enters the head of the pool. Often this is only yards from the bank. A prime holding area for steelhead is where the swifter currents of the riffle or rapids join the quieter water. In a river, if you had only one kind of water to fish, working the seams with your offerings would deliver more fish than testing any other part of the water.

Finding Fish on the Flats

The time of year often influences how well you can see fish in the shallows. The best light is when there is a cloud-free sky and the sun is high overhead. The lower the angle of the sun, the more difficult it is to see into the water. One reason that Christmas Island is so ideal for bonefishing is because it is located on the equator. For most of the day, the sun is high above the horizon. Fishermen who travel to Florida or the Bahamas during winter may be disappointed because they are rather far from the equator. The sun doesn't get high enough until about 9 A.M., and by 4 P.M. spotting fish becomes difficult again. But in the summer months you could fish two or three hours earlier and later, simply because the angle of the sun is higher.

If you are fishing from a boat, try not to stare at the water—you will actually see very little. Scan the area constantly, and not just the waters in front of you. Examine the water as far away as you can locate fish. Look for bonefish to a distance of at least fifty yards. Tarpon will often roll and break and surface, and you can see them as far away as two hundred yards.

When wading in the shallows, once again try to look as far ahead as possible to see the fish. As you move along, keep the sun at your back or side. If you look into the sun's glare, many fish will escape your notice. You can often improve your chances on days when the light is low or overcast. Try fishing along a shoreline with dark foliage, where the fish will be detected more easily. You can also see them better if there is a storm in the background. Poling toward a bright cloud on the horizon can ruin your ability to see well. But poling toward a dark cloud improves your ability to locate fish. Another good time to fish shorelines is when they are leeward and the wind is blowing, because calm water aids greatly in seeing the fish.

Night Fishing

At night, docks and bridges with lights will attract small bait and shrimp in salt water. These foods in turn draw predatory fish. Learning to see these fish is easy and can produce some excellent fishing. The predatory fish will always be holding on the uptide side of such a lighted area. For example, if the tide is flowing from north to south, the fish will be on the north side. To locate the fish, examine where the shadow line falls on the water. The fish will be just inside that shadow line, facing into the current. They will appear as a dark shadow. Once you know what you are looking for, they are easy to see.

Bonefish like to hide out on flats where the color of the sea floor varies.

Reading the Tides

Perhaps the greatest adjustment that a freshwater angler will have to make when moving to salt water is learning about tides. Even people with some understanding of this natural phenomenon think that tides are caused entirely by the gravitational pull of the moon. In fact, there are other elements involved. The wind also plays an important role. If there is a prediction for a high tide at 6:00 P.M. but there is an exceptionally strong west wind blowing against the shore, high tide will occur a little earlier, and it will certainly be higher than originally predicted. The warming of northern seas in summer can also cause higher tides. Similarly, atmospheric pressure can affect a tide's height, as can a "flexing" of the earth's surface.

One point that is predictable is that it takes twenty-eight days (scientists say the time is actually a little less), or roughly one month, for the moon to travel along an elliptical path around the earth. At points in its orbit the moon is farther away, and this reduces the tidal effect. The moon actually exerts nearly two and a half times as much gravitational pull on the earth as does the sun. As the moon goes around the earth, the water is pulled toward it. Naturally the "bulge" in the earth's water always lags behind the pull of the moon as it orbits the earth.

There is a seven-day period when the moon is closer to us than at any other time during a twenty-eight-day span. During this time both the sun and the moon are in near direct line with the earth. The corresponding positions of the three bodies increase the gravitational effects, causing the tides to rise higher and to fall lower than at any other time during the month. These are called spring tides. At this time the moon is said to be in perigee.

One of the reasons it is important to know about tides is so you will understand the baitfish on which the predators feed. Unlike many saltwater species, baitfish do not have a "home." They may be here today and gone tomorrow. They don't fight tidal currents; they allow the tide to take them along. Predator species know this and ambush the baitfish in places where the tide will make them available.

The tide causes many changes for baitfish, including the temperature of the water. Shallow water that has been lying under a hot sun will become uncomfortable for fish. As the tide rises, it brings cooler water from the deeper area, and with it will come the larger fish. Conversely, during a cool night and a low tide, the flats become chilled. As water flows in over these chilled banks, they act like refrigerator coils, drastically cooling the water. This drop in temperature will force fish into deeper water. Sometimes it can be severe enough to actually cause a fish kill.

An area at low tide.

The same area at high tide.

Two bodies of water at different speeds or temperatures have come together here to form a well-defined seam.

The tide can also have an enormous effect upon the water clarity. A flat can be so stirred by the wind that the water looks like soup. Yet a tidal change can suck all that dirty water away, exchanging it for clear water on the next tide. On a high tide, grass, small sticks, and other floating debris are carried in among the mangrove roots or deposited along the shoreline. Should a higher tide occur, it will free all this debris, which is then drained away on the next falling tide. This is a condition that can ruin fishing until the debris is washed out of the area.

Rising tides can cause fish to move into a specific area or to be widely scattered. Low tides can force fish to concentrate in deep pools in the shallows for safety. Common sense helps in analyzing tidal effects: If there are wide, shallow flats with a deep, narrow channel cutting through them, on low stages of the tide you would certainly expect most of the fish to be in the channel. Another basic tidal situation that any fly fisherman can easily understand and take advantage of is an inland bay or lagoon. If such a body of water is tide-drained through a narrow creek, fish will obviously feed on the bait funneled through the creek. The place to fish is on the downtide side of the mouth of the creek—or at the mouth of the funnel.

River mouths are in most cases best fished on a falling tide. Some have underwater bars that become feeding stations for predator species when

These anglers are working an incoming tide for bonefish. In most areas this is the best tidal phase to fish for these elusive speedsters.

the tide rises. Baitfish will go with the incoming tide, seeking the shallows and safety. When the water falls, the baitfish try to remain in the security of the shallows as long as possible. Any ditches or drainages on the lower stages of a tide are the places they will finally have to come out. Predators establish feeding stations at such outlets.

8

APPROACH AND PRESENTATION

Once you have scouted the waters, your next task is to approach the fish and present your fly. No matter what rod, reel, line, or fly you use, unless your presentation is correct, the game is over. At this stage anglers often emphasize presenting an exact fly pattern. But I know many trout fishermen who carry only three or four patterns in their fly box, yet they catch more fish than their friends. The same could be said of fly fishing in salt water. These anglers, of course, have learned the lessons of good approach and presentation.

These principles are about more than dropping your fly in the best position in relation to the fish. They involve the clothes you wear, the way you rig your tackle, how and where you approach the fish, the types of fly lines and reels you use, the direction of the light, the type of cover you use, and your retrieving method. I know a number of fly casters who catch few fish simply because they so often use the wrong cast, or do not understand how to present the fly. I also know fishermen who will make the proper cast but don't know how to correctly retrieve.

Successfully catching fish with a fly rod begins before you leave home and ends when the fish is either landed or released. Those 10 to 20 percent of anglers who consistently score do so because they have mastered certain techniques. Any fish that is alerted to danger or is suspicious is going to be more difficult to catch. First, you need to be concealed from the fish, if possible. If there is even a hint of your presence, the quarry will be more difficult to deceive. It follows that when you approach any fish, whether you are wading, stalking from shore, or in a boat, if you can get near it without giving even a hint of your presence,

Wearing bright clothes and casting in the bright sunlight means trout will see you.

By wearing clothing that blends with the background, and by standing in the shade, this angler will be less visible to trout.

When you're fishing on flat, calm, clear water, it's imperative to use long leaders and a light fly line.

you better your chances of success. Use patience and don't rush. Take time to figure out your approach, what fly is needed, and how you'll present it to the fish. Remember, the first cast is always the most important one; every succeeding cast tends to decrease your chances.

Once you have approached close enough to make a presentation, other factors take over. The angle at which you approach, and the direction in which you cast and retrieve the particular fly are vital to success.

When the cast is made, how the line lands on the surface, and the impact of the fly—all are important.

Finally, the fly must come to the fish in a natural manner. Even novice dry-fly fishermen know that drag will spoil their chances. But there are other factors, such as how the fly drifts or is brought to the fish, that cause the fish to strike or turn away.

The approach, what flies to use, where and how to cast, use of the proper fly line and leader, and the correct retrieve are all vital knowledge for successful fly fishing. To make things a little more complex, the environment where the fish is caught (lake, stream, saltwater flats, open sea) will create special problems, too. Let's take a look at each of these factors.

Motion

Approaching fish without alarming them is a learned art. The two things that alert fish to danger more than any others are motion and sound, and they are more sensitive to the first. The sight of a looming fisherman or a waving fly rod—or even a shadow—will easily spook a fish and send it scurrying away from you and your fly. They are used to watching for ospreys, herons, or eagles swooping down from above, so it behooves fishermen to make as little visible motion as possible. If you can approach from behind brush, a rock, or any structure that prevents your prey from seeing your movement, the chances of your catching a fish will dramatically improve. And approaching fish while highlighted against the sky is not as effective as having a solid background behind you. In fact, there are even times when it is best to crawl to your fishing spot.

Clothing and Tackle

Wearing the proper clothing can also be critical to success. For example, trout streams in the East usually have green foliage along their borders. Wearing a brightly colored shirt here is like carrying a beacon. The fish are going to quickly see any movement you make in clothing bright enough to contrast with the background vegetation. In vogue among many fly fishermen these days is the wearing of flashy hats—some even made of bright fluorescent materials. I watched a fly fisherman sneak down a Pennsylvania stream a few years ago. He stalked quietly and appeared to be aware of the need for a cautious approach. However, he caught nothing during the time I observed him. I think the reason was that he was wearing proper green clothing—but a hat of brilliant fluorescent yellow. I'm sure all the trout saw him long before he got close.

This angler is wisely staying low and downstream of the dam. Many trout will lie at the breast of a dam when feeding. By dropping his fly line across the rocks on the right side of the stream, he avoids getting line drag during the time his fly floats past the trout.

The background is what you want to match. On a western U.S. stream, where the vegetation is often brownish or tan in color, a light tan fly-fishing vest and clothes would blend in well. However, the dark green clothing that worked so nicely in eastern streams may do poorly out West—and vice versa. Many saltwater fly fishermen work from boats. The guide poles the boat across a flat, and the angler stands either in the bow or on a small platform. This added height helps the angler see the fish—but it also makes it easier for the fish to see the angler, particularly if his clothing contrasts with the background sky. For such fishing, it's best to wear white, pale blue, or some other shade that blends with the sky and clouds. Dark colors would create a silhouette, warning the fish.

Experienced trout fishermen know that wearing highly reflective items while fishing can also give their presence away to the trout. For example, the hemostats used to remove hooks are generally chrome plated. So are zingers—small retractable devices that hold clipper and other small tools. This chrome plating gives off flashes of light as you move around. Fortunately, some manufacturers now offer these tools in a dull black finish. If you already have such chrome-plated tools, keep them inside your jacket or paint them a dull color. Some anglers also buff the fine finish on their fly rods to dull any reflective flash made while casting. (Frankly, I don't think this is a problem; I can't recall a time when I believed a reflection from my rod caused me to lose an opportunity.)

Most fly fishermen use a rod eight and a half to nine feet in length. With such a long reach, however, you may find that on some streams the bank on the far side is too close; your rod will prevent you from making a good cast. A simple trick that often works is to slide your hand up the rod to just below the butt or stripping guide. Now you'll have no trouble

When you're using a long rod in a tight corner with little space to cast, you can often slide your rod hand up the rod by as much as 18 inches. After the cast, hold the handle as you normally would to fish.

making a tight-quarters cast. When the cast is finished, return your rod hand to the handle.

Here's another problem during the approach that can cause a lost fish, but it's easily remedied. If you wear hip boots, they're often supported by straps attached to your belt. The ends of the straps dangle down outside your boots. During a cast, and sometimes when fighting a fish, your line can tangle in this dangling strap. How can you fix this? Simply remove the strap from the boot. Reverse the position of the buckle so that the top is at the bottom. Insert the strap again, and the end will go inside your boot instead of dangling on the outside.

Sound

Sound is the other factor that alerts fish. It's not quite as important as motion, but it can surely doom your chances. Crunching your boots on gravel, creating tumbling debris in front of you as you crawl down a rocky bank, or roaring into a location in a boat—all these errors will alert and frighten your quarry.

A simple example can illustrate the problem. Many streams are bordered by fences that you have to climb to reach the water. I've watched some fly fishermen carefully climb the fence—then jump to the ground on the other side. If you do this with a fence close to the stream, be assured that every trout nearby will hear you contact the ground, and they will know there's danger present.

I prefer to walk on a bank of grass or soft dirt as I approach a trout stream, rather than treading on a gravelly one, which crunches underfoot and sends signals to the fish. If you use a wading staff—and it's a good idea—I recommend a wooden one. It doesn't clang against the bottom like a metal one (it also floats). When moving from one location to another, don't let the wading staff drag on the ground behind you. Once, in the Delaware River, I was fishing with another outdoor writer. I never had to wonder where he was. He allowed his wading staff, which was an aluminum ski pole, to drag on the ground as he walked. I could trace all his movements as the pole clattered over the gravel bars. I'm sure trout a long distance away knew that he was approaching, too.

As I've noted, water transmits sound about four and a half times faster than air does. Salt water transmits sound slightly faster than fresh water. This is a very important factor in making a good approach. Whether you're wading a bonefish flat or a calm pool on a small trout stream, always be aware that water will send sounds you make quickly to the fish. For this reason, never wade when you don't have to. Too many anglers fishing small streams will get into the water to make the cast. This

Slide your feet along the bottom when wading to avoid stingrays.

can be a mistake. Only when you can't otherwise make the right presentation should you consider stepping into a stream. Your feet grinding on gravel, slipping off rock, and making other warning sounds will often defeat your efforts.

When wading, I like to think of the water in front of me as a balloon. If you hold up a balloon full of water and poke against one side, all of the other side of the balloon will surge away from you. This is exactly what happens when you wade, especially if the water is calm. (The noise you make is reduced when the water is moving swiftly.) As you wade, notice

Don't make waves.

the small waves moving out from your legs during your forward strides. For some reason, many anglers seem to think this is only a surface disturbance. It isn't! Just like when you poked the balloon and the water surged away, the entire water column directly in front of you is affected. Waves are moving outward from top to bottom because of your disturbance. The lateral line on a fish tells it someone is approaching. The calmer the water, the slower you must move if you hope to get close to wary fish. This is true both on a redfish flat and when fishing a calm spring creek for brown trout.

When you wade on calmer waters, if you see small waves radiating out more than eighteen inches from your legs, you're wading too fast! When I approach wary trout in a calm pool, I move my forward foot so slowly that it may take several minutes to progress just a few yards. I've spent ten minutes wading slowly just to get into position to cast. If you are going to wade, consider speed and make it on the slower side. This is an important concept many fishermen disregard.

A long time ago I learned about which direction to wade when fishing meadow streams for bass, bluegills, and other warmwater species. In Maryland, where I've lived most of my life, many small streams meander through the lush countryside. Many of my most pleasant fishing trips have involved grabbing a 3- or 4-weight fly rod, a floating line, a small box of flies, and a companion, then driving a few miles from home to one of these streams. It's not high-profile fishing, and a minimum of gear is needed. Early on I switched from tennis shoes to regular wading shoes. But since I fish this way only during the warm months, the water temperature is in the eighties and very comfortable. All I need is a rigged rod, a small popper, streamer, or wet fly, and a pair of wading shoes.

At first a companion and I would drive to a bridge and park the car; one angler would go downstream while the other went up. Such streams

Some of the most enjoyable fly fishing the author does is on small meadow streams like this one.

Flip Pallot wades upstream when fishing smaller meadow creeks; wading downstream reduces your catching chances.

produce about the same number of strikes in either direction, unless the character of the water is very different. But I soon realized that one of us would always catch more fish than the other, unless there was a great difference in our skills with the tackle. Who caught the most? Invariably it was the fly fisherman who waded upstream. I'm not sure why; my friends and I learned to wade cautiously and make a good approach. The only reason we could figure out is that the mud and debris kicked up by wading always traveled downstream. In front of the downstream wader, this apparently alerts the fish.

Such meadow streams have bridge crossings every two or three miles, so we eventually altered our method of fishing them. I would drive my friend to a bridge, dropping him off with an extra key to the car. Then I'd drive to the next upstream bridge, park the car, and wade upstream. My friend, upon reaching the car, would drive to the next upstream bridge to pick me up. This is a great sport for two fly fishermen to enjoy.

Motorboats

I'm continually amazed at serious bass fishermen, some considered professionals, who roar in a modern high-speed bass boat into a cove they plan to fish. Then they chop the motor. These heavy boats, which run almost out of the water when at high speed, on the stop will suddenly sink deep into the water. This causes huge waves to radiate outward from the boat. The waves race to shore, washing debris back into it, and often muddying the area near the bank. Saltwater fishermen are also guilty of this action. Aside from dropping dynamite overboard, I can't think of a more effective way to disturb the peace and silence of a cove or any water you plan to fish.

I have an aluminum seventeen-foot johnboat, rigged with a sixty-horsepower jet engine. It's a dream boat for getting around on the rocky rivers of the mid-Atlantic where I fish. When I approach a favorite fishing location, I shut off the big jet engine a good distance away. Then using either the electric motor or a pole, I quietly move into my fishing spot. I'm positive this delivers more hookups for me.

If you fish on saltwater flats with experienced guides nearby, you will very quickly learn that running motors in shallow water close to other anglers can start a fight. One of the quickest ways to get into an argument on a tarpon or bonefish flat is to operate your motor at high speed near someone who's fishing. Experienced guides know that this puts down local fish, and they won't tolerate it. The same ethics apply when you're leaving an area where others are fishing. On occasion I've been tarpon fishing, especially in the Florida Keys, at spots where there were a number of guides either staked out waiting for moving fish, or poling

Early or late in the day is often the best fishing time. Here Bill Anderson helps launch the author's boat as early morning mist shrouds the bridge pilings. The target is smallmouth bass.

quietly along. I've watched good guides leave an area by poling more than half a mile away from other anglers before starting their engines. It's an indication of how seriously these guides take their engine noise.

Again, fish survive by danger indicators that come to them. While they aren't brilliant, anything that's out of the normal pattern of their lives they regard as a threat until they're satisfied it isn't. Motion and noise are two factors that fish use to alert them to danger. We need to constantly keep this in mind.

Let me cite another good example. One well-known outdoor writer, when fly casting, rocks his body back and forth in a most pleasing manner; it looks so smooth. Several times when we fished together, though, I felt his beautiful casting motion was detrimental. If you're in shallow water, such as the backcountry of the Ten Thousand Islands, the bottom is soft and mushy. Step out and your foot will sink a foot or more before it contacts solid turf. I've watched this great caster rocking back and forth while false-casting, and in turn the boat rocked with him. If I looked carefully, I could see the small waves radiating outward from the boat. Even the bottom nearby would become stirred. I'm certain fish feel the pressure created by a boat as it rocks back and forth like this—or when you push it too fast through the shallows. I believe that when

Flats boats are designed for fly fishing. They have no line-tangling devices, and John Zajano and his Bahamian guide are able to work in water only inches deep.

you're in a boat in the shallows, the slower the boat progresses and the less it rocks, the better.

Another factor is important when fishing from boats. The boat is like a giant drum, resonating any noise made within. Remember how much faster water transmits sound than air does? A slight noise made in a boat sitting on the water is communicated rapidly to the fish. If you want to prove this to yourself, snorkel with your head underwater and have someone make a noise with a nearby boat. You'll be amazed how well you hear it—and the fish will certainly hear it better than you do. In deep water you can get away with some boat noise. But in shallow water all noises are detrimental to fishing success.

There are a number of things you can do to reduce or eliminate this problem. The most important is to be constantly aware of the noise factor. Anything you do to avoid it will help. Don't jump from the boat platform to the bottom of the boat. Try not to drop anything on the deck, and when you're moving around in a boat, plan how you'll do it without making noise. Take care to store things so you can move around freely. If you carry tackle boxes or other containers, glue a section of outdoor carpet on the bottom. In a boat I prefer to carry most items in soft bags. I also place a section of outdoor carpet between the mount on my electric

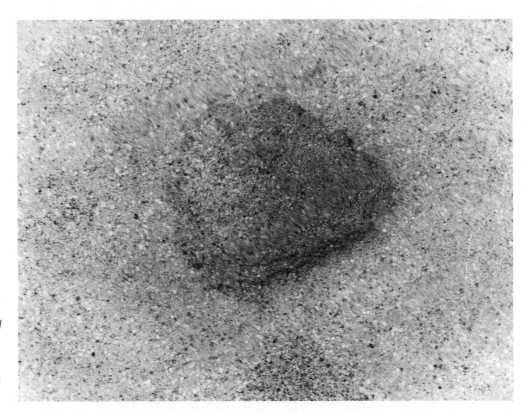

The circular hole in the sand is a tip-off that bonefish have been feeding recently. The hole is caused by bonefish squirting a blast of water to flush out food.

Mike Wolverton points his rod at the place where the guide says there's a fish. Pointing the rod like this is the fastest way to locate a difficult-to-see fish on the flats.

motor and the boat. This padding further reduces any vibrations that are sent to the fish.

Years ago I was told by experienced fly fishermen that loud talking didn't bother fish in the shallows. From my own experience, I know this isn't true. When fishing in shallow water, keep your voice low—or you'll suffer the consequences. You can easily test this. Locate some fish in very shallow, calm water. Then make a loud shout. Even if the fish don't scatter, they'll definitely change their attitude, and you'll know they've been alerted.

Approach

The clothing and equipment you wear mean a great deal in terms of how close you can get to fish. In England a number of years ago I fished with John Goddard, one of Europe's most famous angling writers and a fine trout fisherman. He taught me a lesson that has resulted in my catching more fish. Our first day was to be on the wilderness section of a famous chalk stream, the Kennet. Arriving there, we opened the boot (car trunk) and pulled out our tackle. Rods were rigged, and I put on my fly vest.

"I'm not sure you should wear that. Have you anything else?" John said.

"What's wrong with it?" I asked.

"It's the wrong color and I'm afraid it will frighten the fish," John answered almost apologetically. "This is the color I use," he added, pulling out of the car a medium green one. Mine was a bright khaki color, similar to most vests used in the United States.

Having no other fishing vest with me, I fished that day with mine. John had a spare at home that I wore the rest of the week. On several occasions I switched jackets, and I became aware that trout would seem to sense me quicker when I was wearing the khaki one. The country and streamsides of England are a rich, lush natural green. My khaki vest was so bright by comparison that I felt it did alert many trout.

When I came home I realized that all my vests were the same khaki color. Using Rit dye, I tinted a summer mesh and a standard jacket green for eastern U.S. streams, which are usually in wooded areas. Out west, where much of the habitat is brown or tan, I use the khaki jackets. I now use several colors of jackets and also wear clothing that blends in with the local environment. I am certain that doing this has increased my ability to sneak up on fish.

Many years ago I decided to paint my Grumman aluminum canoe. I did so because I had been fishing with two friends who were in another, similar model on a small pond of the Eastern Shore of Maryland. The sun was low in the sky, just peeking over the trees. One angler was fly casting in the front; the other paddled him along the shoreline. As the angler moved his arm back and forth to make his cast, the canoe rocked in unison with his motion. Each time the canoe tilted back, a bright flash of light bounced off it. It reminded me somewhat of a channel marker light in the dark, giving off periodic flashes of light to alert boaters of danger. I felt that the bright side of the canoe was doing the same thing for the fish. Since that time, all of my boats and canoes have a dull coat of paint. I feel that the popular bass boats with a metallic finish can also sometimes alert fish. Any boat with bright, reflective sides that is in shallow water, attempting to sneak up on fish, can at times frighten fish or at least alert them to the angler's presence.

Rubber-soled waders and hip boots are treacherous. I recommend felt soles. In some areas even felts are not enough, and some type of soft, aluminum cleats are worn either on a special shoe or embedded into the sole. But these metal cleats do make a grating noise when you wade over rocks. Unless they are absolutely necessary, I don't use them; I use felt soles instead. My favorite sole for wading shoes is not felt or cleats, but the material used on the soles of mountain climbers' shoes. This tough rubberlike material makes little noise when wading. For safety and the ability to wade quieter in deeper, swift water, I also prefer a wading staff. If it has a metal tip on the end, place it against the bottom as quietly as possible.

Positioning

The basic approach to the fishing spot is also important. All sorts of factors should be considered. When trout fishing, you need to know if there is room for a backcast. You need to establish where the fish may be lying in the pool. You will want to know if they are nymphing or taking dry flies. If you are lucky enough to hook the fish, how will you fight and land it? All of these factors will decide how you can approach the pool.

In a bass fishing situation, some of the same questions will have to be answered. Here's a good example. Many years ago I was offered a job in Florida. I lived in Maryland and fished the Potomac River for smallmouth bass—still my favorite form of freshwater fishing. During the last early-fall month that I lived in Maryland, I determined to get in as many trips for smallmouths as I could. In that month I caught twenty-nine bass larger than three pounds; a number of them were more than four pounds. That would be considered a significant accomplishment in this region. Most of the bass were taken on a fly rod.

Not rushing, and taking the time to study the situation, selecting the right fly, and easing my way into the proper casting position allowed me to take this gorgeous rainbow. This careful approach is vital for success with big fish.

What was amazing was that I caught almost all of these trophy bass from about ten very specific locations, even though I was fishing miles of the river. What was even more interesting was that in almost all of these hot spots, I determined that the big fish took the fly or lure only when it approached from a certain direction. That meant it was important to get into the right position, make the correct cast, and then bring the lure or fly back in a very specific manner. When all this was accomplished, the bass would strike.

When you approach a stream for trout, if you are a novice you may have no idea just where you should retrieve the fly, be it a nymph, streamer, or dry. Similarly, if you are fishing a stream that you have

The current doesn't flow at the same rate all through a pool; instead, there are narrow currents that travel much faster. These are what the author calls food highways—they transport most of the insects that come downstream. To recognize and fish these, look for flowing, thin lines of foam.

never tested before, you may not know the best places to fish. Here is my advice. In a trout pool the food lies mainly among the rocks and smaller stones in the riffles. We often refer to this portion of a trout stream as the grocery shelf. It is where the nymphs, small minnows, crayfish, hellgrammites, and many other types of organisms live. These are the food supply for the trout living in the deeper water below the riffles. Such food is often washed downstream by the current. Mayflies, in the process of emerging or laying their eggs, float on the surface and drift into these pools, where hungry trout are looking for them.

Understanding this, you should then realize that the insects don't just drift through the pool in a random manner. In almost every pool there are several major currents that flow faster than most of the other water passing downstream. These currents are well defined, if you know where to look for them. I call them food highways, for they are the areas of the pool that will carry the bulk of the insects drifting through it. Fortunately, these are easy to locate. The water rushing over the rocks in the riffles creates tiny air bubbles that collect into lines of foam. (I am not referring to foam that collects in a static state along the shoreline, but flowing lines of foam.) The bulk of the foam lines will be carried (just as the insects are) through the mini currents or food highways of the pool. So when you approach a pool, study it carefully. You will find that these food highways are clearly indicated by the foam lines. These are the most productive places to fish and should be thoroughly searched with your flies.

When working a field, bird dogs seeking quail will begin on the downwind side of the field, moving into the wind that hopefully will carry to them the scent of the birds. Bonefish act in the same manner most of the time. They usually will move up on a flat on the downcurrent side and work into the current, sniffing out shrimp, crabs, and other prey. This tells you the likely direction the fish will be swimming.

Giant tarpon, when in the shallows, prefer to roam the waters from six to twelve feet deep. That's the first place to seek them. But they also like to follow underwater walls or banks. In tarpon country, locate water of that depth that has a drop-off and you stand a good chance of finding these prized gamefish.

Lighted bridges at night in the tropics, especially in Florida, lure in baitfish, attracted to the glare of the lights. This in turn brings in snook and tarpon. To locate these two species, carefully examine the water just inside the shadow created by the structure. The fish will always be holding on the uptide side of the bridge, pouncing on any prey being swept along.

When you are searching for many kinds of fish, a pair of binoculars can be invaluable. Offshore skippers have used them for years. They aid in seeing distant birds, checking debris to see if fish are near it, and seeing free-jumping fish or bait being chased to the surface. They can also be handy to check for bonefish muds and to locate tailing redfish, permit, and bonefish.

Binoculars are most useful to freshwater trout fishermen, particularly those working smaller streams. A surprising number of larger trout quickly become aware of an approaching angler. Often a larger fish will be lying out in the open, and as the footfalls of the angler are sensed

Jim Finn is using field glasses to help him locate trout. But binoculars can be helpful for spotting fish in many situations, in both fresh and salt water.

through vibration, or the fish sees the angler's movement, it eases silently under a rock or moves to cover. Many large brown trout, for example, will ease out from an undercut bank, searching for food that may come their way. If the angler stands back and uses binoculars to check out the pool, there is a good chance that the fish in the open, or that big brown along the bank, will be located, and a proper approach and presentation can be made. When trout fishing, I use a pair of four-power glasses that are ample for what I need. Such glasses should be small enough to fit into a fly vest or jacket so that you can carry them easily. For most saltwater work I prefer at least an eight-power set. I am really enthusiastic about the new types that are autofocus—they save me time adjusting them.

In addition to a silent approach, the angler should avoid a visible approach. A common fault among many trout fishermen is to come to the stream and stand on a high bank or gravel bar. To any fish in that pool, the angler must look like a skyscraper. It would be much better to use the brush along the stream to hide in while observing the pool. It is very important to keep your body as low as possible when approaching a pool. The same thing is true when wading for bonefish. If the fish approaches you, kneel down. I have caught a number of bonefish with both knees resting on the flat, just to keep my profile low. If you are on

Here, Amy Cerrelli demonstrates the correct approach, keeping herself low and concealed behind the brush.

the bow of a boat that nears a bonefish, tarpon, or permit, and it gets too close, kneel or bend low. It has been said many times that the best trout fishermen on small streams will wear out the knees of their hip boots before they do the soles. If you fish small streams, you know that kneeling, crawling, and keeping low are key to catching many fish.

Presentation

If you have finally located and approached your quarry, you now must make a proper presentation. And there is more to this stage than simply casting to the fish. It is vital to understand several points when offering a fish your fly. First, if the fish has even a hint that you are nearby, getting it to accept your fly becomes more difficult. So it's important to make as careful, silent, and unseen an approach as possible. Second, whenever a fish approaches the fly, or the fly approaches the fish, this approach should be as natural as possible. All its life the fish has seen prey act in a particular way. Anything that differs from the natural act may alert or alarm the fish, reducing your chances. These two principles should always be paramount in your mind as you offer your fly to any fish. Understanding and considering these principles as you look for fish, approach them, and then make your presentation are vital to consistent success.

We have already covered locating and approaching the fish. The second principle—that a fly must approach in a natural manner—is something that even many experienced anglers fail to appreciate. Because of this failure, success often eludes them.

Let's look at a natural situation, with a fish facing into the current, looking for food. The prey comes drifting toward the predator in the current. As it nears the fish, it is suddenly aware of the danger, so it darts off to the side, and hopefully to safety. The fish sees the prey as it approaches and as it bolts away. The predator surges forward and grabs it. All of this is a natural situation.

Now let's take several examples of how anglers often fail to appreciate this and thereby lose an opportunity to hook a fish. Wading against the current, the angler sees a nice fish holding upstream from him. Positioning himself below and to the side of the fish so that he doesn't have to throw his fly line directly over the fish, he makes a cast. The streamer fly lands far enough upstream from the fish so that it doesn't alarm it. Allowing the fly to sink to the fish's level, the angler makes a retrieve. The fly comes directly at the fish, which suddenly sees its approach. As the small fly gets nearer, the fish moves forward to strike. But the tiny fly doesn't flee at the sight of the predator. Instead it continues to come

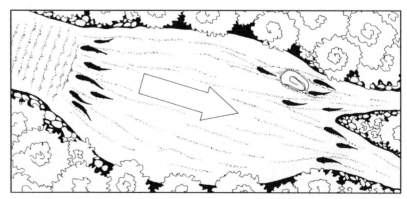

Trout hold at the head of a pool, ahead of rocks or behind them, and at the tail of a pool.

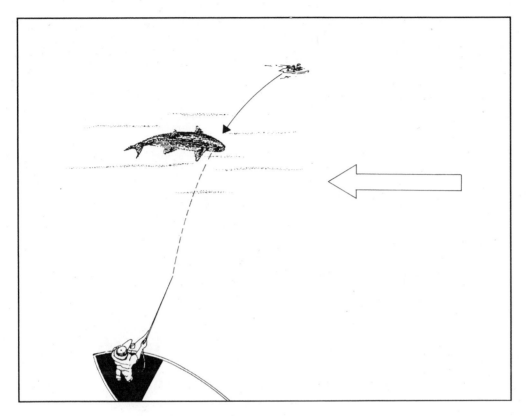

Fly swimming at fish—incorrect presentation.

directly toward the fish. Suddenly the fish realizes instinctively that something is wrong (it's never happened before), so it flees until it can assess the situation. An opportunity for the angler has been lost.

Here is another situation that often occurs when sight-fishing from a boat. For the purposes of illustration, let's assume the angler is proceeding due north. A fish is seen approximately west of the angler, holding in the current or tide. A cast is made in front of the fish in approximately a northwesterly direction, and the fly lands well beyond the fish. As the retrieve begins, the current sweeping south carries the fly toward the fish, even though the fly is also being brought back toward the angler on the retrieve. As it nears the fish, the fly is actually even with or slightly downstream of it. The retrieve continues, causing the fly to come directly at the fish or, worse, to approach it from slightly downstream as the current sweeps the fly farther south. To the fish, again something that resembles prey is attacking it, and so the game is lost again.

And here's one more example. The angler sights a fish directly in front of him and casts directly over it. Even if the fish was not spooked by the line or leader falling on top of it, the chances of success are radically reduced. The angler will be forced, from this position, to retrieve the offering directly at the fish. There are some cases where nothing else is possible—so you take a chance. But if there is any way that you can

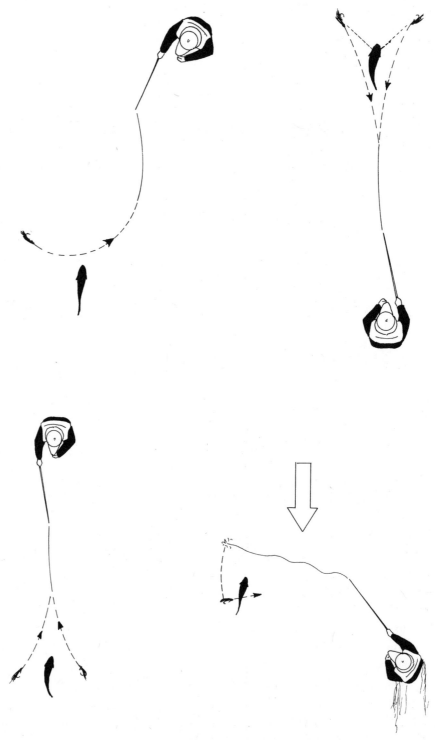

This illustration shows that flies don't attack fish.

get off to one side and offer the fly so that it doesn't come at the fish in an attack position, hookups are far more likely to occur.

There is another basic problem of presentation that often ends in defeat. Somehow you get very close—less than twenty-five feet away—to a fish before you see it. You might be wading and suddenly spot a bonefish, a trout, or any other species holding in front of you. The normal reaction, if you are offering an underwater fly, is to crouch, make a cast, and try to get the fish to follow and hit the fly before it sees you. Usually that doesn't happen.

Solutions

What needs to be evaluated here is what you are trying to do, other than get a hookup. You need to realize that the fish will follow the fly some distance before it grabs it. Once this is understood, you can accommodate the situation by making a different cast. Suppose you make a curve cast to the right or left (whichever you do easily). The fly lands to one side and in front of the fish. The leader and forward part of the line are in a big curve on the water. As the retrieve starts, the fly swims at right angles to the fish, but well in front of it. The fish moves in to inspect the offering. The fly passes by the fish and continues on (at right angles to the fish and to you) until the curve is lost and the fly begins

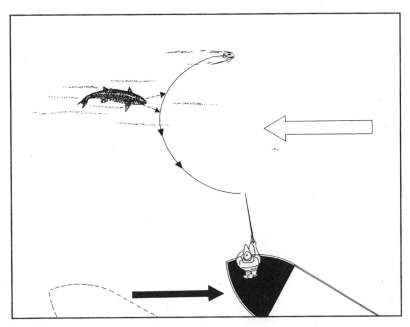

Fly swimming in front of fish—correct presentation.

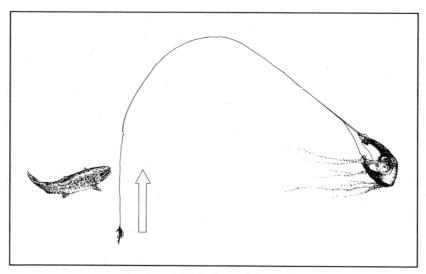

Curve cast: fish in front of the angler.

coming back toward you. With a curve cast, the fish may follow a fly ten to twelve feet without getting any closer to you. Such a cast under these conditions means an infinitely better chance of drawing a strike from a fish that's too close.

Another basic principle of presentation and retrieve is the angle of the rod. It is recommended for some nymph fishing that you hold the rod fairly high, with the tip often above your head. But for almost every situation in which you are stripping a line to manipulate an underwater fly, the rod should be kept very low, always below the belt. When bass bugging, retrieving a streamer, bringing in a bonefish fly, or anytime you retrieve an underwater fly, the rod tip should be very close to the water, or with the tip actually an inch or two under it. This is a basic rule that will get you more fish. The fly is retrieved with the line hand and the rod pointing at the fly.

Here's the reason. With the tip at the surface or slightly beneath it during a retrieve, no slack occurs, and even slight nibbling at the fly can be detected. Because no slack occurs, the fish will often hook itself; this certainly makes it easier for you to strike more effectively. Bass buggers and those who fish streamers have been guilty for years of using the rod to manipulate the bug or fly. The cast is made. The angler flips the rod tip up and down, which activates the bug or fly. As the rod tip drops each time, slack falls into the line. If a fish hits when the slack has accumulated—and this often happens—the strike is often missed.

Another problem occurs when fishing a popping bug. The purpose of stripping the line and then pausing before making another pull on the line is to allow your fly or bug to stop briefly, hopefully exciting the quarry. But when the rod is held high, as most anglers do, or the tip is used to manipulate the fly, little or no pause ever occurs with your offering. Tie on a popping bug and cast it out on the water, and you'll be better able to see what I mean. Flip the rod up and down, activating the popping bug, but keep the rod tip above the level of your waist or belt. Watch the bug; it will keep moving for an extended period after the rod tip has stopped. When the rod flips up, the line is pulled taut, dragging the bug nearer. As the rod stops but is held a few feet from the surface, a sag occurs in the line between the rod tip and the surface. This gradual sagging of the line continues to drag the line toward you. But if you hold the rod tip at or slightly under the surface, each pause during the stripping routine guarantees that the fly or bug also stops moving.

Another basic rule of retrieve is that the line being stripped in should always be controlled by the line hand from behind the rod hand. What

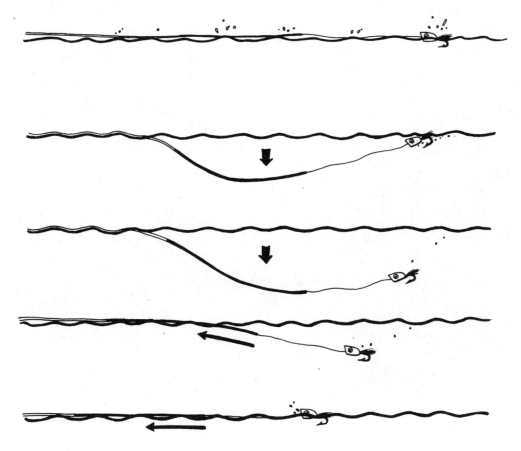

Here is an effective and fascinating way to tease bass with a popping bug and a sink-tip line, with the sinking portion shortened to five feet, and a leader of about six or seven feet. Make a cast and allow the sink tip to drag the bug underwater. If you start to retrieve, the bug will swim underwater, but the retrieve also makes the line loft upward. Eventually the line and bug will surface. Stop retrieving and the bug will sink again, and you can repeat the whole process.

Keep your partner's line tangle free before he or she loses a fish.

often occurs is that you make a cast, grasp the line behind the rod hand, and pull backward, activating the fly. But if the line hand reaches up and grabs the line in front of the rod hand, this requires letting go of the line in the rod hand, then repositioning the line in the rod hand so that it can be trapped under a finger for another stripping motion. If the line hand strips some line in, then reaches behind the rod hand and grabs it for another stripping motion, the rod hand always has the line under control. The same technique applies when you are fighting a fish. Always retrieve line from behind the hand holding the rod—so that you always have control of the line.

Another basic of good presentation comes when you pull off a good amount of line and stand ready to make a cast. This occurs when angling for bonefish, tarpon, or permit. You hold a small amount of line and leader outside the rod tip, and the boat moves along, searching for the prey. The fish is sighted and a quick cast is made. But unless you follow one basic technique, the cast will often end in disaster. As you first strip line from the reel and drop it on the deck, the forward end of the line falls to the deck first. All subsequent line stripped from the reel falls on top of it. If you make a cast with the line in this condition, the forward portion (underneath the pile) often tangles on the shoot. To make sure that you're going to get a good cast, always cast all line pulled from the reel and then bring it back. This way the back of the line is on the bottom of the pile—where it belongs.

Patience

Among the rules you want to follow when presenting a fly to any fish is never to be rushed. Many saltwater guides will rant and rave if you don't instantly throw the fly. But taking an extra two or three seconds often means the difference between a controlled cast and one presented so sloppily that it spooks the fish. If you see a trout rise or a bass pursuing a minnow, and you rush your cast, you'll probably throw a poor one. Just slowing down means only a second or two more to make the cast, but it can make a considerable difference in how well the fly comes to the fish.

Another basic premise of good presentation is never to fish farther than you can cast well. Many impatient anglers will throw the fly before they are at a comfortable casting distance. Cast only as far as you can do so comfortably and accurately. To try to throw even a few feet farther means relinquishing control. Some anglers place a one-foot mark with a permanent marking pen at the point where they can make their longest cast. They strip only that much line from the reel.

Nevertheless, I am a firm believer that you should fish a long way off for many species. Most anglers and many guides feel, for example, that you should not cast to a bonefish until it is within thirty or forty feet. This gives you one opportunity. But if you can cast accurately at seventy to ninety feet, I urge you to try it. If the bonefish refuses or misses the fly, strip and make another cast, and repeat this several times. Instead of one presentation, you often get two or more. I have hooked many trout on my dry flies at forty to sixty-five feet. If I can see the fly (often against glare on the water), I have no hesitation about fishing at these distances. The advantage of fishing this far away is that you have less chance of alerting a wary fish. There are exceptions. Tarpon and billfish are two. Their mouths are so hard inside that you need to have the fish close so you can really set the hook.

If you fish smallmouth bass in a river, seatrout in a grassy basin, steelhead in deeper pools, bluefish, or many other species in open water, make as long a cast as you can and search as much water as possible. So long as the hook is sharp and the rod is held low with a taut line, you'll have no trouble properly hooking the fish. My longest hookup was in Los Roques with my guide, Alex Gonzales. Returning to the boat at the end of our last day, Alex insisted that I cast to a cruising bonefish. I pulled off the entire fly line and some backing, and with a mild breeze behind me made the cast and hooked the fish at what we estimated to be 125 feet. There was no trouble hooking the fish with a taut line and a sharp hook.

When you are presenting a fly, another good rule is never to allow the fly line to fall on top of the fish. A heavy butt section crashing to the water will frequently spook fish. The angle at which you deliver the fly is also important. Many people cast at the surface target. But that often causes the fly to drive heavily into the water—ruining the cast. Most of the time the fly should be cast at or just above eye level. Thus the energy is expended above the target and the fly falls softly to the surface.

If a dry fly floats over a fish and the fish shows no interest, you need to pick up the fly and make another presentation. The fly is often air-dried by false-casting before it is dropped again to the surface. In rough water there is little concern about where you air-dry the fly. But if you lift a dry fly from a calm surface and the false cast is over the fish, two things could happen to alert or spook the fish. First, it may see the line in the air. Second, at the end of the back- and forward casts, as the line's direction is reversed, water is snapped out of the fly. False-casting over a fish holding in calm water causes miniature raindrops that are flushed from the fly and fall to the surface. It's pretty much the same as throwing pebbles on a tin roof.

There are many situations where a side cast is far better than an overhead cast. In very clear water, if you have to false-cast several times, keeping the line very low to the water often is an asset. By false-casting at a low side angle, you keep the line, leader, and fly out of sight of the fish. This is especially true when you are very close to a fish.

Special Situations

When fishing small farm ponds from the bank, a correct position will help in making better presentations. As you are walking around the pond to locate fish, then, always have the pond on the same side as your casting hand so that all your back- and forward casts will travel over water. Walking in the opposite direction will inevitably place your fly in jeopardy: It will be traveling along the shoreline over brush and trees upon which it can easily snag.

When fishing in a boat offshore or on a lake, if you spot predator fish feeding on baitfish on the surface of the water, there is also a correct casting position to assume. Pay attention to your line first. The line that you plan to shoot toward the target should not be left lying on the deck where it can blow all over the place during the chase, but in a large bucket. Then, to give you a right-handed example, take a position at the stern of the boat on the starboard (or right) side, facing forward so you can keep your eyes on the fish.

I usually take this position and, as my boatman and I are making our run at the fish, strip off about 30 feet of line and let it dangle off the rod tip. The speed of the boat will normally keep this much line and the fly aloft as we dash toward the feeding fish. Upon our arrival at the target area, I will ask the boatman to turn the bow of the craft slightly to port as he chops the throttle, so that from the starboard side I have a clean shot over water to make my cast and shoot line into the feeding fish.

When fishing from a canoe or a small boat on a river or lake, the direction that the craft is moved in relation to the shoreline can make a difference. Assuming that you are right-handed and sitting in the bow, the boat or canoe should be moved along the left bank so that you can make accurate casts entirely over the water without having to worry about hanging your fly up in brush along the bank, and without being concerned about your fishing companion in the stern being hit or hooked by your fly. If it's possible, start your fishing sequence by having the boat moving in the correct direction before casting. On small lakes, this is simply a matter of whether you start paddling in one direction or the other.

You can use a canoe to reach hard-to-find saltwater fishing opportunities.

Position Yourself for Fighting and Landing the Fish

Good positioning also means that if the fish takes the fly, you'll be able to continue the fight to a successful conclusion. It does you no good to make a perfect cast, have the fish take your fly, and then be trapped along a streambank unable to follow the fish. I've occasionally seen people hook large trout at the upstream lip of a rapids bordered by rocks too high for them to climb. In such situations, when the fish is hooked and in its panic swims upstream into the rapids, the angler is unable to follow his line upstream, and a broken leader and a lost fish are the result.

I confess I've made this mistake myself many, many times. I remember once spotting a terrific cutthroat trout on the Yellowstone River. The cast from the side I was on would have given me a drag problem that I might have had trouble with. By wading to the other side and climbing down a steep bank, though, I could make an easy cast with a good drift. Upon doing this, I successfully hooked the fish. But as soon as it bolted downstream, I was trapped on the cliff, unable to follow, and consequently lost it. This experience strengthened my conviction that you will increase your chances of success if you anticipate the various positions that you may have to take in fighting and landing the fish before you make your cast.

Position Yourself for Safety

For reasons of safety, positioning is also important when fly fishing from a boat. If you are being poled across a flat for bonefish, tarpon, permit, or other shallow saltwater species, you should make it a firm rule never to cast directly in front of the boat. Remember, the person poling the boat is directly behind you. Since your back-and-forth casts must travel in the same plane, the chance of you hooking your friend (at least he was your friend until you began casting) on casts aimed directly forward of the boat is very real.

When a fish is spotted, wait until your companion handling the boat can swing the rear of the boat around to an angle from the fish at which you can safely cast. For example, if you are moving due north and see a fish approaching, don't cast immediately. Allow the boatman to sweep the boat at right angles to you (or the east or west, depending on whether you are a right- or left-handed caster) in order to position the rear of the boat to the side opposite your rod hand. This will allow you to cast back and forth over the water without any chance of hooking your companion.

In summary, here are my basic rules for approaching and presenting to a fish:

1. Make your approach so that the fish is never aware that you are there.
2. Only wade when you have to.
3. False-cast as little as possible.
4. Approach slowly.
5. Approach quietly.
6. Approach lowly.
7. Approach darkly.
8. Approach patiently.
9. Plan the direction of your approach and casting position in advance.
10. In salt water be sure you factor in the tidal action and underwater holding points for fish, and be aware of the sun position.

Retrieving Methods for Better Results

Fishermen are like everyone else: We get into habits that we tend to follow unthinkingly. However, one of the most important rules of retrieving is to change your retrieving technique if your current method is not producing results. This is especially true if you can see a fish following your fly and it refuses to take. It's time to do something different! Frequently this means imitating the behavior of a crippled fish.

Observing predator fish in the open sea is instructive in this regard. When they discover a school of baitfish, they don't just dash in and try to gobble the bait. Instead, they look for any small fish that may seem to be ailing or weak. If a baitfish appears to be crippled or unable to swim at top speed, the predators streak in and grab it. Similarly, when fish are consistently refusing your underwater offerings, you may be able to tempt a big barracuda, snook, redfish, or numerous other saltwater species by switching to a popping bug or streamer. These patterns will help you give the impression to the fish that your offering is a crippled creature, resulting in a higher percentage of strikes.

In many of these situations, the popper is preferred, because you can easily manipulate a popper to make it appear to be struggling on the surface, as if it were a fish injured or in trouble. Conversely, a streamer swimming below the surface—no matter how large it is—must appear to the fish as if it were in good shape and would offer a harder chase if pursued.

Another advantage of popping bugs is that you can create an illusion to attract fish. You can make the prey you are attempting to imitate seem much bigger than it actually is, whereas a streamer or other underwater pattern worked in front of a fish can be clearly seen by the fish. They can determine how big it is, which may not be large enough for their appetite.

Where this tip really proves its worth is whenever I am fly fishing for two saltwater species in particular: amberjacks and cobia. I have never been able to tie a fly large enough to tempt amberjacks or cobia in excess of fifty pounds, unless the fish was properly teased beforehand. So after casting even twelve-inch streamers to amberjacks and cobia with no luck, I have switched to a big popping bug (maybe only half or two-thirds as long as the streamer pattern) and achieved a strike. I believe that the loud splashing and continuous noise of the popper make the amberjacks or cobia think that there is something really worth taking.

Popping Bug Techniques

There are wide ranges of opinions about how to retrieve a popping bug. Sometimes a quick retrieve works well; sometimes a very slow retrieve, combined with a speed-up of the bug now and then, is best. What usually governs the speed is the species sought, what the fish is doing at the time (is it chasing bait or lying in wait?), and the environment of the fish.

Retrieving for Bonefish

Changing your retrieving method is a good idea when you are getting numerous refusals from bonefish. In bonefishing, a series of short strips, with the fly falling over and over again to the bottom, is normally most effective. But when that is not working, you can change a lazy bonefish into an aggressive predator that will tear into your fly by using a few long, fast pulls of the line. With this type of retrieval, apparently the bonefish thinks the fly is escaping. When it sees the bug swimming swiftly, it moves in and attacks.

Whatever technique you adopt, remember that if there are fish in the area and they are not responding, your best bet is to change your fly offering or dramatically alter your presentation. With aggressive saltwater fish, you will soon know if you have caught the fish's attention.

9

CASTING

Tradition is a fine thing, and it's the part of fly fishing that many people revere the most. Yet at times tradition stands in the way of obtaining more pleasure or increased skill levels from our sport.

Several hundred years ago in England and other parts of Europe, anglers began fishing with flies. These were small wet varieties, fished on narrow streams. The equipment of the time consisted of a wooden rod (often more than twelve feet long) to which was attached a very short, braided line of fine strands from the tail of a horse. The average casting distance was just across a small stream. Using this antiquated equipment, the rod was brought from about the nine o'clock position to about one o'clock. Stopped sharply, it threw the line—only a few feet in length—behind the angler. Then the rod was returned sharply to nine o'clock, completing the cast. It worked fine, and as a result many trout fishermen began to write about and adopt the nine o'clock to one o'clock method. This technique became a part of tradition.

Today most instructors still teach this method. Yet we no longer use a wooden rod, a short horsehair line, or gut leaders. We also don't fish just for trout in small streams. To be successful, the modern angler must be able to cast distances considered impossible two hundred years ago. The flies are often larger and more wind resistant, and we fish in not only tiny streams but also large rivers and even the oceans of the world. Yet people are still using a method developed for a totally antiquated type of equipment and under a vastly different set of fishing conditions.

Almost all fly fishermen should and could cast better. In fact, I believe the nine to one o'clock instructional method is why we have so many poor fly casters today. It should be obvious that we need to consider another method of casting—a modern way. But tradition remains strong, and anyone who offers something different from the clock face method is often criticized and even ridiculed.

Over the past forty years I have been teaching fly casting professionally all over the world. In the beginning I also taught the universal method: Start at nine o'clock, sweep the rod upward, make a power stroke, and stop at about one o'clock. Then sweep the rod forward to eleven o'clock and make another power stroke. I soon learned that with this method, only the strongest men could throw a long line or get any distance under difficult conditions. A strong man may be able to false-cast sixty feet of fly line. But a small woman does not have the strength to cast the same way. What we need is a method that accommodates the physical characteristics of all fly fishermen. Gradually it dawned on me that the old method was inefficient. It was also evident that few women or children enjoyed the sport, except for fishing conditions where small flies were thrown a short distance.

Let's backtrack for a moment. My favorite form of fly fishing in my early years was to catch smallmouth bass from large rivers, such as the Susquehanna and Potomac, where long casts and retrieves produced many more strikes. Then a subtle change came over my casting. I began to bring the rod back farther on the cast, and things went more smoothly. Casting was easier, even at a distance. And so began the transformation of my casting technique.

The best way to learn anything, of course, is to teach it. Over the years I realized that several basic principles apply to any cast made with a fly rod. These are not "my" principles. They are basic physics that applied to the first person to pick up a rod and to someone who will begin casting a hundred years from now. Regardless of anyone's casting style, we are bound to these principles. They are the basis on which every cast is built. Understanding them allows you to become a better caster, and encourages you to review your efforts and improve them. When something goes wrong, one or more of these principles were violated. You shouldn't try to cast exactly like your instructor, rather, use these principles and adapt them to your own physical make-up.

What is so wonderful about this method is that power strokes are eliminated. In fact, pure muscle is no longer required. A woman of 110 pounds with slim wrists can cast nearly as far as a muscular 200-pound man. But the method flies in the face of tradition. For this reason, many people who have spent a great deal of time learning the old way will have difficulty accepting this new practice. However, what is so rewarding to me is that most people who have never fly fished (and have no preconceived notions about the sport) become accomplished casters in two to three lessons. Best of all, they are not working at it, and they can even critique their own efforts.

Principles of Casting

According to the dictionary, a *principle* is a "fundamental truth, law, doctrine, or motivating force, upon which others are based." Here are my cardinal principles of fly casting, on which every cast is based. And it's important to realize that they apply to whatever method or style of casting is used. This means a frail person has to obey the same principles as a 250-pound man.

1. You cannot make any cast until you get the end of the line moving on either your back- or forward cast. So you don't frighten the fish, it is a good idea also to lift all the line (but not the leader) from the surface before you make a backcast.

Here the author demonstrates that the line always travels in the direction in which the rod tip speeds up and stops. In a cast as flat as this one, virtually all the energy of the cast is directed ahead at the target.

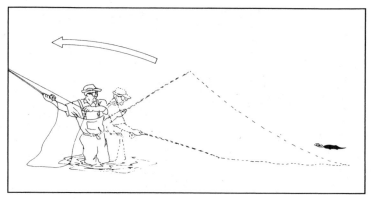

Good line pickup technique.

2. Once the line end is moving, the only way to load the rod is to move your casting hand at ever-increasing speed and then bring it to a sudden stop. This action is usually called a power stroke. Applying power often spoils the cast, however. Instead of calling it a power stroke, I prefer to call the final sudden stop a speed-up-and-stop. The faster you speed up and stop at the end of a cast, the faster the line will travel. The size of the loop is then determined by how far the rod tip moves during the speed-up-and-stop. The tip travels in a gentle arc, and the longer the speed-up-and-stop stroke, the larger the loop.

3. The line will go in the direction in which the rod tip speeds up and stops. If on the backcast the tip stops while it is going up, a straight backcast occurs, which is what you want. But if the tip stops going back and down, a sag occurs and it must be removed before you can make another cast. With almost all forward casts, the rod tip should speed up and stop parallel to the water or slightly climbing.

4. The longer the distance the rod travels on the back and forward casting strokes, the less effort is required for the cast.

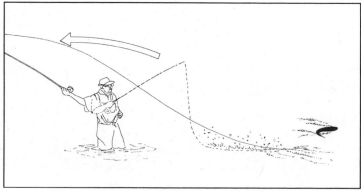

Bad line pickup technique.

Lefty's Method of Fly Casting: These drawings show the proper stroke for a strong backcast. Rotate the rod hand about 45 degrees away from the body, as shown. Use only the forearm! If you use the full arm the backcast will be faulty. Keep your hand at a 45-degree angle as it moves up, straight back, and away from the target. Try not to bend the wrist.

Lefty's Method of Fly Casting: These drawings show the proper stroke for a strong forward cast. As soon as the backcast ends, the rod hand starts coming forward. The forward cast begins with the rod at a 45-degree angle away from the body, but as the rod moves forward, the hand comes around in an oval. When the shoulders are back where they were at the beginning of the backcast, the rod should be vertical, and the thumb pointing up and directly behind the rod handle from the target. At this point, make a very brief acceleration in the direction of the target (with no wrist movement). This, combined with a quick stop, will form a tight, fast-moving loop. As soon as the rod is stopped, draw the tip "just a frog's hair." Tilt your thumb toward the water just enough to know you have moved the tip. Too much downward movement will cause the loop to open up too much.

The rod is a lever (an expensive one, but still a lever). If the rod is brought back with the thumb pointing up, the body will only allow it to bend just in front of the shoulder. This is why people bend or twist their wrists. This results in the line *not* flowing straight away from the target. It is important that you unroll the line directly away from and back to the target for the most efficiency. To take the rod and hand as far back as you can reach, without elevating the elbow, you must use only the forearm and *not bend the wrist*. Use of a full arm will cause the rod tip to travel in a small arc, causing a loss of energy. With the thumb in the proper position, tilt the bottom of the reel inward, so that the side plate is at a forty-five-degree angle. Make a side cast using only the forearm. You can now move the rod directly away from the target, and the fly line will follow.

Rule #1

Let's begin with the basics. The rod is a lever. The longer you move the rod through the casting plane, back or forth, the more likely it is to aid in your cast. Now, many people have misinterpreted this rule. I'm not suggesting that you move the rod through a long distance when you're only throwing a small, easy-to-cast fly a short distance. For example, if you're tossing a small dry fly to a sipping trout no more than thirty feet away, the rod only needs to move through a short distance on the back and forward strokes. But if you need to push a big bass bug into the

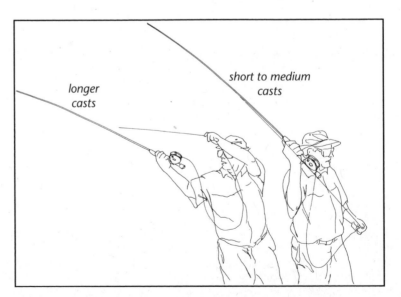

The rod is a flexible lever, which moves through varying arc lengths depending upon the casting distance required.

breeze, or deliver an air-resistant fly to a distant target, then bringing your rod back a longer distance will help immeasurably. The more help you need, the longer you should move your rod back and forward during casting. In fact, with an extremely difficult or long cast, the rod should be nearly parallel to the water behind you.

Rule #2

You can't make any cast until you have the line end moving. And you should lift all the line from the water before making a backcast. You *must* get the end of the line moving before you can cast. That doesn't mean the line end is drifting on the current; you actually have to get it moving. A good analogy is someone dragging a water hose over the lawn. The sprinkler on the other end isn't going to move until the end of the hose does. Likewise, you can't cast your fly until you have the end of the line moving.

I believe that one of the greatest faults of fly fishermen is to start the backcast with the rod held high. It's possible to make a decent short cast this way. But when a longer cast is required and you hold the rod high, the line end doesn't get moving until the rod has passed the vertical. Then, because the rod is now descending down and back behind you, a large sag develops in your backcast. Since you can't make a forward cast until you get the line end moving, most of your forward cast is wasted just removing slack or sag from the line. What little forward rod motion is left often can't deliver an efficient cast.

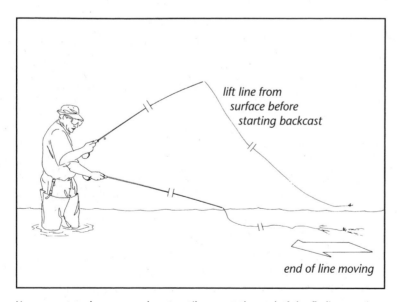

lift line from surface before starting backcast

end of line moving

You cannot make any good cast until you get the end of the fly line moving; and on the first backcast, the end of the fly line should be lifted from the surface of the water before the cast is made.

The second part of Rule #2 is important for catching fish as well as making a better backcast. Surface tension grips the line as it lies on the water. Perhaps one of the main reasons why many fly fishermen don't catch trout with dry flies, or connect with bonefish and tarpon, is that the backcast is made while some of the line is still on the surface. Even if only a few inches of line lie on the water when you make a backcast, you must rip it free. The noise made as the surface tension releases the line will frighten or alert any nearby fish. An important technique in making a good presentation to wary fish in calm water is making sure all of your line is elevated above the water before you make your first backcast.

A major reason why many anglers can't lift a long fly line from the water is that they don't get all their line off the water when they make their final backcast. Then the surface tension gripping the line will cause them to waste casting energy just to get it loose from the water.

Rule #3

The line will go in the direction that the rod tip speeds up and stops during the final moments of the cast. Remember, all casting strokes, whether short or long, can be divided into two parts. The first portion is relatively long; it gets the line moving and the rod bending. Then, at the last instant in a cast, the rod tip is accelerated rapidly and stopped. I call this portion of the stroke the speed-up-and-stop. It's vital to understand what the speed-up-and-stop does to your casts—for it has a major influence on direction and distance.

Many instructors use a clock face to explain when to perform certain casting functions. I think this is misleading. The position on a clock face where a function is made has nothing to do with the direction in which the fly and line will ultimately travel. Let me give you an example. Make a paper airplane from a sheet of typewriter paper. Throw the airplane three times, but concentrate on what would be eleven o'clock. First, holding the airplane in your hand, bring it forward at a climbing angle, and then release it at eleven o'clock. Of course, the plane will soar upward. Repeat the experiment by moving your hand straight ahead and then releasing the plane—and it will travel straight ahead. Now hold your hand above your shoulder, bring the plane forward and downward, and let it go. The plane will soar down into the ground. All three planes were released at eleven o'clock, yet all three planes traveled in a different direction.

Eleven o'clock had nothing to do with where the planes traveled. It was the direction in which you stopped and released the plane that determined the outcome. The same is true with a fly rod. If you stop the rod tip while going straight ahead, the line will go straight ahead. If you

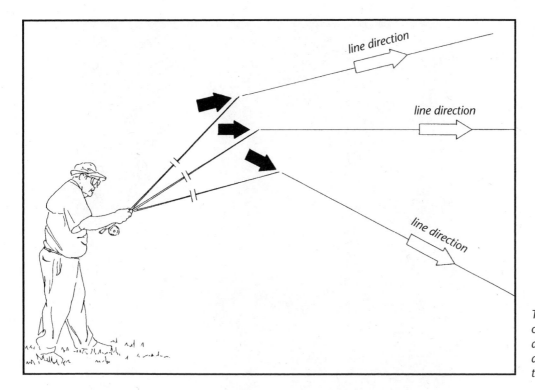

line direction

line direction

line direction

The fly line and the fly are only going to travel in the direction in which you accelerate and stop the rod tip at the end of the cast.

stop the rod (at any hour on the clock face) while going forward and down, then the line will travel forward and down. A major reason why most people have a big sag in the backcast is that the rod tip stopped while going back and down, hence the line went back and down. If you want to throw a straight backcast that travels in a slightly upward plane, you must stop the rod tip at an upward angle, speeding up and stopping while going away from the target.

As we discuss various casts, try to remember that the line is going in the direction at which you speed up and stop the rod tip at the end of the cast. Every efficient backcast should travel in the opposite direction from the target. For example, when fly fishermen make a cast across a stream and then allow the fly to drift downstream, most have to make a series of backcasts before they can place the fly back upstream. The reason for the backcasts is to work the fly line around during each false cast so that eventually the backcast is traveling in the opposite direction from the target. When this occurs, the angler directs the final forward cast at the target. It's important to understand that if the backcast is in a direct line opposite the target, the forward cast is more efficient.

Your thumb should be behind the rod handle from the target at the beginning of the cast. Never twist your wrist throughout the back- or forward cast. Instead, move your forearm to change the casting angle, but never twist your wrist. If your thumb on the stop has rotated slightly to

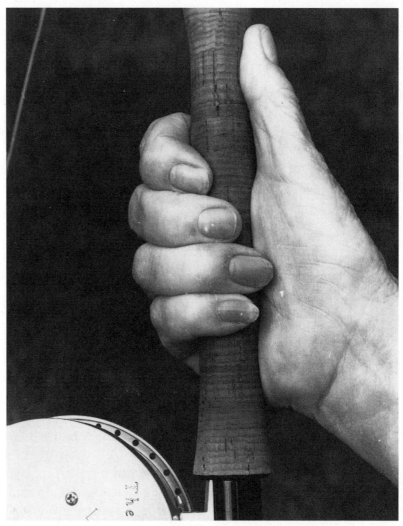

The importance of the thumb in casting is not often fully appreciated. At the end of both the back and forward casts, the thumb should be positioned directly behind the cork from the target.

the left, the line will rotate to the left at the end of your cast. But if your thumb is positioned directly behind the cork from the target, you'll deliver the fly and line straight to the target. This is true with a vertical, slanted, or side cast. I can't emphasize too strongly how much this simple trick can help you obtain a more efficient and accurate cast.

It's also important to understand that a minor movement of your hand on the handle results in a major movement of the rod tip. Try a simple experiment. Hold the rod parallel to the ground. Brace your upper arm against your body and rock the rod back and forth with just the hand. Look at the label immediately in front of the rod handle (Sage, Orvis, Loomis, whatever). You'll notice that this label is moving maybe two inches. Now look at the rod tip—and you'll see that it's probably moving eight to twelve feet. This means that any motion made with your rod hand will be greatly magnified at the tip. Failing to understand this principle can result in not throwing the line straight behind you, opening your loops too much, and many other casting errors.

Rule #4

The size of your loop is determined by the distance your rod tip speeds up and stops at the end of the cast. The shorter your speed-up-and-stop, the smaller will be your loop. And the faster you move the rod tip through that distance, and the more suddenly you stop it, the faster and farther your line will travel.

It is not hard to understand why a large loop doesn't go very far. For decades we've heard it said that large loops cause air resistance. While this is a factor, it's not the main reason. A large loop means you're throwing the fly line around a big arc or curve. The energy of your cast is being directed around a circle. A tight loop, however, means that most of your energy is directed at the target.

As I mentioned earlier, all casting strokes are divided into two parts—a relatively long motion and then a short speed-up-and-stop. When you make a speed-up-and-stop, your rod tip actually travels in a very slight

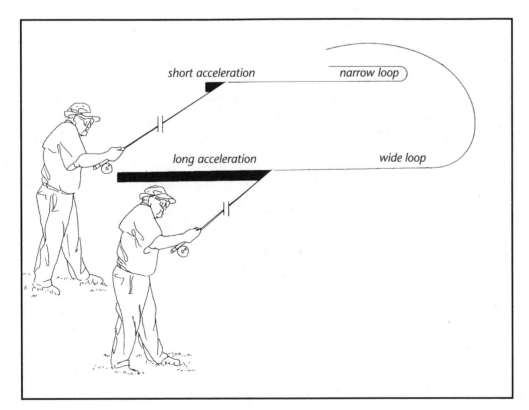

The size of the fly line loop is determined only by the distance that you accelerate the rod tip at the end of the cast. And the faster you accelerate the tip, combined with a quick stop, the farther the cast will travel.

arc. The distance that your fly rod descends from the beginning to the end of the speed-up-and-stop determines your loop size. For example, if you make a long speed-up-and-stop—one in which the tip drops three feet from the start to the end of the stroke—you'll have a three-foot loop. If your stroke is incredibly short and your tip only drops four inches, your loop will be four inches in size. This often seems difficult for people to understand, but it's true.

Why do most people make large and inefficient loops? The reason is that they move their wrist too much during the casting motion. The more the wrist moves during the speed-up-and-stop, the larger the loop will be. Worse, large loops direct energy around a curve, and the final part of the cast is made down toward the water. Remember, the line goes in the direction the tip stops at the end of the cast.

You can easily test the big loop–small loop concept as it relates to wrist movement. Make several false casts, allowing your wrist to move a lot during each. Note how large your loops are. Now try making the cast with your forearm only (not your whole arm, which would cause you to move in a greater arc). Your loops will diminish immediately. Forearm-only casting reduces the distance that your tip speeds up and stops, so if you stop the tip going at some awkward angle behind you on your backcast, you'll improve your cast immediately.

How far your cast will go is determined by four factors. You need to stop the tip going in some upward direction on your backcast, and ahead of you—or slightly climbing—on your forward cast. You also need to make the shortest speed-up-and-stop that you can. Add two more factors and distance will increase even farther. The faster you speed up, and the more abruptly you stop the tip over that short speed-up-and-stop distance, the faster the line will travel—and the farther you'll be able to cast. I can't emphasize too strongly how important it is for efficient casting to stop quickly. The lower portion of your loop is coming out of the tip of your rod. If you stop the cast and immediately lower your rod, you'll tear apart any loop you were creating. Instead, stop while going toward the target and then mentally count to three before you lower your rod.

To understand how important it is to stop quickly, use the analogy of a brush loaded with paint. If you sweep forward in a long motion, little paint will be thrown ahead from your brush. But if you move forward and then suddenly, over a short distance, speed up rapidly and stop abruptly, much more paint will be thrown from your brush—and straight ahead! The same is true with a fly rod. Speed up rapidly over a short distance at the end of your cast, then stop abruptly, and you'll throw more of the cast's energy toward the target.

Remember, for years we have called the final portion of a cast a power stroke. It is not a power stroke. It is a really a speed stroke, coupled with an abrupt stop.

And Furthermore . . .

To make a backcast directly away from your target, your rod tip and hand must also travel in a straight line at an upward angle and in a straight line away from the target. More important, the speed-up-and-stop of the backcast must also be directed in a straight line away from the target and stop in an upward direction.

Rule #1 explains why you want to move the rod through a longer distance on the cast when you throw heavy flies, make longer casts, or need more help on any cast. If you hold the rod in a normal manner, with the thumb pointing up or vertically, moving the rod behind you in a straight line with the tip stopping at an upward angle is very difficult; it takes long hours of practice. People who hold the rod handle with the thumb up and then move the rod well behind them usually cause the tip to travel down and back behind them. This forces the line to go down and back (remember, the line goes in the direction that the tip speeds up and stops).

To move the rod well behind your body, and still travel in a straight line away from the target throughout the cast, is relatively easy. Lower the rod until the tip is below your belt. (You can't make this cast if your rod is held high before starting.) Turn the rod so you can make a side cast. Be sure your thumb is behind the handle from the target and never twist your wrist during the backcast. Remember, use only your forearm—never

For long, or more difficult casts, you will need to bring the rod well behind your body on the backcast. To do this, rotate your casting thumb away from its normal position on top of the rod about 45 degrees away form your body before initiating the backcast, and then take your forearm (never the wrist) straight back 180 degrees from the target.

use your whole arm to make the backcast or the tip will travel in an arc! Move the rod tip back as far as you want, while traveling at an upward angle and straight away from your target. The motion is similar to hitchhiking. To help you do this correctly, make sure that the rod tip is below your head during all of the backcast. This will ensure a better backcast. Allowing the rod tip to go back well above your head will often put a deep and undesirable sag in your backcast—which you'll have to remove before you can make a forward cast. If you twist your wrist, it will divert energy and prevent the line from traveling away from the target.

You can then come forward and make either a side cast or a vertical cast. But keeping the rod tip well below your head on the backcast enables you to travel in a straight line and complete your speed-up-and-stop going away from the target—ending with the rod tip as far back as you desire.

There are a number of elements that need to be combined with the basic principles and incorporated into your cast to achieve advanced casting proficiency. I will explain how to master each of these elements, but I obviously cannot cast for you. You're going to have to do some work and pay some dues to join the elite corps of fly casters. Take the time to carefully think through some of these elements (and, as you will see, I will sometimes demonstrate both the correct and incorrect ways of doing something). Incorporate them into your own casting routine and devote a sufficient amount of your time to practicing them. Then you can become a proficient advanced caster. In addition, you will have the competence to master all types of advanced casts, and to make those casts with greater efficiency and at far greater distances. So let's get to work!

Footwork or Stance

Footwork is very important in almost all sports, and it is certainly vital to good fly casting. Footwork, or stance, helps you get better accuracy. But the proper stance also permits the body to move fluidly through extended motions, which in turn permits the rod to travel through a long arc, aiding considerably on longer casts.

While short casts can sometimes be made with improper footwork, longer and more difficult casts will demand detailed attention to how the feet are used. As you will recall, the first principle explains that the longer you move the rod through an arc, the more it contributes to the cast. Proper footwork permits the body to move through longer motions; thus the rod can travel a greater distance on the back- and forward casts. It also produces smooth, fluid body motions; improper footwork restricts the body's fluid movements and thus interferes with graceful casting.

Here are some illustrations that will help you understand these technical matters.

Because the feet remain even, the body muscles will not allow the angler to reach well back with the rod. With this stance you will find that your body motions are very restricted.

This is the best foot position for casts other than long or difficult ones. The foot opposite the rod hand is placed about eighteen inches forward of the other foot. Thus if you are right-handed, the left foot would be forward.

When the feet are in this position, you can rock back and forth easily, permitting the body to flow smoothly with the cast.

When you have to make a longer or more difficult cast, you will want to place your feet much farther apart. In fact, on a very long cast, as the rod lifts the line from the surface, I will often pick up my rear foot and drop it well behind me. The main purpose of all of this is to get the rod back as far as you can before the forward cast is made. This, in turn, permits the rod to move through a much greater arc, and contributes more power to the cast. Note how the angler's weight has shifted to his hand and rod, and also note his new body position at the end of the backcast.

At the end of the backcast, the angler now faces the target with the rod almost parallel with the water.

The rod hand is drawn forward in a straight line. Whatever the elevation of the rod hand at the end of the backcast, it should stay at that level to complete the forward cast. The angler's weight is gradually being shifted to the front foot. If the rod hand is kept below the shoulder on a long cast, you can more easily attain more distance.

The weight continues to be shifted to the front foot as the rod is brought forward.

As the line is shot toward the target, almost all the weight has now shifted to the front foot. On some long casts the rear foot will actually be lifted off the stream bottom.

Rod Grip

A proper rod grip helps to make your casts accurate and efficient, but comfort is perhaps its most important contribution. Many people get blisters when they cast. The problem is that they are gripping the rod firmly during all of the cast. The only time to grip the rod firmly is during the speed-up-and-stop phases of the back- and forward cast.

The best grip, I believe, is to hold the rod as shown here, with the thumb on top and the fingers wrapped around the handle.

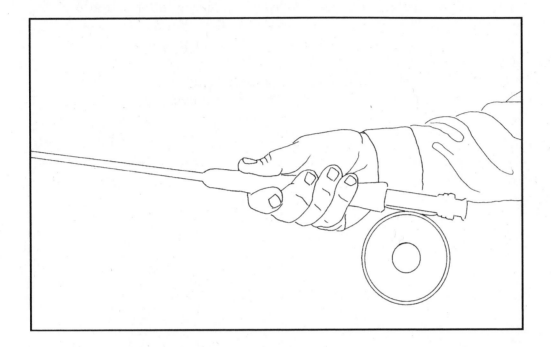

Here is the correct "index finger on top" grip, one that is often favored by trout fishermen who fish mainly small streams. It is a poor grip if you ever want to make longer casts, or want to fish the heavier fly rods, such as 10-weights or higher.

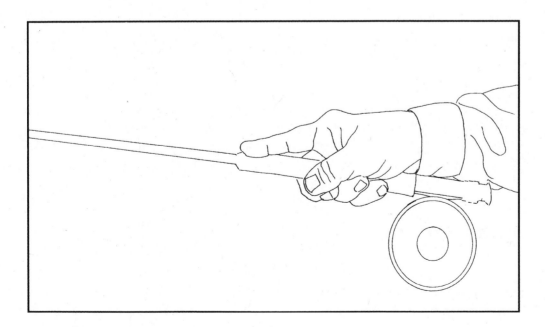

Thumb Position on the Rod Handle

At the finish of the back- and forward casts, the thumb should be positioned behind the rod handle in the direction of the desired target.

It is important to think about the position of the rod hand in the instant after the cast ends. This, to a large degree, will affect your accuracy. As shown in the illustration, the rod handle should be between the thumb and the target as the cast ends. This concept applies to both the back and forward casts.

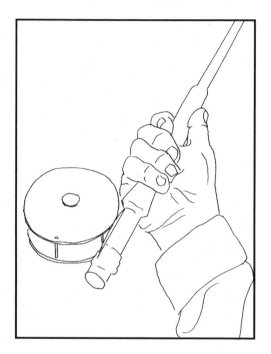 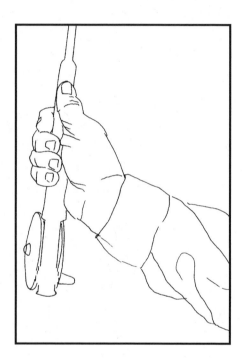

But if the hand turns, as shown here, so that the thumb is not on the other side of the rod handle from the target, you will find that your loops will open. Some of the energy of the cast will now be wasted by moving the line in a circular direction, rather than delivering all of it, most efficiently, directly at the target.

Rod Position at the Start of the Cast

To lift a considerable amount of line from the surface or to make a longer cast, the rod tip should be positioned well below the belt before beginning the backcast.

Rod Tip Distance on the Backcast

The distance that the rod tip travels to the rear on the backcast is dependent on how far the angler wants to cast, or upon existing fishing conditions.

Direction of the Rod Tip on the Back- and Forward Casts

Every backcast should travel at some upward angle (it may contact the water behind you if it doesn't) and, if possible, at 180 degrees or directly

The first time, as shown, I will move my hand forward and go straight ahead, stopping at 10 o'clock as I release the airplane. The plane will sail straight ahead.

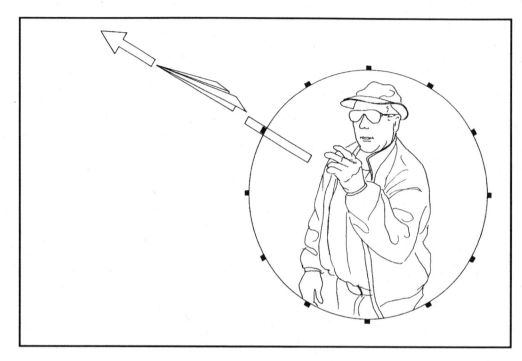

The second time when I release the plane I will have my hand traveling at a climbing angle as I stop at 10 o'clock. Again, of course, the plane goes in the direction in which my hand was traveling as it stopped.

away from the target. With just a few exceptions (which I will discuss later), forward casts should almost always travel either straight ahead or at a slight climbing angle. This means that on most casts the rod hand should stop in an upward direction on the backcast and should stop going either straight ahead or slightly upward on the forward cast.

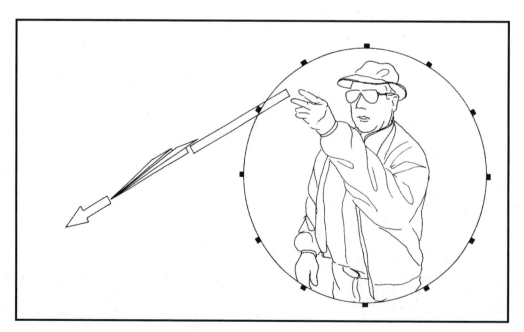

On the third attempt, I will have my hand traveling downward as I stop and release the plane at 10 o'clock. Of Course, the plane will crash into the ground.

What this experiment attempts to do is make the reader realize that where you stop on the clock face has absolutely nothing to do with where the paper plane (or the fly line) is going to travel. It is not the position on the clock dial where you stop the rod tip that determines where the fly line will travel. Instead, it is the direction in which you stop that governs where the fly line will go.

Putting the Elements Together

The style of casting I teach greatly differs from the standard method used over the past three hundred years, principally because I believe that the longer we move the rod through a casting stroke, the more the rod contributes to the cast. Therefore, to execute longer or more difficult casts, on the backcast it is vital to get the rod tip well behind you, permitting the rod to move through a longer arc and assisting you in making a more accurate cast.

Many fly fishermen instinctively realize that getting the rod tip well behind them aids the cast. But more often than not, in an effort to do this they create a lot of undesirable slack in the backcast, generally in one of two ways.

In the first faulty method, from the beginning to the end of the backcast they grip the rod with their thumb up. While this thumb position is correct for short casts when the rod tip never needs to be brought beyond the vertical position, it becomes a flaw when it is maintained on the long or more difficult casts that require that the rod tip travel to a position behind the angler. With such a hand position, when these anglers attempt to move the rod tip well behind them, their forearm is naturally blocked by the anatomy of their upper arm and shoulder, resulting in the rod (and their thumb on the rod) being forced to stop at exactly or just slightly past the vertical position. When they encounter this problem, to get the rod even farther back, they break their wrists and tilt the rod back and down. (Remember: The line is going to go in the direction in which the rod tip stops.)

I have seen some anglers who have learned to make a stop in the correct direction while letting the rod drift backward in this manner, yet they are still able to keep the line going up and back. However, these anglers have mastered this technique only with years of practice. Most anglers who stop their rod and let it drift backward will invariably place some or a good bit of slack into their backcast—slack that must be removed from the line before the rod can begin to transport the fly on the forward cast.

The other method of getting the rod back well behind the angler when the muscles of the upper arm and shoulder prevent the hand from traveling farther to the rear is to turn the rod hand outward (away from the body) in a pivoting motion. This does permit the rod to move behind the angler. But since this pivoting motion occurs just before or simultaneously with the speed-up-and-stop phase of the backcast, and since the line is going to go in the direction of that speed-up-and-stop, this outward pivoting motion of the hand will generally cause the line to unroll behind the angler in an undesirable wide horizontal loop. This is wasting casting energy, and the fly line must be realigned for the forward cast.

It is vital that the line and fly travel in the exact opposite direction from the target on the backcast. If you want the line to be 180 degrees, or exactly opposite, the target, the rod hand must travel in a straight line away from the target on the backcast. And the speed-up-and-stop motion must travel at some climbing angle directly away from the target. The plane of the cast is unimportant. That is, you could make a low side backcast and then a vertical forward cast. What *is* important is that from the start to the finish of the backcast, the rod hand should travel in a straight line away from the target, and that you never twist your wrist. Here is my recommended method.

Grip the rod as you would naturally for a short cast. The thumb will be on top of the rod handle. Before you initiate the cast, move your forearm outward into a position for making a side cast, as shown in the illustration. Incidentally, the farther back you want the rod to travel on the side cast, the lower the side cast should be. The higher the angle of the side cast, the less distance the rod can travel behind you. Therefore, when you want to move the rod as far back as possible, the side cast should be made low to the water and at only a very slight climbing angle.

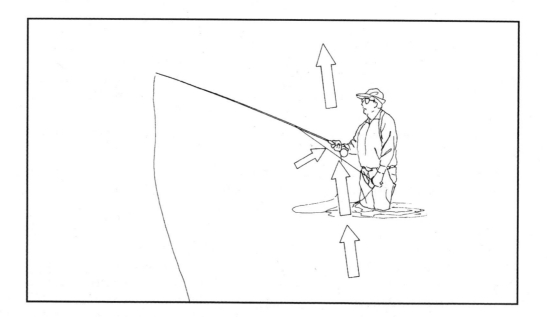

Sweep the rod hand back at some upward angle, making sure that the thumb stays behind the rod handle from the target throughout this entire motion.

A tool that I often use to help people make a tight, straight backcast when the rod is tilted to the side (in the manner I have described for making longer casts) is a smooth board with an arrow taped to its center. This tool helps emphasize that you need to make the backcast in one continuous, climbing motion—while moving the rod hand back in a straight line. Place the back of the rod hand flat on the board and begin to use the forearm (using *only* the forearm) back and up.

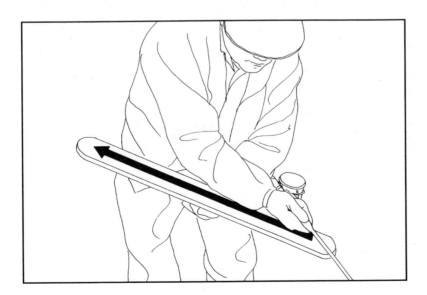

The back of the hand should remain flat on the board as the hand rises and travels straight back and away from the target.

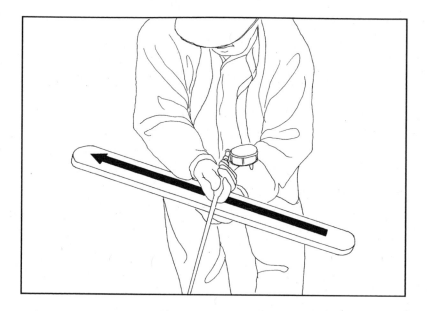

If the backcast is made properly, the back of the hand will stay flat on the board, and the hand, during both the backcast and the speed-up-and-stop, will travel as the arrow indicates—straight away from the target.

You may not want to make a side cast as you come forward. This can cause the fly to curve to the left in front of you at the end of the cast. Remember, the line and fly are going in the direction in which you speed up and stop the rod tip. Therefore, you want to make the forward cast with the rod tip traveling vertically. To perform this, at the end of the side backcast, drop the elbow slowly as the rod hand is moved forward and in toward the body to prepare for the forward cast. It is important that whatever elevation the rod hand was at on the backcast stop, it remain at that same elevation throughout the forward cast. If the rod hand drops as it comes forward—which is a fault of many casters—a tailing loop may result.

Continue to bring the rod hand forward in the direction of the target (making sure that you stay at the same elevation).

A speed-up-and-stop motion of the rod tip in the direction of the target is made to complete the cast. During the entire back- and forward cast, the rod hand has traveled in an oval—out to the side on the backcast and then forward in a vertical plane.

Incorrect Way to Make the Backcast

It is impossible for the rod tip to travel at 180 degrees away from the target when using my fly-casting method if the whole arm is held straight on the backcast. The backcast should be made only with the forearm.

If the arm is held straight when the backcast is made, the rod hand is forced to travel in an arc or half circle, as shown.

As shown here, since the line is going to go in the direction in which the rod tip speeds up and stops, a straight moving arm will consequently cause the line to form a large loop. Even worse, the rod tip will stop going back and to the side of the fly fisherman. Energy will now be wasted on the forward cast to get the fly line straightened and going in the direction needed. Thus a straight arm ultimately results in a very inefficient cast.

Correct Way to Make the Backcast

To make the correct backcast using my method, the rod must travel exactly opposite the target (at 180 degrees) and, most important, the speed-up-and-stop must also be made directly away from the target. This desirable motion can be accomplished only if the side cast is made with the forearm.

The elbow is bent, and the rod will be moved rearward with the hand traveling straight away from the target. If you bend the wrist, you will spoil the cast. As shown in the illustration, the cast is made by moving the rod rearward with only the forearm and an immobile or stiff wrist. The lower the slightly upward angle of the side cast is, the farther back the rod can go. Remember that the thumb is behind the rod handle throughout this backcast. The motion is quite similar to the action made when hitchhiking ("thumbing" a ride).

Note how the rod hand continues to move straight back away from the target and at an upward angle. The speed-up-and-stop of the rod handle is made directly away from the target. Throughout the backcast the rod hand has traveled in a straight line. At the end of the cast, look at your thumb, and do not twist your wrist.

Hand Elevation on the Backcast

The lower the hand travels on the backcast, the less likely you are to develop casting problems on the forward cast. Ideally, on almost all casts, the rod hand should never rise as high as your ear. If the hand is kept below the shoulder, the energy of the cast is more likely to be directed toward the target, more distance can be obtained, and casting mistakes are lessened.

Wrist Position

The more you bend the wrist during the speed-up-and-stop motion at the end of the forward cast, the larger the loop will be and the less efficient the cast. In my experience the size of the loop is determined by the distance the rod speeds up and stops at the end of the forward cast. Bending the wrist will open the loop, and the more the wrist is bent, the larger the loop becomes and the more energy is misdirected away from the target.

This is easy to demonstrate. Without any line strung through the guides, bring your rod forward as if you are actually making a cast. When the rod is in a vertical position over your head, make a short speed-up-and-stop with your wrist immobile, using only your forearm. Do this several times and you will note two things. First, the distance the rod tip moves during that brief speed-up-and-stop motion is very short, which will always create a small, tight loop. Second—and very important—the rod tip is going to stop in the direction in which you want the cast to go.

Now bring the rod to the same vertical position you did before—but this time quite deliberately bend your wrist to make the speed-up-and-stop motion. Now you have two problems. First, you will see that the rod tip has traveled a considerably longer distance than when you moved only your forearm, which creates a larger loop. And second, the rod will stop in a downward direction. As a result, not only is the loop a large one, wastefully throwing energy around a circle (with only a portion going toward the target), but some of the cast's energy is also being directed uselessly down in front of you.

You will find some fishing situations in which you need to create a larger loop deliberately: when you are casting heavy flies; when you are using a very long leader, perhaps with one or more dropper flies; or when you are using split shot or a large strike indicator. Throwing a tight loop for these different casts generally results in a hopeless tangle of your leader. It is obviously important that you know how to throw a big loop in certain fishing situations. However, most of the time you will want to throw the most efficient loop—one that is rather small or tight.

Hand Elevation and Direction on the Back- and Forward Casts

A common casting mistake occurs when you raise your hand on the backcast. This causes the hand to travel in a downward direction on the forward cast. To avoid tailing loops as well as many other casting and presentation problems, the rod hand should travel directly at the target in a straight line from the beginning to the end of the cast.

Many anglers actually raise their hand on the backcast until it stops at an elevation even with or higher than their shoulder. It takes an accomplished caster to begin a forward cast from this high hand position and make a good presentation beyond forty feet. In fact, stopping the hand on the backcast so that it is higher than the shoulder automatically handicaps the forward cast. These consistently high backcast stops will stretch the shoulder and upper arm muscles, and you will tire easily. Second, when the elevated hand and arm are carried forward to make the cast in front of you, the hand has to travel either in a downward direction or, worse, in a circular motion (just as the hand will travel along a circular path when a side backcast is made with a straight arm). Third, the higher the arm stops on the backcast, the more there is a tendency for the cast to fly down in front of you, instead of out and toward the target. Fourth, a high hand stop on the backcast is one of the two most common ways to develop a tailing loop. These illustrations show the mistakes.

Here the backcast has ended with the hand well above the shoulder.

Now the rod hand sweeps forward as well as downward.

The cast ends. The line and fly will go in the direction in which the rod tip speeds up and stops. Because the hand has been traveling downward, the fly line will be traveling downward at the same angle. In addition to the problems already mentioned, the line is also driven into the water with a fish-frightening splash.

If, however, the rod hand is brought back low, and then carried straight forward, most of the energy of the cast will be directed at the target. The following four illustrations show the correct technique.

The backcast has ended. Note that the hand is below the shoulder. It is important to remember the rule about hand elevation. When making a cast that travels parallel to the surface (as most casts do), at whatever elevation the rod hand stops on the backcast, the hands should stay at that elevation throughout the forward cast. I can't overemphasize this point. This factor alone will make a big difference as you develop better control and longer casts.

The angler begins to move the rod hand forward, being careful to keep the hand at the same elevation.

The rod hand continues to move forward in a straight line.

Note that the speed-up-and-stop at the end of the cast is being made with the rod still going straight ahead. And as soon as the stop occurs, the rod is tilted slightly downward to eliminate a tailing loop.

Angle and Elevation of the Forward Cast

The angle at which you direct your forward cast can be an incredibly important contributor to your fishing effectiveness. Yet I am constantly seeing confusion among fly fishermen on this subject. Perhaps the problem started during their early casting instruction. Some teachers say that you should throw the cast downward toward the target. Others recommend that the cast be thrown at eye level, or parallel to the water. And others don't even deal with the subject of casting angles. Most of the time, a cast should be directed at eye level or slightly above eye level. However, for certain types of specialized casts and fishing situations, you will want to aim your cast at a low or high angle.

When you think about it, there's nothing particularly complicated about this question, even though there really is no single correct casting angle. In most cases, you will have to experiment and decide for yourself at streamside, based on what you are trying to do with the cast. Ask yourself some basic questions. What kind of pattern and fly line are you using? Where do you want the fly to go? What do you want to do with the line while it is in flight? What direction do you want the line and the fly to go? And how you expect the fish to react to your presentation?

Eye-Level Cast

Perhaps 90 percent of all of your casts should be directed parallel to the water's surface—or climbing slightly. I often advise people to imagine that their target is not actually at water level, but more at their eye level, and to cast as if it really were there. While it apparently makes good sense to cast downward toward the surface of the water where the fly is ultimately going to land, there are two reasons why this may be a mistake.

First, the impact of the leader, fly, and the fly line on the surface can often be disturbing enough to frighten the fish. Second, keep in mind that the cast is going to go in the direction in which the rod tip speeds up and stops. If you want to cast, say, fifty feet and your rod tip stops going in a downward direction, the possibility exists that the cast may actually travel a shorter distance and not reach your target. If you see this happening, there's nothing you can do at this point to add more distance to your cast.

This is very much like firing a rifle. If you aim it at the ground out in front of you, that is where the bullet will strike—it certainly isn't going to go farther. But if you aim the rifle at an upward angle, the bullet will travel a long distance. With a cast that is canted upward, you are observing its flight path and have the option of stopping its flight at any point along its trajectory. For a fifty-foot target, you can cast slightly upward and with enough energy for the fly to travel seventy-five feet. Then, when the fly is over the target, simply stop its flight and it will fall on the right spot. A cast that is directed downward will never give you this option.

On this cast, it's important that you make your speed-up-and-stop motion going straight ahead, parallel to the water, as shown. Then, when the line completes its forward motion, the leader will fall softly to the surface.

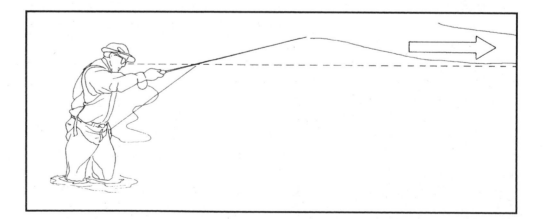

Although this is the least used of the casting angles, throwing the line in a downward-slanting angle—directly toward the target—can be advantageous. Use this technique when you need to drive the fly under overhanging bushes, boat docks, bridges, or other obstructions; or when you want to drive a streamer or popping bug under brush to attract the attention of such species as bass, snook, or redfish that are hiding underneath cover. Most of the time it makes good sense to present your fly quietly so it will not alert or alarm the fish. But in these special situations, the rapid turnover and hard and loud splashdown of a fly that has been cast in a downward direction are ideal. They will definitely bring a fish out of cover to investigate what has fallen to the water's surface.

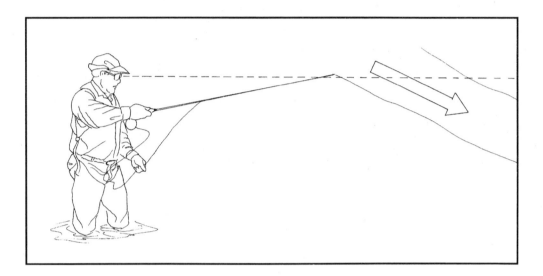

Climbing Cast

Sometimes it is absolutely necessary to direct your cast above eye level. For example, you will need to use a climbing cast for a long-distance cast. In this instance, the upward direction of the line will help offset the effects of gravity as the line travels out a long distance. You'll have similar needs with the reach cast. Here the increased height of the line above the water will allow you time to lay the rod and line over in an upstream direction. For the tuck cast, you'll need to get the line high enough to allow room for the fly to sweep back under the line and fall to the surface. And for the slack line cast (also known as the pile cast, stack cast, stutter cast, puddle cast, and more), the dry-fly angler wants to put slack in the forward end of the line and leader to create soft S curves for a drag-free float.

The principal disadvantages of the climbing cast are that if it is directed too high, when the loop and the line is fully extended it will fall with considerable slack in the forward end. And of course, throwing high into a wind generally causes line to be blown back a considerable distance.

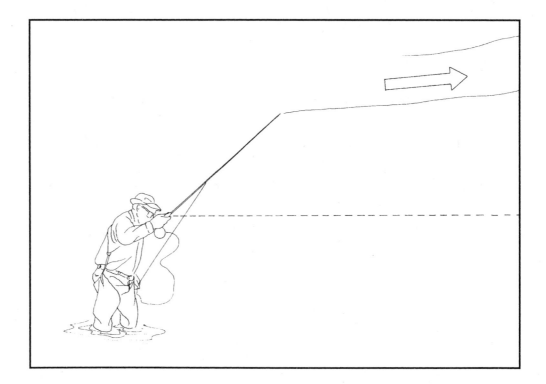

Reducing the Number of False Casts

Here is one of my cardinal rules. Try to make as few false casts as possible. A sure indicator of a good caster is how few false casts he makes before the fly lands gently on the water. Like many aspects of fly fishing, it's all about preparation. The advanced caster understands how to properly prepare everything before making the first cast. This eliminates many wasted motions or mistakes that won't have to be removed by false-casting during the casting sequence before making the final forward motion.

Although the advanced caster can remove faults with false-casting (and many times even the very best casters cannot correct a cast that simply got started badly), just the reverse is true for most people: False casts can actually create new faults that did not exist on the first cast. It is true that every false cast has the potential for going wrong: Your line hand may slip; too much slack can creep into the cast; the loop can become too open; a gust of wind can direct the line off course; and so on. Thus the more false casts you make, the more chances you create for faults to sneak into the casting sequence.

One of the major reasons why so many fly fishermen make extra and unnecessary false casts is that they retrieve too much line from the surface of the water after their last fly presentation. Of course, you always need a certain amount of line weight outside the rod tip to properly load the rod and shoot line to the desired target. This line length can vary as a function of your individual casting skill. (No matter how well you can cast, you still need a requisite amount of line as well as line weight outside the rod tip.) So be careful as you retrieve line that you do not retrieve too much. If you do, several false casts will be required to extend enough line to properly load the rod for your next cast.

Take the time to watch a really good fly fisherman and you will quickly see one of the secrets of fly fishing. Advanced casters are able to make just a single backcast and then come forward and shoot line back to the target in one fluid back-and-forth motion. And the main reason is that they start their backcast with a sufficient amount of line outside the rod tip.

Eliminating Slack in the Cast

If there is any slack in the back- or forward cast, it will have to be eliminated with rod motion before the fly can be moved. This principle is best demonstrated by a simple experiment. Place a garden hose on the lawn. Then position it so there is a deep sag or single wave in it. (Try to make it resemble a backcast with a deep sag.) Pick up one end of the garden hose and begin walking, while looking at the other end of the hose. You will quickly see that you won't move the far end of the hose until the entire length straightens.

Now conduct a second experiment. Position the hose so that one end runs straight and true for a considerable distance. But at the other end, form a large U shape with the hose, so that it resembles a backcast with a huge loop. Again, pick up the straight end and begin walking. Note that the tip of the other end of the hose will not move until the large curve (representing a big fly-line loop) has been removed.

The same principles apply to casting. If there is a deep sag or large loop in the line, all this slack must be removed (or the line straightened) before the rod can begin to move the fly.

Understanding Tailing Loops

Elimination of the tailing loop from your cast is, I believe, one of the most important things you must do to become an advanced fly caster. Perhaps 99 percent of all fairly good casters (those who can throw forty-five feet or more of line) have problems with tailing loops. Usually, the longer the cast, the more likely a tailing loop will result.

A tailing loop is a cast in which, near the completion of the forward cast, the leader and/or the front portion of the line run into the main portion of the line, creating a tangle or knot. A common explanation is that a "wind knot" has developed in the leader or line (or both). But casters get wind knots even on dead calm days. The wind usually has nothing to do with a tailing loop.

In fact, maybe the reason so few fly casters understand what creates tailing loops is that instructors have been giving their students all sorts of faulty explanations, almost none of which really causes the problem. For example, "shocking" or jarring the rod to a stop is supposed to cause a tailing loop. This is not true. A tailing loop only occurs if the rod is shocked while going straight ahead at the speed-up-and-stop. Other casters cite applying a power stroke too soon or too late at the end of the cast. And there are many other reasons that have been offered by instructors, almost all of them incorrect.

Tailing loops are caused by five distinct imperfections in fly-casting technique. Let's start with the basics. All casts are divided into two parts or motions. First is the relatively long rod motion to get the line moving and the rod loaded. Second is the short motion of the speed-up-and-stop of the rod tip at the end of the cast. Regarding this second motion, it is vital to understand that the line and fly will go in the direction in which the rod tip speeds up and stops at the end of the cast. Once this is understood, it is rather easy to understand the various reasons why tailing loops are created.

Perhaps half of all tailing loops are caused by directing the rod tip straight ahead during the speed-up-and-stop phase at the end of the cast. Remember, the line is going to go in the direction in which you speed up and stop. If you sweep the rod forward and at the end of the cast make a stop with your rod hand while going straight ahead, the tip of the rod is going to travel in the same direction. This is going to cause the line coming from behind you to travel in the same straight line. As a result, it will crash into the line in front of it—and create a messy tailing loop.

As suggested above, some instructors claim that if you "shock" the rod, a tailing loop results. Again, keeping in mind that the line is going to go in the direction of the speed-up-and-stop, let's look at this explanation. A tailing loop does occur if you sweep the rod forward and then make the speed-up-and-stop going straight ahead with enough force to shock the rod. However, make another forceful cast and use the speed-

If you make a short speed-up-and-stop of the rod tip straight ahead, you will develop a nice, tight loop like this one.

up-and-stop motion—but don't stop going straight ahead. Regardless of how much you shock the rod—even though this will cause the rod to dip downward slightly and likely produce numerous shock waves in the line—there will be no tailing loop. What caused the tailing loop was not shocking the rod, but going straight ahead on the stop.

Let me illustrate the steps involved in this common way of producing a tailing loop. Here, a fairly good caster makes a series of false casts, each one beautifully executed.

During his false cast, his hand stops near his face and no tailing loop occurs.

But then, note that on the final throw, the caster's rod hand sweeps well out in front, with the hand and arm fully extended to obtain more distance (a mistake!) before the stop is made . . .

. . . and he ends up with his final cast trailing. The same principle applies if you cast too soon. If the speed-up-and-stop is made too soon, there is a great tendency to shove the rod hard (and the rod tip) straight forward, causing the line behind to run into the line ahead of it.

The second most common cause of tailing loops is changing the elevation of the hand during the forward cast, as shown in the next sequence of illustrations.

Note that the caster's arm is not traveling at the same elevation during the stroke toward the target as it sweeps the rod forward. It begins at one elevation and drops downward as the hand is brought forward to complete the cast.

Anytime the rod hand travels in a downward and forward direction like this, you are really stopping the tip from going in a straight line.

Now you are causing the backcast line to be pulled down on top of the portion of the line that is unrolling toward the target.

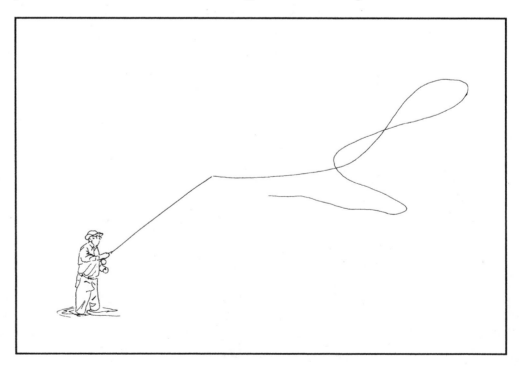

Here is the third cause of a tailing loop. In this instance the rod begins at one elevation and then is directed to travel upward.

Note that if the rod hand travels from a low position . . .

. . . and climbs upward on the forward cast, but travels in a straight line . . .

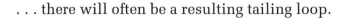

. . . there will often be a resulting tailing loop.

I find that this third problem occurs much more frequently with anglers in the West than those who live in the East, perhaps because westerners fly fish more often by wading in deep water or from a bellyboat. In either of these situations, when the trunk of your body is close to the surface of the water, you will have to throw your backcast higher so the line doesn't hit the surface of the water behind you.

I should add that there is a common misconception about this casting problem: that is, the higher you elevate the rod hand on the backcast, the higher you keep the line off the surface behind you. This is simply not true. Remember, the line is going to go in the direction in which you speed up and stop the rod tip (and rod hand). So elevating the rod hand does not cause you to throw a higher line. Indeed, it can cause just the reverse!

And unless you are a really excellent fly caster, elevating the rod hand on the backcast will almost certainly result in a tailing loop.

Here is the fourth explanation for these problem loops. Occasionally, a tailing loop happens when a trout fisherman who is used to casting at very short distances, and who is in the habit of stopping the rod at about twelve o'clock or the near-vertical attitude, tries to make a longer cast. When he stops his rod in a position almost straight up on the backcast, he can throw the line about twenty-five feet and no tailing loop will occur. But if he attempts to throw a longer cast from this same position, a tailing loop will almost certainly occur. This is because his line has been cast straight back and then brought forward in a straight line on the same plane—and the line simply runs into itself.

The final explanation for a tailing loop is a low, weak backcast. This is an uncommon error, but it can result in a tailing loop, even on a short cast.

If a backcast is made so weakly that the line falls down well behind the caster . . .

. . . and then is swept forward . . .

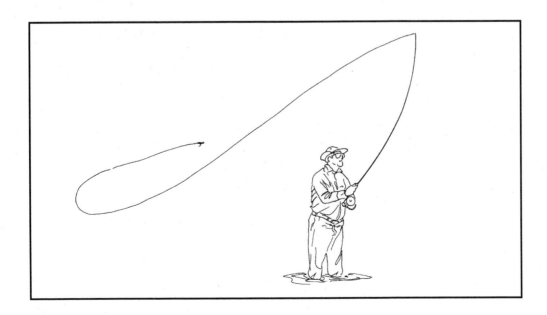

. . . the line is in a tailing loop attitude even before the forward cast has begun.

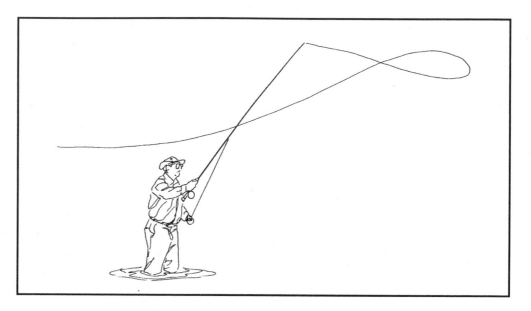

Correcting Tailing Loops

Throughout this section of the book I have been stressing that stopping straight ahead at the end of the cast causes a tailing loop. But there is a paradox here. Because the line goes in the direction in which the rod tip speeds up and stops, and because you want to cast in a straight line to make an accurate cast to the target, you need to throw the line straight ahead and at the same time stop the rod tip going straight ahead. But you have learned that at this point in the cast, if nothing else occurs, you will get a tailing loop. The key to understanding how to eliminate tailing loops is to visualize the relationship in time and space between the speed-up-and-stop action of the rod tip and the unrolling characteristics of the fly line in flight.

Let's first look at the speed-up-and-stop of the rod from this perspective. Imagine what happens when a rifle is fired. If you throw the gun aside the moment the bullet leaves the barrel, the bullet will still go where it was aimed. In a similar fashion, as soon as the rod stops at the end of the cast, if you could magically detach your line from your rod, just like the bullet your line would go in the direction in which the rod tip stopped. Here's the secret: After the rod stops, almost nothing can influence or alter the direction that the fly line and fly are going to travel.

Next, try to visualize that when the rod stops and the line is being propelled toward the target by the power of the forward cast from its position in the air behind you, the end of the fly line is unrolling and forming a loop that has a bottom as well as a top. The top of the loop consists of the front portion of the fly line, and the leader and fly that are attached to it. The bottom of the loop consists of the balance of fly line behind the front portion. As I have already discussed, a tailing loop is one in which these bottom and top portions of the fly line (which in unrolling have formed into the configuration of a loop) crash into each other and become intermingled or tangled.

But if you can't alter the direction of the line, how can you prevent a tailing loop? What you are going to do is something that takes place after the speed-up-and-stop. You are not going to alter the direction of the fly line to do it, because, just like the bullet that has been fired, that is no longer in your power. Instead you are going to alter slightly the configuration of the loop, as shown in the following sequence of illustrations.

Speed up and stop in the direction you want the line to go (usually straight ahead) . . .

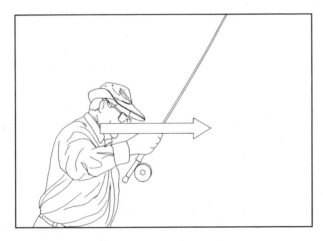

. . . and the moment the stop occurs, briefly tilt the rod tip downward with thumb pressure just a fraction of an inch. Here's what happens. The line is directed at the target straight ahead on the stop, and if the tip is immediately ducked or lowered a few inches, then a tight casting loop is maintained . . .

. . . but without a tailing loop. By lowering the tip after the stop, you have not altered the direction of the cast. Instead, you have slightly altered the configuration of the loop by ensuring—with this slight and brief thumb movement after the stop—that the bottom of the loop remains on the bottom, and the top remains on the top (in a tight loop configuration) so that they cannot crash into each other.

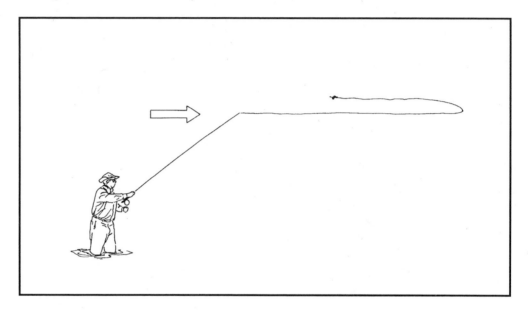

To summarize, all your tailing loop problems will vanish if you take the following steps:

1. Make a positive backcast that will cause the line to unroll behind you.
2. Carry the rod forward in a straight line.
3. Speed up and stop the rod in the direction you want the line to travel.
4. As soon as the rod tip stops, tilt the rod downward very slightly with your thumb.

And, as with most skills in life, practicing these skills will bring—if not perfection—then at least fewer frustrations while you're on the water.

10

SPECIAL CASTS

If you are going to make good presentations, you need to be versatile so you can make a variety of special casts. Mastering these advanced techniques will enable you to catch many more fish. Just remember that the casting rules outlined earlier will—with practice—allow you to make every cast that is possible with a fly rod.

Roll Cast

Next to the conventional overhead cast, the roll cast is used more than any other. There are hosts of fishing situations in which this cast is beneficial; in some cases it is essential. Its most frequent application is in spots where there is little or no room for a backcast. Another case would be when you need to lift a dry fly silently from the water. Or if your fly is snagged on something, here's my solution. Make a roll cast, allowing your leader and a small amount of the line to roll beyond the snag. Then make a backcast. This trick will often free the fly. If you are fishing with a fast-sinking line or lead-core shooting head, here again you need the roll cast to lift your line from the water so you can make a backcast.

There are vertical roll casts, and side roll casts, and so many situations for using both that I could write a whole chapter on the subject. The shame is that so few fly fishermen can make an efficient roll cast. Even worse, some instructors teach what I regard as poor technique, which only complicates the problem of learning what is really an easy cast to master.

The inefficient method of roll-casting is to position the fly rod as shown here. This allows a minimum of rod movement to aid in your cast.

The line follows the direction of the rod tip, speeds up, and stops. Loop size is determined by the length of the speed-up-and-stop stroke. By driving the rod tip downward, as shown by the arrow, you throw the largest loop possible and direct the cast down toward the surface. This is why so many roll casts pile up.

To deliver a good roll cast, consider several important but easy-to-understand tips:

1. Do not forget that you are modifying only the backcast. Instead, most fly fishermen try to modify the entire cast. If you already know how to make a good forward cast, don't change this when you roll-cast—only your backcast needs to be altered.
2. The line on any cast will go in the direction in which the rod tip stops at the end of what most people refer to as the power stroke, but what I have been referring to as the speed-up-and-stop of the rod tip. (This is an extremely important point, which I will explain in more detail later.)
3. The size of the line loop as it unrolls on the cast is determined by only one factor: the distance the rod tip moves during the final part of the cast, referred to above. After the rod moves forward, the speed-up-and-stop occurs. The rod tip is traveling in a slight arc or curved path (it's very difficult to make the tip travel straight ahead during the whole speed-up-and-stop motion). The distance that the rod tip drops from the beginning to the end of the speed-up-and-stop (or arc) is exactly the size that the loop will become. For example, if your rod tip drops two feet on the speed-up-and-stop, your loop will be two feet in size.
4. The longer the rod moves through the cast, the more it helps with that cast. Watch great casters: In some manner they always manage to get the rod well in back of them. This is true even if they stop the rod in an elevated position. They have learned that the farther the rod tip moves during the cast, the farther and easier the fly and line will go.

Why Most People Have Trouble Roll-Casting

Here's how the typical fly fisherman makes the roll cast. The rod is brought up until it is nearly vertical. Then it is swept forward and downward. But reexamine the four important points I made above and you will see that this roll cast violates all of them. Point 1 suggests that you should not modify your forward cast. If you can make a good forward cast, there is no reason to alter it.

Try this experiment to prove my point. Make several conventional false casts by sweeping the rod forward and downward—the way most people roll-cast. This will drive the line down in front, causing a piled mess in the fly line and leader—just as it does when most people roll-cast. This should convince you that when roll-casting, you need to make your forward cast just as you would a conventional forward cast. To monitor this technique, observe your forward cast. If it travels in a

This is an inefficient way to begin a roll cast. The rod is held vertically and the line often sags behind the angler.

large circular loop, you are not casting it efficiently. If the loop is rather oval in shape, you are doing it right.

Point 2 indicates that the line and fly go in the direction you stop the rod tip. Most people end a roll cast by driving the tip toward the water. This is one reason why the line usually falls in a heap on the surface in front of them. At the end of the speed-up-and-stop, the rod tip should be traveling forward, not downward. Point 3 explains that the size of your loop is determined by the distance you speed up and stop the rod tip at the end of the cast. Most people begin a roll cast with the rod tip held vertically, then sweep forward and downward in one continuous motion. This forces the rod to throw the largest loop possible, which means that you are throwing the energy of the cast around the largest circle

This is an inefficient way to execute a roll cast, thrusting the rod tip forward and down. The loop is large and sloppy.

possible. Your rod's movement will be vastly restricted if you hold it vertically at the beginning of the cast.

Roll-Casting the Efficient Way

Improving your roll cast is really very easy, and here are the steps to follow. Slowly bring the rod back as far as you can. The best results for longer roll casts occur when the rod tip is behind you and pointing directly away from your target—parallel to the water. The longer you move the rod tip behind you, the more the rod helps in the cast. When you need additional help, move your rod and hand back as far as the fishing condi-

An efficient roll cast. Position the rod as far back as conditions allow. Note that the rod hand should be held low to help form a small tight loop.

tions allow. It is very important that during all of the backward movement, your rod hand does not rise above your shoulder. Indeed, for longer roll casts, if you can bring back your rod hand at about belt level—that is even better. Now, with the rod parallel to the water, it is vital that at this point, you stop. If the line in front of you does not stop, you will not make a good roll cast. What happens when you stop (and you only have to pause for a heartbeat) is that surface tension grips the line. Your rod can then load or flex against this tension when you sweep forward.

There is no need to hurry at this point. After the line stops, make a normal forward cast. Throughout this forward cast you should keep your rod hand at the same height as when you started. If your hand travels at a downward or upward angle, a poorer cast will result. But if you

An efficient roll cast. Keep the rod hand low and on the same plane as it travels straight forward. The arrows show the hand positions at the start and end of the cast.

make a normal forward cast with your rod hand moving straight ahead, you will be directing almost all the energy of your cast at your target.

At the final moment in the cast, you reach a critical instant: The shorter the distance of your speed-up and the faster your rod tip stops, the tighter will be your line loop and the farther it will go. The same happens when you make any good forward cast.

There are several situations in which a modified roll cast can be extremely helpful. One is when you need to make a forward cast that stays very close to the surface and has to travel back under overhanging brush. Here you need to bring your rod back to a vertical position and then, just before the start of your forward roll cast, drop the rod over so that you can make a side roll cast. Make the stroke as you would a nor-

The result of a good, efficient roll cast. Try to make this a normal forward cast with the tip stopping straight ahead, and the cast will travel fast and far.

mal, vertical roll cast—but move the rod tip parallel to the water, even during the speed-up- and-stop.

If you want your cast to remain parallel to the water, then your speed-up-and-stop must be made parallel to the water. Otherwise your line and fly will end up in the brush. For example, if you begin the speed-up-and-stop stroke with the tip twelve inches off the surface, the tip must travel at twelve inches off the surface and stop that high above the water, too. It is also important to make a very brief speed-up-and-stop; a long one would create a large loop that might not go back under the brush.

Another situation in which a variation of a roll cast can be helpful is when you have impaled your hook in a log or other obstruction. Make a roll cast with a large loop—so large that it will unroll and go beyond the spot where the hook is impaled. As soon as the loop passes beyond the fly, make a hard backcast. The line in the air that has passed beyond the fly will usually pull it free.

The roll cast is also handy when you are fishing a short line and want to change direction. Make a roll cast roughly in the direction you want to throw the fly. If you then make a backcast opposite your target, it will be easy for you to throw the fly to the target. And you can often get a wonderful drag-free drift by using a modified roll cast. Try this technique. Make a downward roll cast with the rod tip directed at the water where you want your fly to drift. What you are doing is deliberately causing the leader and front portion of the fly line not to straighten out, but to collapse. This, of course, produces a great deal of slack in your leader and the front of your line—which allows you to obtain a long, drag-free drift.

The roll cast can lift a popping bug or other fly from the surface with minimal disturbance, too. Make a roll cast that is angled upward and your line will roll out and lift the bug or fly almost vertically from the surface. As soon as the fly leaves the water, make a normal backcast. The result is a lift and backcast with almost no surface disturbance. I use this cast constantly when I want to pick up a dry fly without frightening the fish. The same technique can be used to lift a sinking line from the water so a backcast can be made.

You can also use a roll cast to free almost any grass that snags on the fly. Near the end of a retrieve, make a roll cast directed upward. This will lift your line above the water. Now watch carefully. When all of the line is above the water, but the fly is still underwater, make a hard backcast. In fact, make an extra-hard backcast. Use a single haul to generate additional line speed. What occurs is that the water grips the fly loaded with grass, creating enough resistance on the vegetation that the hook acts like a shear. Remember that the backcast must be made while the line is in the air and the fly is underwater. About 90 percent of the time this frees the grass and you can continue to fish.

Aerial Roll Cast

The aerial roll cast is used only for short-range work in spots where almost any other cast with a fly would be impossible. It is especially useful for trout fishing on small streams. Here is the common problem. You want to deliver your fly to a target—but there is no room for a back- or roll cast. Worse, there may be overhead obstructions, too. The aerial roll is effective to about fifteen or twenty feet, but works better at slightly shorter distances.

First, extend your leader and approximately six to ten feet of fly line outside your rod tip. Hold the fly in your hand. (Be sure to hold the hook by the end so that the point will not impale you.) Lower your rod tip to the water until it points at your target. It is vital to begin with the rod tip just inches above the water and the tip directed at the target.

Sweep the rod tip swiftly up and directly away from the target. Keep a firm but not-too-tight grip on the fly. How high you bring the rod tip before making a forward cast is dependent upon any overhead obstructions. Ideally, if you can sweep the rod tip at least to a vertical position, the cast is easier to make. However, you can cast fifteen feet or more if you bring the rod just past forty-five degrees from the surface.

Quickly bring your rod as high as conditions will allow, keeping a grip on the hook bend.

The instant it has reached its highest point, the rod tip is immediately swept forward. Do not make any stop between your back- and forward casts! It is vital that you change the rod's direction without a stop.This keeps your line and leader in a tight loop. Up to this point, you should be holding the hook firmly enough that it will not skip out of your fingers. This permits you to load your rod with the line and leader that are sweeping through the air. The instant that the rod begins to sweep forward, reduce your grip on the fly, but allow the tight, fast-moving leader and line to pull the fly from your fingers.

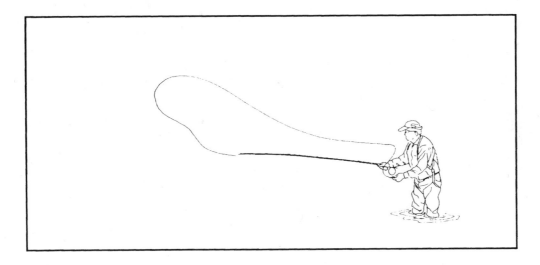

On the stop in your forward cast, be sure to direct the rod tip well above your target. This will cause the leader and line to unroll in the air in the target's direction. If you drive the rod tip downward at this stop, you will throw the line down and short of the target.

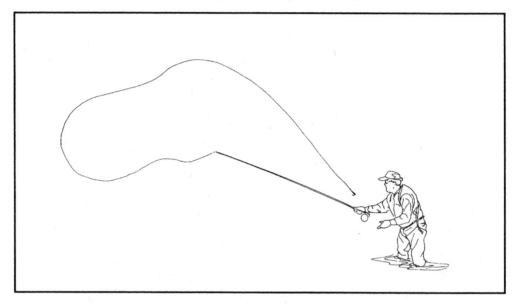

After the stop, lower your rod to the fishing position. If you speed up and stop your rod tip above and in the direction of the target, the line will unroll and the fly will drop exactly where you want it.

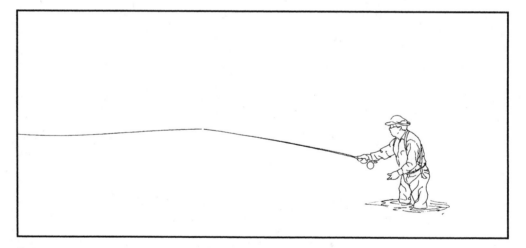

Side Cast

In some situations a side cast, with the line traveling parallel to the water, is best. Where there are overhanging obstructions such as boat

As shown, the side roll cast is set up on the backcast just like any good basic roll cast. The rod hand is drawn well back behind the body, so that much of the line falls in a gentle curve behind the fisherman, as it would on any conventional roll cast.

As soon as the rod stops on the backward motion, the rod tip is lowered to the side so that the rod is parallel to the surface of the water. It is extremely important that the rod be parallel to the surface before the forward roll cast is begun! Note that if the rod is tilted at a high angle, a bad cast will certainly result.

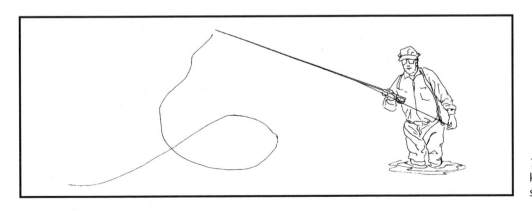

The rod is swept forward, keeping it as parallel to the surface as you can make it.

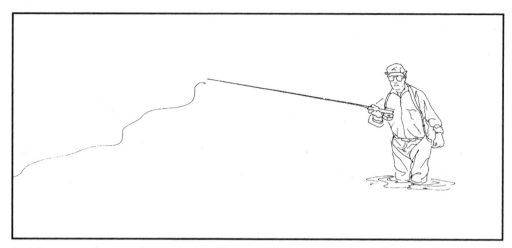

And then, a very fast speed-up and a quick stop will cause the line to unroll parallel to the water in a tight loop toward the target.

But if the rod is tilted high above the parallel plane as the speed-up-and-stop occurs, the loop will be tilted at an angle and the fly will unroll and jump and into the bushes. I am often successful in getting my casting students to better understand this by emphasizing the relationship between the rod tip and the surface of the water: if the rod tip is 2 feet and 2 inches off the surface at the beginning of the speed-up-and-stop, the line will then unroll throughout the entire cast at 2 feet 2 inches off the surface. No more, no less. Unlike very long casts, since the side roll cast is a short one, not enough time expires on this cast for gravity to pull the line down toward the surface.

docks, trees along the shoreline, or bridges and you want to get your fly well back under them, a properly thrown side cast will do better than a vertical one. Also, when you want to throw a wide curve to the left or right, a side cast will throw a larger curve than any other method.

When I am casting to spooky trout, bonefish, tarpon, snook, redfish, permit, and other species, I always try to use a side cast. There are two advantages. One is that the line remains low and is unlikely to be seen by the fish. The other is that at the end of the cast, the fly falls from just above the surface. An overhead cast would drop the fly from a height of at least several feet, and often more. The line crashing to the water usually scares a fish more than the impact of the fly itself.

Properly Controlling Line on the Shoot

Failing to properly control your line when you shoot it on the final forward cast can result in inaccurate casts, missed strikes, and other problems. This control is especially important when you are shooting a great deal of line—but it is also essential when fishing dry flies, nymphs, and other patterns that are generally cast a short distance.

When you're fly fishing for difficult-to-see fish such as bonefish, a major fault is releasing the line on the shoot, as shown here.

Instead, when you shoot the line toward the target, form an O-ring with your thumb and first finger, allowing the line to flow through.

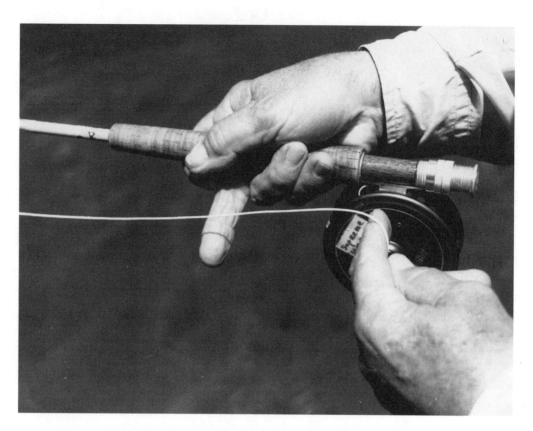

Observe your fly, in flight. When it's over the target, trap the line flowing through your O-ring fingers, then move the line over to your index finger holding the rod.

What almost all fly fishermen do on their last forward cast is release the line after the speed-up-and-stop. Control of both the cast and the retrieve is now lost until the line can again be trapped in the hand.

To achieve accuracy, a spin fisherman will overcast the lure toward the target, and then feather the line with his forefinger to slow it down. When the lure is over the target, the finger traps the line, stopping the flight and dropping the lure. A plug caster does the same thing, but instead of the forefinger he presses his thumb against the revolving spool to stop the lure at the desired distance. Fly fishermen have the same option—but not if they release the line at the end of the forward cast, which takes away their control of the line's flight.

Also, when the line is released like this and the fly falls to the water, it will be nearly impossible to hook any fish that might strike. When you are targeting difficult-to-see fish that are rapidly moving (such as bonefish and tarpon), you always want your line hand to be in control. What drives a good guide on a tropical flat crazy is to see his client cast, release his line, and, at the end of the cast, look down to find his line. Only after he grasps it in his hand does the angler look up to locate the fish. But because these fish are difficult to see, he frequently has no idea where that might be. This usually means a lost chance.

This caster has kept his concentration on the fly and never looked down. As his index finger gathers in the line he lowers the rod, and when the fly touches the water the retrieve can begin.

Only when extreme distance is necessary and you don't expect the fish to strike immediately should you ever consider letting go of the line in your hand. For almost all fly-fishing situations, a better presentation can be made if, on the shoot, the line remains under the control of your hand.

Double Haul

I have observed thousands of fishermen in my lifetime of fly fishing. With only a few exceptions, most casters use the double haul incorrectly, or at least inefficiently—and this includes many of the great ones with whom I have been lucky enough to share a river. Next to the proper casting stroke, the double haul is the single most important tool you can possess. It will permit you to throw a longer line—even against the wind—and to toss heavier flies and lines with less effort. Once you have mastered it, you will use it to some degree on almost every cast.

What exactly is a *haul*? A single haul is a downward pull on the back-cast or on the forward cast. When you pull swiftly on the line in your hand, you cause the rod tip to flex. Here is another experiment to try. Toss a short cast out in front of you and then hold the rod slightly elevated. With the rod still, yank downward on the line in your hand. The rod tip will flex rapidly and cause the line to leap upward. A haul bends the rod and flexes the tip. This is the most important factor to understand about hauling—single or double.

Most fly casters are taught to make a long downward pull during the backcast and again when coming forward. In my view this is an inefficient use of the double haul.

First, remember that when you make a haul, you bend the rod and flex the rod tip. Now, it is important to good casting to make a very small loop. The angler who makes long and continuous hauls causes the rod to flex over a greater distance than the fly fisherman who makes a shorter haul. Remember, the shorter the haul, the shorter the distance the rod tip will flex, and the tighter the loop. Long hauls will develop wider and less efficient loops.

Second, the faster you stop the rod tip at the end of your cast, the more the energy of the cast will be catapulted toward the target. Since hauling causes the tip to flex, it is vital to efficient casting to stop the haul with the speed-up-and-stop. Ideally, the haul should begin when the speed-up starts, and it should end when your rod hand stops. Your rod hand's speed-up-and-stop and your line hand's haul should be simultaneous—both starting and stopping at the same time.

For example, if your rod hand moves three inches at the end of the cast for the speed-up-and-stop, your haul should be no longer than three inches. There are fishing situations in which you may have to draw your line hand well away from your rod hand to remove slack or help flex the rod. But the actual, brief haul should occur only during the speed-up-and-stop.

Long downward pulls on the backcast cause several problems. The rod flexes deeper, so the loop is larger. Pulling on the line after your rod

Throughout the double haul, keep the line hand close to the casting hand. At this stage of the backcast, the haul should be accelerated simultaneously with the speed of the rod.

hand stops causes some of the cast's energy to be directed downward instead of directly away from the target. Fishermen who make long hauls on the backcast frequently find that on the forward cast, the line has become wrapped around the rod butt. This will not happen with the shorter haul strokes I recommend. Finally, if you make a long downward pull, your line hand must then rise toward the reel so that you can make another haul. And unless you have developed great line speed on the backcast, as your rod hand begins to move forward and your line hand travels toward it, some slack will be pushed into the system. This slack will have to be removed before the forward cast can proceed.

To make the most efficient double haul, the hand holding the line should follow the reel on the backcast. Try to keep your hands close together—no more than twelve inches apart. Watch the end of the line on the water; after this has been lifted from the surface, you can make the haul. Make the speed-up-and-stop motion with your rod hand and the haul at the same time, beginning and stopping simultaneously. During the forward cast your line hand should travel in front of the reel, staying at the same distance from your rod hand. Then make both the haul and the speed-up-and-stop motion again, together. And make sure that your rod and line hands stop together as the cast ends.

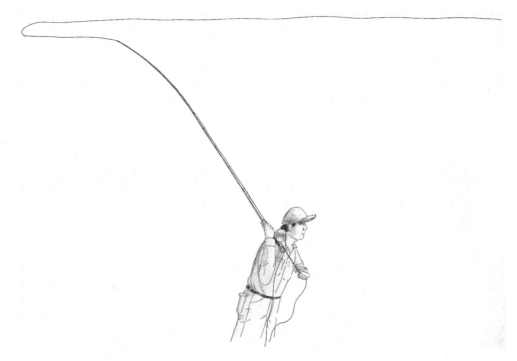

At the moment the rod speeds up and stops, the haul likewise accelerates and stops. Note the distance between the line hand and the casting hand: To haul effectively you must haul quicker, not longer.

There may be times when, as you lift the rod for the backcast, your line hand must move downward to eliminate unwanted slack or to flex the rod. If this is necessary, your line hand may well be below your belt when you make the speed-up-and-stop with your rod hand. Make the brief haul from this position. Do not raise your line hand toward the rod. Maintain

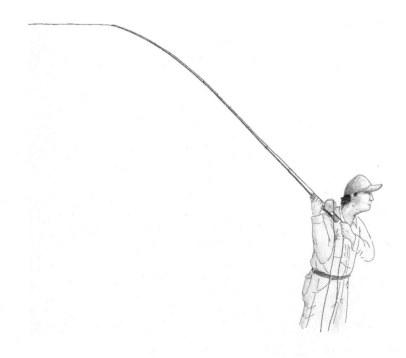

During the time that it takes for the line to unroll behind you, reposition the line hand close to the casting hand in preparation for the forward haul.

The moment before the speed-up-and-stop, the haul is at its quickest. Again, note that even at the peak speed of the haul, the line hand is relatively close to the casting hand.

the same distance between your rod and line hands as you sweep forward and no slack will occur. When the rod hand makes the speed-up-and-stop, the line hand (down by your hip) makes that brief haul.

Of course to make a good backcast, especially a long one, remember that the lower you position your rod before beginning the backcast, the more efficient this cast will be. To summarize, a line falls when it opens. To reach a target, the line must get there before it opens or unrolls. And

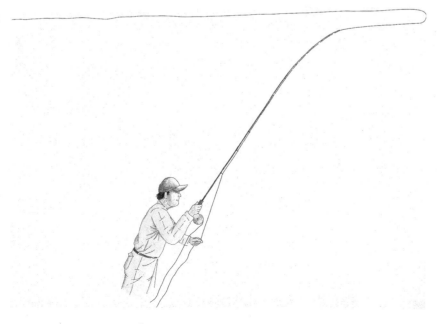

The moment when the rod stops, the haul is stopped.

the only way you can accomplish this is to form a small loop, and to make the rod tip move faster and stop quicker.

Learning the Double Haul in Fifteen Minutes

Because there are so many different motions involving both hands in the double haul, it is very difficult to learn while actually casting on the water. The method I've developed to teach the double haul has the average caster learning the technique within fifteen minutes. Some have learned it in five. I want to emphasize that the slower you do this exercise, the faster you'll learn the double haul. The faster you do it, the longer it will take. Here's the method.

On a lawn, work out about twenty feet of line. It is important that you make side casts low and to the ground, not vertical casts, during this exercise. With the line stretched out in front of you, begin to slowly move the rod back and to the side. Make sure your line hand follows the reel and that your two hands are no more than twelve inches apart. Make a normal side backcast with your rod hand. At the same time you complete the speed-up-and-stop, give a fast one-inch tug on the line with your line hand. Try not to tug more than one inch, and concentrate on making your rod and line hands move through the casting and haul motions at the same time. If you have made the moves correctly, the line will zip back behind you. As it falls to the grass, your hands should still be twelve inches or less apart.

Here is the important part. Do not make your forward cast immediately; stop and think about what you did. Because the line is on the grass behind you, you can also take time to analyze what you are going to do on the forward cast. Bring the rod forward slowly—with your line hand leading in front of the reel and close to it. Then make a forward side cast and, at the same time, a one-inch haul with your line hand.

I will warn you that most people have trouble coordinating the forward cast with the haul. Stick with it and it will soon come. Continue this exercise until you see you are hauling correctly. It is vital that during this learning session you move ever-so-slowly back and forth prior to making the haul and the speed-up-and-stop. Within five minutes most people—if they are making the motions slowly and allowing the line to lie on the grass after each cast—will have the technique pretty well down. Once you feel you have it, try false-casting using the double haul. As soon as something goes wrong, stop and resort to the grass exercise again.

To further improve your double haul, try using a half rod. By working with a short rod, any casting flaws will be more evident. As you learn to make the brief stroke and haul simultaneously, you will find that your casting improves steadily.

Making Your Double Haul Better

Watch fly casters using the double haul under different fishing conditions. Rarely will you see one change the speed of his line hand on the haul. When you haul with your line hand, you accelerate the rod tip. The faster the tip accelerates and stops, the farther the line will travel. Yet once a fly fisherman learns the double haul, he too often makes all subsequent hauls at the same speed.

When you want to make a longer cast, the tendency is to put additional power into your rod hand. This opens the loop, shocks the rod, and creates a poor cast. If you want to make a longer-than-normal cast, try this technique. False-cast until you have a fair amount of line out, but your rod hand is still controlling a nice loop and no shock waves appear in the line. Now do not use any more force with your rod hand. Instead, increase the speed of your double haul. Do not make the haul longer—only faster. When I ask good casters to back off the power in their rod hands like this, they have immediately picked up ten feet on their casts. Think of the double haul as a gear shift. When you need more speed, change gears and increase the speed with your haul. Never increase the length of the haul—just the swiftness. And do not try to obtain additional distance by putting more power or speed into your rod hand.

Curve Cast

I remember a dead calm morning in the Florida Keys. The surface was like oiled glass—not a ripple anywhere. The sun had just risen. Laid-up tarpon were resting in the deep-water basin, their bodies suspended just below the surface. Here and there I could just see the tip of a tail or a dorsal fin, pinpointing their locations. Such fish are as spooky as a pickpocket at a police convention. My guide quietly, very quietly, pushed the boat ahead. At the same moment we both saw a nice tarpon facing toward us, maybe twenty-five feet away. Invariably, under such conditions, if a cast is made to the fish and it follows only a short distance, it sees the boat and flees.

A curve cast was the answer here. The fly landed six feet to the right of the fish and slightly in front, with the leader gently falling to the surface. But the line had fallen so that the end had curved and lay six feet to the left of the tarpon. I started my retrieve; the fly swam from the tarpon's right, past its head, and then off to the left. But it never got a chance to follow the curve in the line. The tarpon swished its tail, moved forward, and inhaled the fly. Ten minutes later the hook fell free

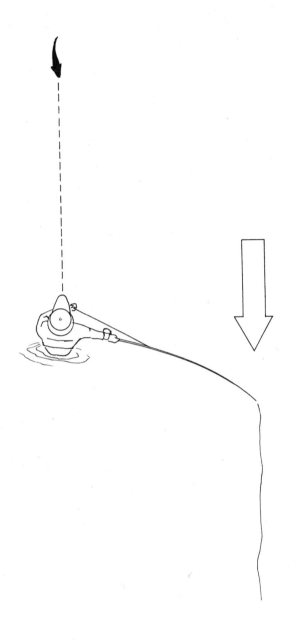

In order for the curve cast to be accurate, you must face the target. You should make the lowest backcast possible; you can't make a curve cast with a vertical backcast.

on a jump and we went looking for another fish. But it was the curve cast that had been responsible for that hookup.

There are two ways to make a curve cast. One way is to bring your rod forward into a vertical position, permitting a curve to the left or right. I find this is the most difficult of all the casts I teach. If you are right-handed, it is easy to understand and master making a curve to the left. Of course, the reverse is true for a left-hander. While this limits you to curving the line in one direction only, the ability to make even this cast offers many advantages when fly fishing. The curve cast gives you a tool

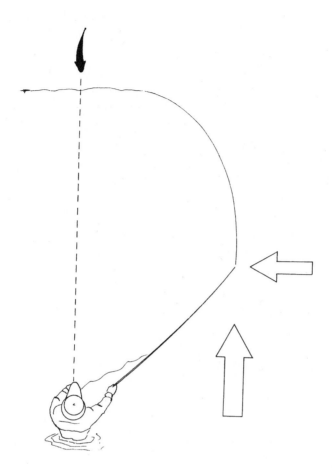

Keep the rod parallel to the surface of the water as you sweep it forward. Then, while still facing the fish, stop the rod abruptly at 45 degrees. The line will go in the direction that the rod tip speeds up and stops. If you make a very abrupt stop, the rod tip will curve to the left and the line will do the same. To make a bigger curve, stop the rod tip faster and more abruptly and haul the line. When most people first try the curve cast they don't make the speed-up-and-stop parallel to the water. Instead, the rod tip dives slightly toward the surface, so the line dives to the surface. To hone your skills, make the speed-up-and-stop at a climbing angle and bring it down with each practice cast.

that can do several jobs. On numerous occasions I have used it to drop my fly or popping bug on the other side of a rock, a tree standing in water, a boat dock, or another obstruction. I then began my retrieve but hooked the fish while it was still behind the obstruction.

The curve cast can also be invaluable on a trout stream or saltwater flat. Here, of course, fish will be looking either away from you or toward you (as my laid-up tarpon were). If you cast in a straight line to drop your fly in front of a fish looking away from you, then retrieve the fly, the fish will often refuse your offering. The reason is that a fly that swims directly toward a fish is unnatural. Predator fish expect to chase their prey, not have it approach in an attack mode. On the other hand, if the fish is facing toward you and only a short distance away, as it follows the fly on the retrieve it will all too often see you and the game is over.

The basic problem here is to avoid "attacking" the fish with your fly. Instead, you want to make a cast that will permit the fish to follow your fly a long enough distance to become interested in striking—but not see you. A properly presented curve cast will allow a fish to track the fly for at least six to ten feet without drawing it any closer to you. I cannot emphasize how important this is when a fish is near you.

There is another situation in which the curve cast is helpful: when you want a fly to land parallel to a shoreline or some fish-hiding structure. The general method is to make a cast to the shoreline and retrieve the fly more or less right back to you. But a fish along the shoreline will see your fly much the way that you would see a knife pointed at you lengthwise. In fact, you wouldn't see much at all. Make a curve cast, however, and your fly will swim parallel to the shoreline, giving the fish a side view of it—which is much more effective.

Along a saltwater shoreline bordered by mangroves, for example, you might want to retrieve your fly parallel to the roots. The curve cast is very effective in this situation. Rather than throwing your fly to the root-lined shore and retrieving it directly away, use this cast to make it swim along the roots. Then that fish gets a look at the wide profile of the fly. You can do the same thing when fishing a trout stream, or the shoreline of a lake. Once you master the curve cast, you will find many practical uses for it in your fly-fishing outings.

Since you want your fly line to travel parallel to the water, and to end in a curve, your rod tip must travel parallel to the surface during the speed-up-and-stop. This will cause the rod tip to curve or hook at the very end of the cast. Here's how you accomplish this task. The backcast should be a low side cast, so that at the beginning of the forward motion your rod comes forward low and parallel to the water. If you make a conventional vertical backcast, the curve cast will be very difficult to make. You need to make a low side backcast. Then on the forward cast your speed-up-and-stop must be very swift, and the rod tip must stop dead!

This high-speed motion, coupled with the dead stop, causes the rod tip to flex into a curve to the left (if you are right-handed). The rod tip moves in a sharp bend or curve to the left and parallel to the surface, so the leader and line will do the same—because the line, leader, and fly go in the direction that the rod tip speeds up and stops. The faster (not harder) you move the rod tip during the brief speed-up, and the more abruptly you stop it, the greater will be the resulting curve in your line and leader.

You can increase the curve of your line even more if you use a haul on the forward cast to increase the tip speed. Of course, if your rod tip travels downward (rather than parallel to the water) on the speed-up-and-stop, you will throw the line downward into the water and no curve will appear. It is absolutely necessary that during the speed-up-and-stop your rod tip travel parallel to the surface.

Once you have mastered making the curve cast, getting extreme accuracy with it is easy. Start by facing your target. During the forward cast, if you sweep your rod parallel to the surface and make your stop forty-five degrees from the fish, the curve in the line will land in front of you. Face the target and complete the above operation and your curve cast will be accurate.

Stack Cast

This is one of the oldest of all casts. It is used primarily for those situations in trout fishing when you want to create slack in the leader and forward portion of your fly line, enabling your fly to drift drag-free. Every decade or so someone renames it. I have heard it called the pile cast, the puddle cast, and many other names. Regardless of the name today, it is one of the most important casts a trout fisherman can learn.

I used to go trout fishing with a certain outdoor writer. He threw one of the biggest, ugliest forward-cast loops imaginable. You could have ridden a bicycle through his loop. Yet with dry flies he often far outperformed better casters. It was some time before I realized why. His loop was huge and when it turned over, the leader and forward end of his fly line collapsed into a pile—allowing his fly to drift a long way free of drag.

The purpose of the stack cast is to get a lot of small waves into the leader, and often in front of the line. Only when the leader directly in front of the fly straightens will drag occur. It is vital to understand that if you want drag-free drift, the tippet immediately in front of your fly must have some waves or slack in it.

The stack cast is one of the easiest of all casts to master. It requires only that you understand four simple elements:

1. The cast must be made slowly. If you cast at high speed, nothing will be accomplished!
2. The lower you take your rod on the backcast, the easier it will be to perform the stack cast.
3. The cast must be aimed high and in front of you. The higher the cast is aimed, the more slack will accumulate in your leader. You may have to make several casts in a particular fishing situation to obtain the angle you need.
4. As soon as the cast ends, you must drop the rod. If you leave your rod tip elevated at the end of the cast, the line hanging from the tip to the surface will begin to slowly sag back toward you. As the line creeps backward, it will draw most of the slack out of your line and leader. Many people who make a stack cast fail to realize that by not dropping the rod immediately at the end of the cast, they will pull out the very slack they worked to put in.

For best results, it is essential that you make a low backcast, as shown here.

The low backcast permits the angler to make a climbing forward cast, as shown here. It is very important that this forward cast isn't overpowered: If too much line speed develops, the line will recoil and spoil the cast. It is essential to make the climbing forward cast a very "soft" cast.

As soon as the speed-up-and-stop occurs, the direction of the cast has been determined. As soon as the rod stops, drop the tip toward the surface, and waves will occur (as shown here). Failure to stop the rod immediately after the stop will remove much of the slack.

Change-of-Direction Cast

The change-of-direction cast is invaluable, but it works best when you have less than thirty-five feet of line and leader outside your rod tip. It can be made with additional line outside the tip, but it becomes more difficult.

Here are three typical situations in which this cast is useful. You are standing in the front of a bonefish boat retrieving your fly. Suddenly the guide tells you to change direction fast and cast to an incoming fish. If you make a series of false casts, your fly will not get to the bonefish in time. The same thing can happen in trout fishing. You are fishing over a trout that is rising to dry flies. Out of the corner of your eye you see another, larger fish take a fly from the surface. You don't have time for a series of false casts; what you need is a single back-and-forward cast that will drop the fly right on target.

Here is an even more common situation. You have made a cast upstream and allowed the line to drift through a good-looking hole. Now you want to return the fly to the same upstream starting point. Most people do this with a series of false casts. They make a backcast, then turn slightly upstream on the forward cast. Another backcast is made and, as the rod is brought forward, the cast is directed even farther upstream. Another backcast is made, and the final cast is directed at the target.

If you understand why anglers make a series of false casts, it will be easy for you to learn how to change direction with one back- and one forward cast. The most efficient backcast is one that travels in a direct line (180 degrees) away from the target. The reason for the series of false casts is to allow you to slowly work the backcast around until it is directly opposite the upstream target.

Once you grasp this concept, you can make a change-of-direction cast. Here is the technique. Your fly has drifted downstream and you are ready to cast it back to the starting point. Move your rod tip rapidly until it points at the target, making sure that you keep the tip very close to the water. Remember the cardinal rule that you cannot make a cast until you have the end of the line moving. As you move the rod tip toward the target, do not stop or the line end will stop, and you will have to get it moving again before you can make a backcast. When the rod tip is aimed at the target, make a strong backcast in the direction opposite the target. Often a single haul on this backcast will help you make a good forward cast. Now come forward and drop the fly on your target.

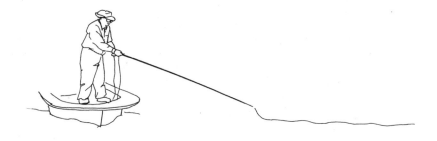

Lower the rod so the tip is near the surface and remove all slack from the line.

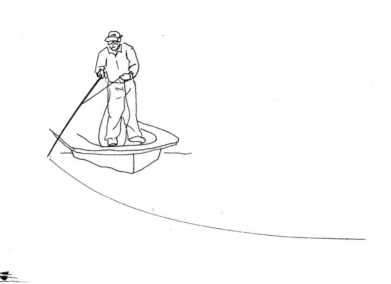

Move the rod tip in the direction of the target with a constant motion and with the rod tip very close to the water. You don't have to move it fast, but you can't stop. If you stop, you won't be able to make a backcast until you move the end of the fly line again. Also, the higher you raise the rod tip above the surface, the less efficient the backcast. Continue to sweep the rod to the side until the rod is pointing directly at the target. Many anglers make the backcast before they point it at the target, which makes the forward cast difficult.

When the rod is pointing toward the target, make a strong backcast. Use a haul to assist the back and forward casts.

Here is a quick summary of the important points. Lower your rod, then move it quickly and low to the water until it points at the target. Don't stop! Make a backcast opposite the target, and then a forward cast to the target.

Right-Angled Cast

There are times when you are fishing with little or no room behind you and a roll cast would be difficult. Here's a typical situation. You are on a stream with a high bank behind you. You have made a cast out from the bank, and your fly has drifted downstream. Now you would like to make another cast at right angles to the bank out in the stream, but you have little room for a backcast. It would be tough to roll-cast in this situation, but a right-angled cast will do nicely. It works well to about thirty feet; beyond this it becomes much more difficult.

Here's how you accomplish a right-angled cast. Make a backcast, being sure to take your rod and hand well behind you. The farther back you take the rod, the easier the cast is to make. As the backcast nears its end, bring your rod hand swiftly forward until it is even with your body. You now have the line end moving. Remember Casting Rule #3? The line always goes in the direction in which you stop. As your hand becomes even with your body, use your rod hand to make a fast speed-up-

Stand parallel to the obstruction and make a normal backcast. Be sure to extend your rod hand well behind your body.

Bring your rod hand forward until it is even with your body. Remember, the line will go in the direction that the rod tip is pointing after it accelerates and stops. So at this point, move your casting hand ninety degrees to the side, so that it points at the target.

and-stop at a right angle to the backcast and ending toward the target. If you make the speed-up-and-stop at a right angle and stop when pointing toward the target, your line will sweep forward, make a right-angled turn, and speed in the direction of the target. If you encounter difficulty in making this cast, remember these three tips:

Don't start accelerating your rod hand until the right-angle turn toward the target is made. Finish the acceleration and stop with the rod tip pointing in the direction you want the fly to go. You'll find the line sweeps forward alongside the obstruction behind you, then turns at a right angle and drops the fly where you want it.

1. Move your rod and hand well behind your body.
2. Bring them forward rather swiftly.
3. If you don't make a right-angled turn during the speed-up-and-stop, you won't be able to perform this very valuable cast.

Long-Line Pickup Cast

There are times when you need to pick a long line up from the water to make a backcast. You may, for example, have made a long cast and suddenly see a fish rise in another direction. Or you may have made a long cast to a cruising fish, which didn't take. Before the fish gets away, you need to make another cast—one that requires lifting a lot of line from the water for a quick backcast. These are just two of many situations when a long pickup is needed.

If you can cast a fairly long distance but have trouble picking up a long line from the water, it will help to know why you are having this difficulty. For almost all casters, lifting a long line from the water is difficult because they never get all the line completely off the water before making the cast. Remember Rule #2? When a lot of line is on the water, surface tension grips it firmly, resisting your attempt to release it as you begin to make a backcast. With practice a good caster should easily be able to lift at least sixty-five feet of line off the water; a really good caster can lift even more line and make a good backcast.

Here is my technique. Touch your rod tip to the surface so that you can get maximum lift with it. Remove all slack, making sure the rod tip remains on the water. Extend the first finger of your rod hand and place it on the first guide (the butt guide). (Once you master the cast you won't have to do this, but as you learn, placing your finger on the butt guide will help.)

You are now ready to lift the line from the water. But first you must realize that lifting the rod will remove only a certain amount of the line. Some of it will still be on the surface, and it must be released before a

Lower the rod tip to the water, pointing it in the direction of the fly. Bend over and lean forward: This allows you to life a little more line that you could from an upright position. Use your line hand to remove all slack from the line.

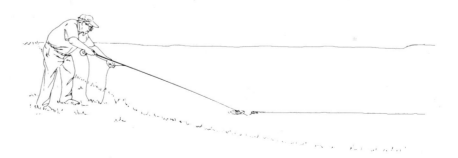

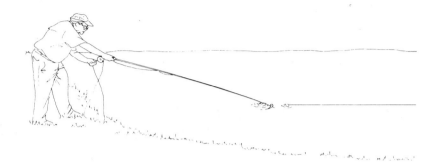

As soon as all slack has been removed, reach forward and grasp the line as close as you can to the butt or stripping guide.

good backcast can be made. That is why you must keep your fingertip on the butt guide. Once you have lifted as much line with your rod tip as possible, a quick drawing down of your line hand should get the rest of it off. In the beginning, if you do not place your fingertip against the guide, you will naturally bring your line hand down as the rod starts to lift line. Also, be careful not to let your fingertip off the guide until the rod has lifted as much line as possible.

Now that you know the importance of starting low (with the rod tip in the water) and keeping your fingertip on the guide until the rod has done its job, let's proceed with the cast. The rod tip is touching the surface at this point. However, do not lift the rod vertically. If you do, before you've lifted all the line from the water the rod tip will be traveling down and back. The speed-up-and-stop will then be down and back, creating a sag in your line that you will have to remove before a forward cast begins. Instead, make a side cast that travels up and back. *If you keep the rod tip*

Raise the rod, but try to keep your line hand in the position you started with—close to the butt guide. When you think you have lifted as much line from the surface as you can, pull downward with the line hand, which will allow you to lift even more of the line. At this point, if you have made all the right moves, most of the fly line will lift from the surface, and only the leader and fly will remain there.

Make a normal backcast. You will need to use a single haul, and of course another haul on the forward cast.

below your head as it travels back and up on the side cast, you will be able to lift the maximum amount of line. The more vertically the rod travels, the more likely it is that a poor backcast will result. As you bring the rod back and to the side, keep your fingertip firmly on the butt guide. And keep watching the line, too. When you feel you have lifted as much line with the rod as you can, draw swiftly down with your line hand until the remainder of the line is off the water—then make your backcast. A single haul will be helpful on this backcast.

One word of caution should be offered here. You must lift the rod rather quickly. I do not mean that you have to jerk the line from the water. But if you lift the rod slowly, the line between the rod tip and the water will sag down, making it nearly impossible for you to pick up a long line.

This may sound like a difficult cast to master, but if you remember the basics—place your rod tip in the water; move swiftly back to the side, keeping the tip below your head; and draw down with your line hand when needed—you will find you can do it effortlessly after a bit of concerted practice.

Back-Forward Cast

There are many times when it is better to throw a forward cast to the rear, and then make a conventional forward cast in front of you, than it is to use the standard back-and-forward cast. For example, there may be trees or brush behind you. But when you turn around and examine the obstacles, you see a hole in the brush into which you can deliver a back-cast. Most fly fishermen who attempt a conventional backcast into this hole will meet with disaster. They look at the hole then face forward and throw a normal backcast, hoping it goes into the safe area. Usually it doesn't. Making a cast like this is like shooting a gun with your eyes closed. Instead, you need to turn around and look at the target area, throw a forward cast into it, and, at the end of the cast, turn around and throw a regular forward cast.

Another excellent use for this cast is when you need to make an immediate backcast to a fish. If, for example, you are standing in a boat fishing for tarpon and suddenly the guide yells that a fish is approaching from behind, the back-forward cast is a much more accurate way to cast. Here is my technique. Look in the direction of the hole in the trees—or whatever target area you need to throw the line into. Then lower your rod until the tip touches the water. It is important that you begin this cast with a very low rod. As you raise the rod, move your body so your weight shifts to your back foot. Also, before starting the cast, turn your hand so your thumb is behind or underneath the rod handle. Continue to move your hand toward the rear. (This is one of the few casts for which I recommend that your rod hand be higher than your shoulder on the speed-up-and-stop.)

Now, as soon as your hand passes beyond your head, make a speed-up-and-stop action with the rod toward the target. But do not make this action too soon; wait until your rod hand has passed well beyond your head! Because you are looking at the hole in the brush and can see the line as it travels backward, you know where you are delivering the cast. As the line enters the hole, turn your hand around and face the water; your thumb is now in the normal position to make a conventional forward cast. Now make the regular forward cast to your target in front of you.

Extra-High Backcast

Almost every fly fisherman has at some point been frustrated because he must make a very high backcast. But within limits, there's a way to solve this problem: an extra-high backcast. Steelheaders know this, as do trout fishermen and surf casters who have had a high wall of sand behind them. With fifty feet of line it is very difficult, but with less line, the following cast will produce remarkable results. It is a back-forward cast with a slight modification. Beginning with your rod tip in the water, follow the directions for the back-forward cast. Here's the difference. You know, of course, that the direction in which you speed up and stop the rod tip determines the direction of your cast. So here, once the rod passes beyond your head, make the speed-up-and-stop in the direction in which you want the line to travel. The line will magically follow your directions.

Touch the rod tip to the water, as shown. Invert your rod hand so that the rod is held upside down, with the reel pointing up and your thumb on the down side. With your thumb underneath like this, you can stop your hand on the acceleration at a much higher angle. And for casting into an opening, you'll essentially be making a forward cast behind you. Almost all anglers make a better, more controlled forward cast than they do a backcast—so this method improves their chances of throwing a fly into an opening behind them.

You should never make a backcast until you get the end of the line moving and all line off the water. Regardless of the amount of line on the surface when you start the cast, if you lift the rod tip smoothly and swiftly, by the time your rod hand has reached the position in the drawing, all line will be off the surface.

Accelerate the rod tip and stop when the tip points in the direction you want to go-either above the obstruction, or into an opening.

As soon as the stop is made, rotate your hand back to a normal position.

Bring the rod forward and get the end moving, as you would for a normal forward cast.

Finish as you would a normal forward cast.

Tuck Cast

The tuck is one of the most useful casts for anglers who fish for trout in the current and offer underwater flies. It causes the leader and line to "tuck" back under the forward position of your fly line. The fly begins to sink upon contact with the water as the slack you have placed in the cast drifts downstream. As a result, the fly can sink deeper than it would if it followed a straight-line cast. Tuck-casting is generally regarded as a technique used when nymph fishing, but it works with any underwater fly that you want to drift naturally and deeper into the current. Almost everyone familiar with the tuck cast regards it as a method of tucking the leader and fly directly underneath the line as it falls to the water—but you can also modify it to obtain curves to the right or left. The curve tuck cast will often catch more fish than a cast in a vertical plane.

The tuck cast is made exactly like the curve cast I described earlier, except that it is made in a vertical, not a side, position. First, make a high vertical cast. The important factor here is that the line attain a very high speed. In fact, you want enough speed to make a cast that would travel two or three times farther than the amount of line you are casting.

Note how high the rod has stopped. The circle indicates where the fly has tucked well back under the fly line.

Without excessive speed, the tuck cast simply will not work. It helps to use a single haul on your forward cast. Then stop the rod at just past the vertical position. The more vertically the rod is stopped, and the greater the line speed, the more of your leader and fly will tuck on the cast. The lower the elevation of the rod on the forward stop, the less tuck can occur. Also, the rod must be stopped dead at the end of the cast.

It is vital to hold the rod motionless until after the tuck—any movement, back or front, will detract from the amount of leader that gets tucked under. The stationary rod and great line speed are the two most important factors in a good tuck cast. If you hold the rod perfectly motionless at the vertical angle, the force of your high-speed forward cast will straighten the line and bend the rod. Then your rod tip will recoil.

It is the recoiling of the rod tip that creates the tuck cast—provided the rod is held motionless at this stage. The line falls to the water with the leader and some of its own forward portion of the line tucked back and under. Remember to drop the rod tip as the line begins to fall to the water. The more tuck you desire, the greater the line speed you need on the forward cast. The fly will begin to sink as your line begins drifting downstream. Because of the slack, the fly is now able to dive deeper before you start your retrieve.

Tuck Cast with a Curve to the Left or Right

As I just noted, you can also make a tuck cast so that the line tucks with a curve to your left or right. This is an advantage if you are wading with the streambank on your left and you would like to get a nymph or streamer deeper on its downstream drift. In this instance, use the tuck-to-the-left cast. First, make a conventional tuck cast, with one exception. During the speed-up-and-stop, lean the tip slightly to the right. This will cause the tuck to occur, but will also whip the nymph around so that it curves to the left. The fly will then precede the leader during the drift. Curve to the right at the end of the tuck cast if you want to get a left-hand curve.

Skip Cast

Sometimes you will want to cast a fly well back under a dock or overhanging brush and a normal cast will not work. The skip cast is the answer. Remember when you were young, throwing a flat stone so that it skipped several times on the water before ending its flight? Keep this in mind when you make a skip cast.

This is one of many casts you will have difficulty making if you bring the rod tip up vertically on the backcast.

To make a good skip cast, you have to set up the forward cast with a very low backcast. It is ideal to bring the line back almost parallel to the surface.

After the low side cast is made, carry the rod forward nearly parallel to the water, with the rod tip only a foot or so above the surface. Aim the cast so that the fly line bounces off the water just in front of you. The arrow in the photo shows where the line hit the surface just in front of my body. The line is now traveling parallel to the surface so that it will skim back under the overhanging branches.

Begin by having enough line outside the rod tip to reach your target. You must make a very low backcast—so low that the line is just above the surface. (Remember how you kept your arm low when you made the stone skip?) On the forward cast you must aim at a spot on the water well in front of your target. The cast won't work unless you develop a lot of line speed, so a line haul helps here. (If you threw the stone with little force it wouldn't skip; neither will the line skip now unless you get it moving fast.) The line will strike the water well in front of the target, then skip low and forward under the dock or overhanging trees. Once you have mastered this unique cast, you will find many special uses it.

Casting and Wind Problems

Wind is perhaps the greatest enemy of the fly caster in salt water. Because there is almost always a difference in temperature between a landmass and the nearby sea, there is usually a continual flow of air from one to the other. On creeks and lakes there are wind breaks in the form of high banks or trees—a luxury not afforded the saltwater fly fisherman. Most freshwater fishermen are appalled at the winds they must fish against when they come to the salt and are often unprepared for them. It sometimes leads to discouragement and a tendency by fly casters to avoid fishing in salt water.

As a result, there are two special demands placed on a fly fisherman in salt water. He must cast accurately, and often quickly at a target that will soon disappear; and he faces almost constant resistance casting into the wind. This challenge, plus cold fronts, means that if you're going to fish the salt you have to know how to handle a breeze. Also, many freshwater situations require only a short cast. But to be successful in salt water an angler often needs to throw a longer distance.

Using the Wind to Your Advantage

Often an experienced angler can actually use the wind to his advantage. For example, on some flats, coves, and bays when there is no breeze, the water is so calm that presenting your offering without alerting the fish can be very difficult. The approach of the boat and motor, or the crashing of the fly line and fly to the placid surface, can often frighten fish. Under such conditions the wise angler waits until these areas are slightly rippled, allowing him to make a better presentation.

Another situation in which wind can help is when you fish shallow basins or bays that feature a narrow opening through which the tide flows to fill and drain the pool. If you know about wind direction and its effect on the tides in such a basin, you can plan your fishing accordingly. When a strong wind blows from a specific direction, it empties the basin on an outgoing tide. At such times the tide forces most of the fish to escape through the basin outlet—concentrating them for your cast.

If there is a stiff wind at your back, you can actually throw more fly line than you can buy. Throw the backcast low behind you then, as you come forward, try to make a much higher-than-normal cast toward your target. This elevated line is caught by the breeze, which turns the fly and line into a kite, carrying it along for a great distance. Under such conditions, anglers who can throw a tight backcast will find that they use the wind to extend their cast and search more water with their fly.

Casting into the Wind

The exact opposite type of cast is used to throw into the wind, because the problems here are compounded. First, the air resistance of both the fly and the line makes obtaining any distance a problem. And a major concern comes at the end of the cast—as soon as the line is fully extended or unrolls—when the breeze can blow the fly, the leader, and part of the line back toward you. To prevent this problem, aim directly at the spot you want the fly to land and try to drive the fly down and at the surface. If this is properly executed, the line will unroll and, as soon as the leader and fly are fully extended, the fly will be in the water, without blowback.

Line Weight

There are some basic rules to observe if you are casting into the wind. The major mistake anglers make when the wind increases is to use the same rod with a larger or heavier line. For example, if a WF9 line is being cast and the wind comes up, many sportsmen will substitute a WF10 line on the same rod. That is exactly the opposite of what you should do. The 10-weight line is much larger in diameter, so it has more wind resistance. And another factor enters here, too—rod action. You need to throw lighter loops into the wind. The size of a loop is, of course, determined by the distance that the rod tip moves through an arc at the end of the forward cast. If you use a 10-weight line on a 9-weight rod, the heavier line causes the rod to bend more deeply during your casting motions—causing you to throw a loop much larger than normal.

If you are a good caster, you should substitute a line one size lighter or smaller than what your rod calls for. In this case it would be an 8-weight. But—and this is important—you need to extend more than the normal amount of line. By having a little additional line outside the guides, the 8 line will weigh as much as a 9 and cause the rod to bend as if you were casting a 9. Tight loops will then be possible. Because more line is outside the guides with the 8, it also has a thinner diameter and will encounter less air resistance. And the increased amount of line held aloft during the false cast means less line has to be shot to the target. This is a lesson that many fly fishermen have never learned, but every serious tournament angler (who measures his casts with a ruler) knows and uses this trick.

Casting Tricks for Windy Conditions

• A common mistake of anglers drifting and fly casting when the wind is blowing is to cast with the wind; this results in the fly falling downwind of the boat. Because the boat is being pushed along by the wind, it tends to override the fly and spoils the retrieve. Either you have difficulty retrieving fast enough to get the desired action, or the length of your retrieve is shortened. Under such conditions you should cast down and across the wind. The fly will land off to one side, but the wind will help carry it to the target. This results in a long retrieve and less effort when tossing a fly.

• When you are approaching a school of fish or a target area in a boat, if you are right-handed have the boat operator approach from upwind. Stand in the right rear corner of the boat (left front if you're left-handed), where you can make your backcast over the water; then use the wind to help make a cast at an angle sideways to it. A left-hander would approach from upwind and stand on the left rear corner of the boat.

• With a stiff breeze blowing, it is best under most fishing conditions not to use a floating fly line, which has the largest diameter of any fly line of comparable weight. Thinner lines allow you to cast into the breeze more easily. If you must fish shallow water, use at least an intermediate line. If possible, a high-density or similar sinking line—which has greater mass for a thinner diameter—will allow you to throw farther with less effort.

• The double-haul technique is vital for casting into a breeze. As I have described, this is a casting technique in which you pull down at the end of both back- and forward casts, causing the line to greatly accelerate. All fly lines stop their forward motion and begin falling as soon as the loop unrolls. A double haul has one more advantage: It makes your line travel faster. Thus if you make a loop that is relatively large (it opens after, say, two seconds to deliver your fly at forty feet) and by using a double haul you can double your line speed, with this technique you could throw the line eighty feet. Every serious saltwater fly fisherman uses the double haul.

• Loop size has a great impact on how well you can cast into the breeze. Smaller loops concentrate your energy in the target direction, while large loops tend to throw your effort over a wider circle. (They also encounter more air resistance.) Thus if you can throw smaller loops, you can be more efficient by concentrating your energy toward the target and decreasing air resistance. The size of your forward casting loop is totally determined by the distance you move your wrist (or rod tip—same thing) at the end of the cast. Learn to load the rod and then, at the last moment in your forward cast, make the smallest wrist motion to form a tight loop. You will drastically improve your distance against the wind.

• Another way to obtain more distance on windy days is to use shooting-taper-style lines (shooting heads). This kind of line has a conventional heavy forward position, usually with a double- or weight-forward taper. But instead of the relatively large running line behind this head (which the head must drag to the target), a shooting taper has a very thin line. This permits the head to travel a far greater distance. While many people use monofilament for the shooting line behind the head, anglers experienced in combating the wind usually prefer commercial shooting line, which is an ultrathin level fly line. There are two problems with monofilament. Since it is so thin, it tends to tangle and kink—and such kinks are often impossible to remove. But the major problem is that when the head is released, the light mono lying at your feet is often picked up in a mass and carried toward the stripping guide—resulting in a snarled mess.

• Another trick to obtain more distance in the wind is to use smaller or lightly weighted flies. Admittedly, some species and conditions call for a fly that is larger, sinks faster, or is bulkier. But if you are going to get your offering to your target, a smaller, less wind-resistant, or lightly weighted fly may be the better choice.

11

HOOKING AND FIGHTING A FISH

During my lifetime of fly fishing, I have found that there are some essential elements when it comes to hooking and fighting a fish on a fly rod.

1. Before you make your presentation, consider how you will fight and land the fish—and make those preparations.
2. When fighting strong fish on fragile leaders, never allow a jerk to occur on the line or leader.
3. The fish's most frantic moments usually happen immediately after the strike. Be aware that the fish may bolt away—so be prepared!
4. When fighting larger fish, you cannot simply reel them in. Use a rod-pumping motion to draw them closer.
5. Rod angle is very important when fighting a fish and must be changed to meet different conditions during the battle.
6. When a fish jumps, throw slack while the fish is in the air, either by bowing to the fish or dipping the rod.

Hooking and Fighting a Fish in Fresh Water

Carefully consider your casting position, not only for a good presentation, but also for when you hook the fish. Is there room to follow the fish as it takes off? Are there obstructions or hazards that you might not encounter if you take a different casting position? Where is the best place to land the fish, and can you get to it easily? Ask all these questions before making the cast. It does no good to hook a fish and then have no way to win the fight. When you are trout fishing, for example, the best place to land large ones is usually at the tail of the pool. Here the river will be shallow, so the fish has less water to fight in, and you have a better chance of bringing the fish close to shore. If you can get the fish into very shallow water, you restrict its ability to swim, and you better your chances of landing it.

Striking

Here are some of my basic rules for striking the fish:

1. When a trout takes a dry fly, the speed of the current will determine how you strike.
2. Whenever possible, keep the rod pointed low and at the fish just prior to setting the hook.
3. Do not strike too hard. You may tear the fly out of the fish's mouth—or simply break your line.
3. With underwater flies in shallow water, never strike upward with the rod.
4. When dry-fly fishing, a slip strike is often best.
5. If the fly is drifting rapidly toward you, slack is accumulating and the rod is usually elevated to get rid of that slack. If a fish takes with the rod in this position, make a roll cast forward with the rod tip.
7. When nymph fishing, driving the rod tip down toward the water is often the best technique.
8. When striking most large or powerful fish, and all tough-mouthed fish, never strike with the rod tip. Instead, use the butt of the rod.

Learn Good Rod-Handling Techniques

One factor to consider in retrieving technique is the angle of the rod during the time the fly approaches and passes near the fish. For many years outdoor writers have implored bass fishermen not to manipulate their underwater flies and popping bugs with the rod tip, because this creates unwanted slack line when the rod tip is flipped upward and then dropped. This faulty rod technique is a major reason why many anglers miss strikes.

Rod angle during retrieve is important in fly fishing for almost all species. A good technique when nymph or dry-fly fishing for trout in fast water, after the offering is thrown upstream, is to strip the line and remove unwanted slack by raising the rod tip. To prevent slack from developing when fishing streamers or other underwater flies, keep the tip in, or almost in, the water. And placing the rod tip underwater keeps the line straight between you and fly, so you can feel the fish take.

Mending the line by rolling the rod in an upstream or downstream arc to create a bow in the line is a technique learned by most anglers at an early stage. A closely related technique—following the fly with the rod tip during the drift to prevent a deep sag from occurring in the midsection of the fly line—is employed less frequently than line mending. However, it is also a very important rod-handling technique for successful hookups.

In almost every kind of fly fishing, the angle at which the rod is held throughout the drift or retrieve makes the difference between hooking fish and not getting a strike.

Striking the Fish

Keeping the rod tip low and pointed at the fish just prior to striking will result in a better hookup in most situations. Many anglers make the mistake of turning their rod at an angle away from the fish during the retrieve, reducing the amount of distance available to move the rod on the strike. But with the rod pointed directly at the fish, the maximum amount of distance is available to move the rod. Therefore, the maximum amount of slack can be removed from the line with your rod motion.

Do Not Strike Too Hard

There is a tendency with many anglers to strike too hard, especially if they see or know that they've hooked into a trophy fish. In most situations, unless there is considerable slack in the line, a gentle lifting of the rod while grasping the line firmly with the line hand is all that is needed to set the hook. A basic mistake made by many dry-fly fishermen is ripping the rod backward on the strike too fast and too hard. This results in broken tippets and lost fish.

Use a Strip Strike with Underwater Flies

When fishing underwater flies, almost all but the very experienced fly fishermen strike improperly. When they become aware that a fish has taken their underwater fly in shallow water, the normal response is to quickly flip the rod tip upward. This is okay if the fish has the fly in its mouth. But if it does not, you will lift the fly from the water. If this happens and the fish is fairly close to you, but did not spook, you may get another chance to throw the fly back into the water—though I would not count on it. Every extra cast thrown near a fish in shallow water lessens your chances of a take.

If you are retrieving an underwater fly in shallow water and think a fish has taken it, never strike upward with the rod tip! Instead, you can either strike by moving the rod to the side, or use what is called a strip strike.

The strip strike is easy. Holding the line in your hand as you are ready to strike, firmly grasp the line and simply pull back on it without moving your rod. This technique is most effective if the rod is pointed at the fish and there is no slack in the line. Its advantage, of course, is that if the fish does not actually have the fly in its mouth (even though you were sure it did), a side or strip strike will only cause the fly to leap a few inches to one side. Thus the fly remains in front of the fish. And frequently this little hop of the fly on the strip strike will, in and of itself, trigger a second strike.

Use a Slip Strike with Dry Flies

There are writers who may have instructed you to gently raise the rod tip when a big trout takes your dry fly. I find this very hard to do. My adrenaline is pumping so fast that I want to rip the lips off the trout, even though I know my fragile tippet is not going to be able to withstand that amount of shock. The gut reaction of most anglers when a trout takes a dry fly is to swiftly raise the rod tip. And this is how we break off tippets. To prevent break-offs and still allow you to follow your gut reaction of striking as fast as you can, you can resort to a very old technique, which surprisingly is known to very few trout fishermen. It is called a slip strike, and with it you will almost never break even a 7X tippet.

Here is the technique. The dry fly comes drifting down toward you, and you begin recovering line. Suddenly the trout rises and takes the fly. Now form a large O ring by cupping your fingers in a curling motion so the first two fingers contact the thumb. The line will then be lying loosely inside the O ring formed by your fingers. The instant that your fingers touch the thumb, sweep the rod swiftly to the side or upward. The drag created by the line moving across your fingers and through the rod guides will be more than enough resistance to drive the hook home. But enough slack remains (because the line is lying loosely in the line hand) so that it is almost impossible to break the leader. After the line flows through the O ring during the sweep of the rod, the line can be immediately trapped after the hook has been set. With a little practice, a slip strike can become a very useful tool for trout fishermen.

The Time to Strike Forward

There is a frequent striking problem that occurs when a trout fisherman is casting upstream into a swift current. After the dry fly lands, in order to prevent unwanted slack and get a drag-free drift, the angler will usually raise the rod as the fly drifts toward him. If a strike occurs when the rod is in this elevated position, it is very difficult to set the hook by sweeping backward with the rod.

In these situations, an exactly opposite technique is recommended. Anytime that the rod is near or past vertical during a dry-fly retrieve, and the fish takes, strike *forward* with the rod. The motion is exactly the same as that of making a forward roll cast. The rod sweeps forward and pulls the line and fly toward you, setting the hook. Best of all, the instant the hook is set, the line continues to sweep forward, falling in slack waves. When the trout reacts to the setting of the hook, the slack in the line will prevent it from breaking off the leader. Don't worry about this slack. I have never had a fly fall out after setting the hook in this manner.

Striking Slowly Is Best

So if you are going to err in making your strike when fishing dry flies, it is best to err on the slow side. It is surprising how long you can take to set the hook and still connect—and how many fish you will fail to hook if you strike too quickly. A slow striking technique also almost always results in the angler using a gentler rod motion, thereby reducing the chances of breaking a fragile leader tippet.

Strike Down When Nymph Fishing

When fishing a nymph, the fly is usually cast straight or at an angle upstream. The fisherman is attempting to get the nymph to drift downstream in a normal fashion, just as if the current were sweeping it along. He watches the line, the leader, or an indicator to see if one of them pauses during the drift. If there is a hesitation in the drifting line, it perhaps indicates that a trout has the nymph and is examining it. This examination will be quite brief, for the trout will quickly spit out anything it believes to be artificial. During the brief pause, the angler needs to set the hook.

The problem this creates is that many line pauses are actually created not by a fish, but by the nymph contacting a weed, stick, log, rock, bottom, or some other underwater obstruction. On such a pause, if you set the hook by sweeping upward with the rod, and it isn't a fish after all, you've removed the fly from the water and will have to make another cast at close quarters. Of course, this is undesirable.

But what if you could strike at every pause, and set the hook well if it's a trout, but not remove the fly from the water if it isn't? This would be an ideal nymphing situation. And it is possible. Make your cast and watch the fly as it drifts down to you. If there is a pause, snap sharply downward with the rod. This will cause the rod tip to first whip upward and then downward. I know this sounds crazy, but assemble a fly rod and hold it out in front of you. Now snap downward and watch the tip. First it goes up, and then down. This action allows you to strike on many pauses that are not fish. And since the downward strike only zips the fly a few inches through the water, if there is no take the fly is not out of the water and out of action but is continuing to drift through the pool.

During the retrieve, whenever possible, watch the fly. You should set the hook only after you are convinced that the fish has taken it well. There are a number of ways to strike, or set the hook, and they vary with the fish being sought, the line used, and sometimes the fishing conditions. But certain rules govern good striking technique.

When you are retrieving underwater flies, most of the time a more efficient strike occurs if the rod tip is held low and pointing toward the fish. The lower the rod on the retrieve—especially if it can be pointed at the fish—the less slack develops in the line between you and the quarry. On the strike, all slack must be removed before the hook can be driven home. A good basic rule for getting an effective strike is to eliminate all slack before you strike. This means a low rod that is pointed at the fish.

There are some exceptions to this rule, of course. When you are fishing with nymphs in pocket water and riffles in a trout stream, the best technique is generally to elevate the rod and keep as much line off the water as possible. When you are drifting a fly for steelhead or Atlantic salmon, a large slack mend is thrown in the line upstream to get a controlled drift, often necessitating a high rod angle. But most of the time when you are fishing underwater flies, it is best to keep the rod low and pointing at the fish during the retrieve.

Adjusting to Water Conditions

When dry-fly fishing, you strike differently under various fishing conditions. Trout live in a variety of environments, which require them to feed differently. Thus you have to adapt your striking technique to score consistently. Here are two examples. A rainbow trout is holding in a swift riffle in a large river. An insect is swept by quickly. The trout sees it and has to make an instant decision. Hungry, it sweeps up, inhales the fly quickly, and dives below, out of the current. It does not take the fly gingerly. It is forced to grab it in its mouth before the fly can sweep away on the current. The other extreme is a second trout that lives in a slow-moving stream (such as a limestone or spring creek) or a lake. The feeding situation is entirely different. A fly settles to the slow-moving surface, and the trout rises carefully and leisurely to inspect it. There is plenty of time to look it over and decide if it should be eaten. And if this decision is made, the trout slowly sucks the fly from the surface, instead of gulping it down.

In the two situations, the trout are forced to feed differently. The rainbow, because the fly was in its vision and soon would be gone on the fast currents, had to make an instant decision. It could get only a brief look at the quarry and then had to open its mouth and gulp the fly in, inhaling it deeply to be sure it did not escape. But the trout in slow water has no need for haste. This fish is more leisurely and has no need to grab the fly. It moves under the fly and slowly sucks it down.

The fish in swift water takes the fly so deeply that an instant strike will usually result in a hookup. Without such a quick strike, the fish will often spit out the imitation. But when fish are feeding on surface flies in slow-moving or still water, the strike must be delayed briefly. As the fish accepts your offering, count mentally, "One, two, three," then lift the rod gently. The English used to say before striking, "God save the Queen." This gives the fish time to suck the fly deeply into its mouth. Of course, you can delay too long, but you will hook more trout in this case by striking too late rather than too early.

I have watched hair-trigger fly fishermen set hooks on fish sipping flies off a slow current who missed perhaps 75 percent of what should have been solid hookups. The reason is that the trout is slowly inhaling the fly and the water around it. Its mouth is open as the water and fly go inside. If you make a quick strike with the trout's mouth open, you stand a good chance of pulling the fly free. The fast-water fish grabs the fly and closes its mouth quickly, so that the insect cannot escape; thus you can strike much faster.

There are times when a "nonstrike" can be very effective, too. Sometimes if the line and leader are taut between you and the fish, it is a good idea not to strike. Instead you firmly grip the line and simply hold on. The rod is usually held at a slight side angle to the fish, but it is not swept away from the fish, as in conventional striking.

You can use this technique when fishing dry flies for steelhead in big rivers. As the floating line and surface fly drift downstream from you, the steelhead pokes its head out of the water and sucks in the fly. The fish is usually pointed toward you, and its mouth is open so that the fly can be inhaled. If you strike as the fish is inhaling the fly, you simply pull it from the open mouth. You have to wait until the mouth has closed to ensure a hookup. The line and fly are being swept downstream and usually to the side as the fish takes the fly. If you don't strike but simply grip the line with the rod pointed at the fish, the current will help sweep the fly deeper into the steelhead's mouth. Some steelheaders are so adept that they actually feed a slight bit of line to a steelhead taking a dry, in order to get the fly deeper into the mouth. That takes experience!

Fighting

The most important thing to do after a strike is to clear any line that remains around your feet. Experienced anglers never pull any more fly line off the reel than is needed to make the anticipated casts. If extra line lies at your feet, it is only a source of trouble when the fish tries to flee. Here is how that line can be cleared using the O-ring finger trick. To do this, as soon as you hook up, form an O ring with the fingers of the line hand, touching the first two fingers against the thumb, and use this as a giant rod guide to feed the line down at your feet so that it comes up through the guides. Often you will see a tangle coming, you can either shake the line to clear it or handle it in some other manner so that it finally clears through the guides.

At the same time that you form the O ring with the line hand, cock your rod hand inward so that the butt of the rod is pressed firmly against your forearm, just in back of the wrist. Then turn the rod hand downward and outward. This places the butt of the rod strongly against the forearm. And by rotating the hand outward, you place the reel on the outside of your forearm, which will prevent the line traveling up from your feet from tangling in the reel or slipping under the end of the rod butt.

Once the hook is set, concentrate on using the O ring to manipulate the line off the many things that tend to grab it, and from under your feet, too. Also, as the final bit of line is being cleared, make sure you feed that line toward the butt guide. Some anglers will keep their fingers forming the O ring near the reel. This can cause the line to catch on the reel or around the butt of the rod.

Frequently the longest and hardest run that a hooked fish makes is the first one. Fear and a desire to get away cause it to flee, burning up vital energy. On this panic run, let the fish go under light pressure. Most fish are lost either at this time or at the very end of the fight. As the fish slows down, you can begin retrieving line.

In most situations, unless the fish is very small, it is best to pump it in rather than trying to reel it to you. *Pumping* means raising the rod, which will draw the fish toward you, then lowering it to recover line by reeling in accumulated slack. But there is a little more to the pumping procedure. Moving the rod farther back does not mean you are applying more pressure on the fish. In fact, the reverse is true. If you raise the lower portion of the rod much beyond the horizontal, you actually begin to apply less pressure. And the more you sweep the rod up or back so it forms a deep bow or horseshoe shape, the less pressure is being placed on the fish.

What you want to do is a series of short, fast pumps, keeping the rod only slightly elevated. This technique is easy to learn if you have a spring scale. Attach the leader end to the scale. Then have someone hold the scale and look at the readings. Begin bringing the rod slowly back. As the rod is raised, pressure will increase the reading on the scale, depending on how hard you have set the drag. As the rod butt passes beyond about a forty-five-degree angle to the water's surface, the readings will begin to decline. Many people bring the rod back so far that the tip is actually behind them. In this case you may be surprised to find that the scale will be registering almost no pressure.

Another very important factor when pumping fish is to reel in slack only as the rod is lowered. Do not pump up and then quickly drop the rod tip. This creates a lot of slack, which might cause the hook to fall out. The key to good pumping technique is to raise the rod, putting a bend only in the butt section. As the rod is lowered and your reeling begins, make sure the tip of the rod always has a slight bend. This will keep the line taut and prevent the hook from falling out.

Three Principles

Once your fish is hooked, you need to concentrate on three basic principles. First, a steady pull rarely breaks a line; it is a sharp jerk that is the enemy. In fact, I tell people it's the jerk on the wrong end that breaks the line! To demonstrate this principle, run the fly line and leader through the rod, and attach the leader (preferably about three- or four-pound test) to a doorknob. With a rod that throws a 2-weight line through 6-weight, raise the rod. You will find it difficult to break the three-pound leader with a steady pull. If you give it a sharp jerk, it snaps instantly.

The key, then, is never to allow a jerk to occur on the leader. Watch the fish during the fight. If it surges away, even in the middle of a pumping situation, immediately drop the rod toward the fish. By pointing the rod at the fish and forcing the fish to pull straight off the reel, you reduce the possibility of a jerk occurring, and the fish will be running against the lightest possible drag. Once the fish slows, you can return to recovering line.

Now you need to be ready to apply the second principle. When a fish jumps, you need to throw controlled slack. A fish underwater trying to escape is somewhat like a person trying to run in a swimming pool. As the fish lunges sideways against the line, it also has to fight the water, which cushions the jerking on the line. But let that same fish rise above the surface and you have a totally different situation. Suppose the fish is lightly hooked in the side of the mouth. Underwater it cannot pull very hard. But when the fish is in the air, it can throw its full body weight against the hook, and probably break the tippet or tear it free.

You need to throw slack as soon as any fish (rainbow, brown trout, bass, sailfish, tarpon, what have you) jumps above the surface. For years anglers were taught to bow to a fish; that is, to stab the rod in the direction of a jumping fish. This creates a lot of slack, preventing the fish from breaking off. But bowing can create other problems. As the fish rocks back and forth in the air, this affects the line. The wavering line can wrap around the fish's head or tangle on the rod tip, causing you to lose the fish. Instead, dipping the rod is recommended. As the fish rises above the surface, stick the rod tip just underwater in the direction of the leaping fish. If the tip is underwater, there is the desirable slack, but the line is under much better control when the fish rocks wildly back and forth. With the dipping method, few fish are lost. Once your quarry is back in the water, return to fighting the fish in a normal manner.

The third thing to remember, especially when large fish are fought on light leaders, is that you must always tire the fish before you can bring it to you. Many people think that the best way to fight a fish (this is especially true of trout fishermen) is to hold the rod almost vertically. In most cases this is a poor way to fight a fish. Let me give you an example. An angler is fishing downstream and he unknowingly hooks a drifting stick. Anyone who has done this knows that the water pressure against the stick will form a deep bend in the rod. Hold the rod vertically and what is the stick doing? Nothing. The same thing happens with any fish lying directly downcurrent if you are holding the rod high. In fact, the fish is probably resting.

What you need is a way to make the fish burn up its energy. Side pressure is the answer. But side pressure only works when the fish is closer than forty feet. Beyond this distance the angle is so small that it really doesn't do much good. Here is how the technique works. If the fish swims in one direction, move the rod at such an angle that it pulls the fish's head sideways. For example, if the fish is moving north, drop the rod to the west. Keep the rod low to the water for maximum side pressure. This will cause the fish's head to be pulled westward. The fish will resist, but it will finally be towed in this direction. If the fish now starts moving west, manipulate the rod so that you are pulling at a right angle (to the north or south as conditions warrant). This will also allow you to bring the fish closer by recovering some line. Proper pumping technique, not allowing a jerk to occur to a fragile leader, and side pressure will help you quickly land many trophy fish in freshwater situations. To apply maximum pressure on any fish try to pull the line and leader toward the tail.

Finally, never chase a fish with a net. Hold the net motionless at roughly a seventy-five degree angle and lead the fish toward the net. Once the head of the fish is in the mouth of the net, sweep forward with a swift, upward motion. Never approach a fish from the rear with a net. If you touch the tail of most fish, unless it is exhausted, it will surely bolt away. And that sudden jerk may break the line.

Hooking and Fighting a Fish in Salt Water

If you have made the transition from freshwater fishing, you will certainly discover soon—if you haven't already—that the denizens of the shallows are tough competitors. They cannot be subdued at will like their freshwater counterparts but will battle with the tenacity and abandon of a barroom brawler. Those anglers who choose simply to hold on and wait it out will invariably lose the fish—or in rare instances—it may die from old age while still tethered to the hook.

Reacting to a strike on the flats takes many forms, depending on the species of fish, the bait or lure, the direction of the take, and your tackle. You must know not only how to strike each fish, but also when to do it. Experience has no substitute, but a series of guidelines may help.

Generally fish are missed on the strike and lost during the fracas because of tackle failure or angler error. Careful preparation will eliminate the first reason for defeat. Experts often say that fish such as tarpon or bonefish are caught "the night before." They are really telling you to take your time in rigging your tackle and to make certain that every element of the equipment is in perfect working order. For example, if there is a question about the performance of a reel, take it apart and fix it. Replace the drag washers and clean and lubricate the moving parts. Lines must be changed regularly and knots tied with extreme care. A knot in monofilament begins to slip just before it fails. You can improve the connections by drawing each one up tightly.

Setting the Hook

Knowing how to fight a saltwater fish helps eliminate angler error. Couple the correct approach with total concentration and you should begin to land a respectable number of fish. So let's begin with the tackle basics. Every hook should be carefully sharpened. Almost all species you will encounter in the shallows have relatively tough mouths that make hook penetration difficult. Tarpon and sharks, of course, place an additional burden on you when it comes to planting the barb. In fact, some fishermen file the barb down for these species to make it shorter and easier to drive into the mouth.

No matter how or when you set the hook, the line between you and the fish must be tight and the tip of the rod must point directly at your quarry. If you set the hook against a loose line, the effect on the fish is negligible. You also stand a better chance of breaking the line when it is slack. Watch a clerk in a bakery break string after he ties it around a cake box. He holds it in both hands and puts a U in the middle. As he pulls his hands apart and the string suddenly becomes tight, it breaks. The force is enough to overcome the impact resistance of the line.

In a typical strike, you wait until the fish takes the fly. Then strip-strike with a series of short, sharp jerks in quick succession. The force of each pull should be geared both to the particular fish you are fighting and to the breaking strength of the line. If you are fishing for seatrout, for example, you know that they have tender mouths, so you merely lift the rod sharply. With tarpon, you really have to sock it to them.

In many situations striking sideways with the rod low and parallel to the water makes more sense. Use short, sharp tugs, but do it with a sideways motion. This involves a natural body rotation that enables you to put force into the strike. Side-striking has a different effect on the bait or lure; the pull becomes relatively straight rather than upward. This means you could put the hook in the side of the mouth instead of the upper jaw.

Equally significant, a side strike keeps the bait or lure in the vicinity of the fish if you happen to miss. Suppose you are working a popping bug. Yank upward and the lure flies out of the water, usually landing some distance from the fish and out of its immediate visual range. Keep the rod low and the offering stays close.

Some leading anglers vary this approach slightly. Instead of pulling the rod to set the hook, they simply hold it to one side and parallel to the water, trapping the line against the rod. They let the surge of the fish set the hook, releasing the line as the tarpon starts to move off strongly.

For fish with seemingly impregnable jaws, fly fishermen often employ the double haul to set the hook. They pull the rod sideways and parallel to the water with one hand while they tug on the line with the other. With species that have less formidable mouths, you need only lift the rod sharply or tug on the fly line. If you are using delicate tippets and do not want to break them on the strike, lift the rod and let go of the fly line. There will be enough pressure from the rod to bury the barb, but the loose line will cushion the strike and prevent a break-off.

Anglers in salt *and* fresh water often make one consistent error, and that is striking too soon. Fish must usually expel the water they take into their mouths before they can swallow a bait or lure. A pause before setting the hook enables them to complete this action. Bonefish and permit actually have crushers in the backs of their mouths. So you need to allow them a chance to toss an offering back there to crush it.

You must also consider the angle of the strike. A tarpon follows the lure directly toward the boat. This is called a head-tail take because your quarry is coming straight toward you. If you watch the fish, you will see it open a massive maw and engulf your offering. The natural instinct is to rear back and set the hook. When you move too quickly, however, you miss the fish. Strike when the tarpon closes his mouth. And you will probably do best to sweep the rod parallel to the water. (Some fly fishermen try to determine whether a fish is going from right to left or left to right when it strikes. Then they sweep the rod in the opposite direction, trying to drag the lure into a corner of the fish's mouth. If you are fishing with a guide and are new to the game, take a moment to ask him how he wants you to strike and when.)

Timing is also critical. A permit, for example, picks up a crab and swims off. If you strike too soon, you will probably succeed in pulling the crab away from the fish. If you strike too late, the fish may spit the fly. I let the line become taut and then set the hook.

Fighting a Fish

There is nothing delicate about doing battle with the husky critters of the flats. You know before you ever plant the barb in their jaws that they will run great distances. Tarpon, with few exceptions, will also jump repeatedly. To win in these situations, your tackle must be up to the task and you must think of yourself as a fighter. Boxers know when to circle the ring marking time and when to step in with fists flying. These same tactics apply to whipping a tarpon, shark, permit, bonefish, snook, or anything else in salt water.

Use of the Reel's Drag Mechanism

A major factor in fighting fish is the proper use of a reel's drag, an adjustable restraining device that prevents the escaping fish from breaking the line. Most saltwater fly reels, as well as the freshwater reels that are used for fighting larger fish such as salmon, are equipped with a drag device. But there are different schools of thought on the correct way to set the adjustable tension or restraint on a drag.

How smoothly a drag releases line is very important. For the release, a drag is said to have a starting and a running drag. *Starting drag* simply means that the drag will not release line until enough pressure is applied. *Running drag* is the amount of resistance needed to keep the spool in motion against the drag. In almost all reels, it will take more pressure on the line to get a drag started than it does to keep it running, just as it is much harder to get a stalled car moving than it is to keep it moving. Drags on fly reels work the same way. Some reels have a much lower starting drag than others, and they are recommended. If you are considering buying a new reel and are comparing several models, check them to see which has a lower starting drag.

Fly reels with drags come in two designs: direct drive and anti-reverse. With a direct-drive reel, when the fish runs the reel handle will turn, freeing line. Anti-reverse reels, however, allow you to hold on to the reel handle while the fish is pulling off line. With either design, how hard the fish has to pull to get line is controlled by the amount of tension you set on the reel's drag mechanism.

There are some fishing situations in which an anti-reverse reel is not recommended. In bonefishing, for example, the light tippets require that you set the drag tension for no more than a pound on a straight pull. But if a bonefish runs off a lot of line, the light drag tension you have set on the slip clutch of the anti-reverse reel may not be enough to retrieve the line and the fish. The drag will simply slip. In such situations a direct-drive reel is much better.

When anglers make a mistake in setting tensions, it is often establishing too much drag, which increases the starting factor and causes broken lines. You can check the amount of drag pressure you have established on your reel by attaching a scale to the line end and then pulling on the scale until the drag releases. Note on the scale what the starting drag is and what the running drag is. A very good guide for most fishing situations is never to set the starting drag for more than 20 percent of the test of the line: a 15 percent ratio is even better.

You may encounter a few situations in which a heavy drag setting may be necessary. In salt water, for example, if you are fishing over a wreck or a coral reef, around a bridge, or anywhere that you must not allow the fish to get into the structure, then a heavier drag setting is advised. But whenever the fish can be fought in relatively open water, if you err on a drag setting, err on the light side. For bonefish my personal way of setting the starting drag tension is to grip the fly line directly in front of the reel as firmly as I can between my lips. Then I adjust the drag until I can just barely pull off line. This is usually less than a pound of direct pull. For giant tarpon, I recommend an initial drag setting of two pounds.

For sailfish, a drag setting of more than one pound of pull is necessary if you are using leader tippets testing at sixteen pounds or less. This is because a sailfish runs off such a terrific amount of line at a very high speed. It creates tremendous water tension against the line, so if there is less than one pound of drag setting, the leader will break.

It is important to understand that there are times when you need to reduce or back off the drag, too. If you have a full spool of line adjusted to a drag of, say, one pound, and then the spool is more than half emptied by the run of a fish, the amount of drag now required to pull line from the reel could easily be three times that much, or three pounds. Therefore, if you encounter a very long run from a fish, it is wise to reduce the drag tension.

And here is an important point about setting drags—one that's worth repeating from chapter 3. Almost all these devices (spinning, fly, or conventional reels) are composed of alternating soft and hard washers. Your drag will function smoothly only as long as the softer drag washers remain soft. If you screw down the adjustment nut on any kind of reel and allow it to remain that way for long periods of time, the tension slowly crushes the softness from the washers, and a jerky drag will result. So make it a habit always to back off the drag tension on any reel at the end of the day's fishing.

Drag Techniques

As a fish runs and the diameter of line remaining on the spool decreases, the drag increases. That is an important point to remember. Most anglers want to tighten the drag if it appears that a fish will take all the line. Actually, the drag should be loosened to compensate for the increased amount of drag. However, if you set the drag initially at 15 percent, there should be enough cushion to withstand the increase without having to reset. I strongly recommend that unless you are very experienced, you do not change the mechanical setting of the drag during the battle. It is too easy to increase the drag too much, and that could cost you a fish.

Additional drag can be applied to a reel with your hands and fingers. If you are using spinning tackle, you need only cup the spool with the hand not holding the rod. A thumb on the reel spool can put more force into a plug-casting outfit. If the fish has slowed or stopped running, you can press the line against the foregrip or push it aside with your thumb to add even more drag. Fly fishermen can palm the flanges of some reel models, reaching up from underneath to put a finger on the spool and clamping the line against the foregrip with their fingers. You can use a cotton glove to protect your fingers while fighting fast-running fish. Again, be careful not to apply too much pressure.

The instant you set the hook, you must expect the fish to run. A bonefish may streak for 150 yards before it pauses. Sharks will go even farther, and tarpon can cover large distances if they don't stop to jump. Your first concern is to minimize the amount of drag on the fish and let the reel spool start turning. Sea fans, coral, and other obstructions on some flats also pose a hazard. Bonefishermen have traditionally lifted the rod high above their heads to keep the line out of the water and create a sharper angle between rod and fish. If the drag is set exceptionally light, this is fine and probably necessary on some flats. However, the primary task is to get line coming smoothly off the spool. Once this is accomplished, you can safely lift the rod.

There is no way to stop or snub a fish on that initial run. If you try, you will probably spend the next few minutes rerigging your gear. The line will pop so quickly that you won't have even an instant for second thoughts. Let the fish go and do not try to stop it even if it seems that all the line will be stripped. In this eventuality, you should have the boat under way to follow or at least take some of the pressure off the fish and hope for the best. Due to the stretching action in the fly line and backing, try to get as much line on the reel as soon as possible.

The precise instant that the fish stops running or even pauses to catch its breath, you must begin your part of the battle. You must give no quarter. The longer the fish is in the water, the greater your chance of losing it. And you must also think about the fish. If you plan to release it, you want to turn it loose as quickly as possible. A fish that fights to exhaustion has a poorer chance for survival because of lactic acid buildup in its blood, which can eventually poison it. In its weakened state it is also easy prey for a larger fish.

Pumping

To regain line and bring a fish toward you, you must learn to pump— just as you would in fresh water if you have a large fish on the line. It should be repeated over and over as long as the fish will come your way.

If the fish is deep, the pumping action has to be slow and deliberate. Actually, you are trying to lift the fish. On the flats, use a faster pump to bring the fish toward you. Experts often resort to a very short and quick pumping technique, refusing to stop until the fish is alongside the boat or decides to run again.

With a light drag setting, you may experience difficulty in pumping, because line may slip every time you lift the rod. That can be overcome easily. Apply additional drag with your hands as outlined above. If the fish should suddenly start to run, simply remove the extra pressure by taking your hand off the reel and dropping the rod tip. When the fish stops, put the pressure back on and keep pumping.

A fish must be fought to the maximum strength of the tackle. If you are using twelve-pound-test line, there are times when you will be exerting ten pounds of pressure. The mistake many beginning anglers make is to "baby" a big fish, thinking erroneously that if they take it easy, they have a better chance of landing their quarry. The reverse is true. You either bully a brute or it beats you. Besides, if you pause to rest, the fish will regain its strength and you will have to start again from square one.

Positioning

There is an old saying that I like: "Where the head of the fish goes, the tail will surely follow." If you are going to beat your adversary, you have to be able to move its head. In deeper water you have to lift it, but on the flats the secret is to tack the fish from side to side like a sailboat going upwind. The easiest way to do this is to put side pressure on the fish. Drop the rod so that it is parallel with the water and then pump to one side or the other, keeping the rod parallel. As the fish goes one way, begin pumping in the other direction. This is an excellent way to close the distance and tire a fish.

During every battle, there are a few test points in which the outcome may be in doubt for a few seconds. The fish tries to power off slowly, and your task is to turn it. Sometimes this can be done by reaching forward with the rod and then pulling back. It is almost like a give-and-take session. Your hand clamps on the reel and you hesitate before yielding line. It is to your advantage to turn the fish, but if the strain becomes critical, remove your hand and let line come off the reel. Try the same procedure again and again until you are consistently successful.

At all times during the battle, you want the fish directly in front of you. Even when you are applying side pressure, the pumping action does not go far and you do not turn too far away from the fish. You want to face your adversary and move with it. If the boat is anchored or staked, you may have to run the boat to stay with the fish. You don't want to find yourself in one spot and the fish somewhere else.

Leaping Fish

Tarpon have earned the title *acrobats of the flats,* but large barracudas also are capable of greyhounding leaps across the water, and snook may jump, too. These fish exert a lot less force on the line when they are in the water than when they are in the air. The effects of the water's neutral buoyancy have been negated and a hundred-pound tarpon weighs just that when it is airborne. You also have to consider its velocity, or the rate at which it happens to be flying through the atmosphere.

Light-tackle specialists came up with the technique of bowing to the fish many years ago, and it still works today. As soon as the fish starts to break the surface, you push the rod directly at it, lunging forward and stretching. This creates controlled slack line and enables the tackle to withstand the sudden shock of the leap. At the same time, it helps to prevent the fish from landing on a taut line and keeps the hook or lure in the vicinity of the tarpon in the event that it is thrown. Those who have fished tarpon for years acknowledge that the fish sometimes gets rehooked after it has thrown the lure. This bowing technique works on all salt- and freshwater fish.

The moment the fish reenters the water, recover the controlled slack line and apply full pressure once again. It is a matter of give and take. When you cannot stop the fish, you must yield; but when you can, you must press forward regardless of how tired you may feel. If you are not exhausted after battling a big fish, you have not been applying maximum pressure or taking advantage of the opportunities.

Near the Boat

More fish are lost at or near the boat than at any other time during the fight. If you have weathered the hook setting and the initial run, the next critical moments occur when the battle is nearing its end.

I recommend that most fish be at the boatside in less than thirty minutes, and that includes hundred-pounders. There are rogue fish that are the exception, but the longer the fight, the more the odds shift from you to the fish. In the final stages of battle, either the fish surges suddenly and breaks the line on impact or it dives under the boat and cuts the line. The shock-absorbing properties of a line depend to a great degree upon how much of it lies between you and the fish. When that last dash for freedom occurs close at hand, there is little to absorb the shock. It is pretty obvious that any fish is going to dive the instant it sees the boat.

Mentally and physically you need to be prepared. One approach is to loosen the drag slightly when the fish is under control and just before it is brought near the boat.

As your quarry darts away from you, do not try to stop it. Pulling back on the rod only compounds the problem and increases the probability of a break-off. Instead, push the rod at the fish just as you would do if it were jumping. Then only the drag that is set on the reel will operate, without the added pressure caused by the bend in the rod. As soon as possible, get the fish back under control.

Anticipation is the greatest aid in preventing a fish from dashing under the boat. By using side pressure, try to steer it away and guide it around the boat. If this fails and the fish does go under, shove the rod into the water as far as you can. This allows the line to clear the bottom and the lower unit of the engine. With the tip still in the water, sweep the rod around the bow or stern until you and the fish are both on the same side again. Then, continue the battle.

Landing a Fish

Long before you are ready to land the fish, you should have decided whether you intend to keep it. If you plan to release your quarry, you must fight it as hard as you can so that you reduce the time it is under stress. (I urge you to release unharmed as many fish as possible, regardless of the species.) No matter what your decision, you must know your quarry before you can land it safely. If you do not anticipate that a fish has sharp teeth, gillrakers, spines, knife-edged gill plates, or other protective devices, you can be painfully injured.

For a complete discussion of landing and releasing smaller saltwater fish, see chapter 12.

Gaffing

For many years it was acceptable to land fish with various types of gaffs. But gaffing is essentially the act of impaling a fish on a steel hook, and many such fish die from their injuries after being released. Today in most situations gaffing a fish is looked upon with disfavor.

You can still use a gaff to bring a fish aboard if you intend to keep it for eating, but for catch-and-release fishing, you should use a hand-held device called a BogaGrip, which doesn't injure the fish. It has a pair of round, spring-loaded steel fingers that open and securely clamp around a fish's jaw. You can handle the fish, weigh it (there is a scale on the device), remove the hook, and release the fish without harming it.

Alternatively, experienced tarpon guides in the Florida Keys have replaced gaffing with a method more kindly to the fish. The guide wears special gloves and when the tired fish is brought boatside, the guide firmly grips the lower jaw of the fish. This allows you to remove the hook and release the tarpon.

Billfish should be neither gaffed nor netted when taken on a fly. The mate should wear gloves because the bill is very abrasive. As the tired fish is brought alongside, the mate should grab the bill and lift it up to be released or brought into the boat. It is very important that the bill be grasped with both hands and the point held away from the body. This way, if the fish surges forward the deadly bill point can be pushed away from the body. I have seen several mates badly hurt when the fish was held so that the bill was pointed toward their stomachs, and the fish bolted forward. Any billfish put in a boat should first be dispatched.

12

HANDLING FISH AND CONSERVATION PRACTICES

Today most fly fishermen release their catch, although some people still ask me why I put fish back. My usual lighthearted answer is, "You don't burn your golf balls at the end of the day, do you?" However, there is a more serious issue at stake. The number of fish in the world may *seem* to be unlimited, but that's not the reality. We can deplete the fish resources in any watershed on earth if we are not careful. Here is my own motto: Any fish not kept for food or mounting should be carefully returned to the water in as good a condition as possible. One of the great satisfactions of fly fishing is that we can have all of the thrills of the hunt and the capture, yet we can still put the fish back so it can live on and provide a thrill for another angler.

Landing and Releasing Fish

Proper releasing technique begins even before a fish is hooked. It is in the fish's best interest, once it is hooked, for you to bring it in as quickly as possible and free it. Saltwater fish will experience lactic acid buildup in their bodies during long fights, which can actually result in a fish dying after it has been released. Freshwater fish often die after being released simply because we fight them for too long. Trout fishermen are especially guilty. Sometimes we use ultrathin 8X or 7X leaders and play our fish for a long time, fearing they will break the leader if we try to bring them in too quickly. As long as you can get the monofilament through the eye of a dry fly or nymph, then the smallest leader you need for almost all fishing situations is a 5X or 6X. Remember that between a 5X and a 7X there is only a 0.002 inch difference, and trout do not have eyeballs to measure this difference. Be kind to your trout and use the largest leader possible for the existing conditions.

As I've mentioned, a net is the most valuable landing tool you have for smaller fish. Even if you are going to release a fish, you can handle it much sooner if you slip a net under it. Otherwise, you have to wait until it is totally exhausted. Have someone place the net in the water and lead the fish into it. Try always to net headfirst, since a fish cannot swim backward and any final lunge will drive it into the mesh. If you intend to keep the fish, lift the net and swing it into the boat with one motion.

If your quarry is to be released, pull the net alongside you or your boat, but try to keep the fish in the water so that its weight is supported. Handle it firmly but gently. A pair of forceps, pliers, or a hook remover will assist you in getting the hook out. Should the fish have swallowed the hook, do not pull it out. Cut the leader as close to the mouth as you can and release the fish with the hook intact. It will eventually come out, and the fish will not be hurt.

Once a fish has been landed, it should be released as quickly as possible. Holding the fish out of the water for more than a brief period is like holding a person underwater. In other words, do not keep the fish out of water longer than you can hold your breath.

Under no circumstances should you hold a fish by its eyes or put your fingers inside its gill covers. And never squeeze a fish you intend to turn loose, nor handle it roughly. Remove the hook quickly and handle the fish as little as possible. If it seems to be exhausted, do your best to revive it. The common technique is to hold the fish underwater in its normal swimming position, then swish it back and forth rapidly. Many anglers hold the fish by the tail to steady it, with its head pointing into the current. However, this technique actually restricts the flow of water across the gills; only what little water enters the mouth will get into the gills.

Instead, with any fish that has no sharp teeth, grasp the tail of the fish and insert your thumb in the mouth, with the first finger gripping the jaw. This forces the mouth open, and much more life-giving water is passed over the gills. Now gently rock the fish back and forth. Each time the fish is drawn backward, the gills flare open, flooding them with oxygenated water. If the fish has sharp teeth, a BogaGrip works well. Also, try to release the fish in shallow water, so that if it is still in distress you can recapture it. And put it back gently in its normal swimming position. Sometimes the fish will start to roll over or be unable to swim well. Touching it with the boat pole or net or rod tip will often stimulate the fish to swim away in a normal manner. Always make sure any fish can swim well before you release it.

Saltwater Fish

Most freshwater fish can be handled safely. The catfish has spines that can give you trouble and pike and pickerel have pointed teeth, but most freshwater fish are relatively safe to pick up. Saltwater fish, as I've noted, are a different matter; almost all species can be hazardous to handle. Most of them have coarser and stronger gill covers than freshwater varieties. You should not put your hands inside the gill flaps of any saltwater fish unless you know what you are doing. The channel bass and many bottom species have extremely rough gills, for example, and they can inflict nasty cuts if the fish flops around while your fingers are inside those gill covers. Snappers have earned that name, so respect them. Some fish present other challenges. Bonefish fight so valiantly that they often arrive at the boat in a state of collapse. If released immediately they will usually sink to the bottom and die. Tarpon often meet the same fate, as do many other species.

When it comes to teeth, saltwater fish are dangerous creatures. Bluefish, for example, have very sharp teeth. As with barracudas, mackerels, and wahoo, not only are the bluefish's teeth sharp at the ends, but the sides are honed to razor edges. If you see teeth in the mouth of a saltwater fish, assume that those teeth will be dangerous.

Other saltwater fish crush their food. Any fish with soft, rubbery lips must do something to its prey so it can swallow it. Such fish usually have strong crushers in their mouths. The fish grabs its victim, flips it back between the crushers—which close quickly with the force of a steel vise—and the prey is reduced to pulp. I have seen a permit pick up a hard-shelled crab, crush it with a gulp, and spit out the shell as easily as you would a peanut. Any angler who sticks his hands inside the mouth of a fish with smooth or leathery lips is taking a good chance of losing a few fingers.

Some fish present hazards that are not really apparent to the angler with little saltwater experience. Members of the jack family, which has many subspecies, usually have soft rays in the dorsal fin. However, some jacks carry a small pair of stiff, sharp spines on the belly near the anus that can cause a painful stab. You can immobilize a jack by gripping the fish across the back of the head and clamping your fingers at the junction of the gill covers.

The snook is another fish that can hurt you. In the middle of the outer area of the gill covers is a transparent cutter blade that is as sharp as a knife. About the size of a nickel, it can slice your finger if you carelessly grab the fish. This cutter is why most snook fishermen use a thirty- or forty-pound monofilament shock leader. Most guides when holding a snook place their thumb inside the mouth and curl their first finger inside the gill at the point where the gills meet the throat. Barracudas, mackerel, king mackerel, and other thin, hard-to-hold fish are best grabbed with either a glove or a towel. One of the finest tools for handling a fish you intend to release is the BogaGrip, a tool that doesn't hurt the fish, but allows you to hold it securely until it is released.

Saving Freshwater Resources

We are fortunate in North America to have so many great river systems that hold bass. The slow-moving rivers of the Deep South, for example, are excellent habitats for largemouths, although they are often too warm for smallmouths. For far too long, however, many departments of natural resources in the more northerly states were vitally concerned with their coldwater trout fisheries, but ignored their bass rivers. Fortunately, this is changing.

For nearly twenty years I worked as an outdoor writer for the *Baltimore Sun,* one of the biggest newspapers in the country. In the mid-1980s I wrote several editorials arguing for a catch-and-return section on the Potomac River. The idea was scoffed at by most state officials. But about ten years later, under pressure from many bass fishermen, Maryland's Department of Natural Resources indeed established a catch-and-return section of good length on the Potomac. Pennsylvania angler Bob Clouser, inventor of the famous Clouser Minnow, led the fight to establish slot limits on bass in the wide Susquehanna River, one of the finest smallmouth rivers in the world. The stretch of river that Bob and his companions worked so hard on is now producing better catches than anywhere else on the Susquehanna. In fact, this stretch is doing so well that much of the rest of the river now has these more stringent regulations about keeping bass. The John Day River in the West is another of the fine smallmouth rivers. But there is a possibility that it is being overfished, and we may soon see the demise of many of its larger bass—so abundant there for decades. Unless we move to put regulations on this fine river, and others, we will lose some of our best smallmouth fishing.

Preserving Saltwater Resources

As you have seen, flats fishing is a one-on-one confrontation in which you stalk your quarry before making a presentation. Equally important, all the action takes place in a fragile ecosystem where you often can see the bottom and the variety of life it supports. Catching fish is only one aspect of this endeavor. You develop an appreciation for the beauty of the environment and its battle to survive. There may be days on the flats when you go fishless and still come away with a feeling of satisfaction simply from being there. The scenery never seems to tire the eyes, or the mind.

But those of us who have pursued flats fishing for decades are concerned. Over the seasons, we have observed a deterioration in fishing for some species and a consequent need to probe farther and farther into the remaining pristine areas. This does not mean that we cannot or will not catch fish, but the bonefish schools are a bit smaller and there are fewer snook around to be enticed by our flies.

For those who doubt the effect of sportfishing pressure, consider that there are at least twice as many fishing guides in the Florida Keys as there were twenty years ago. All of them now have better boats. Anglers use polarizing glasses, GPS units, improved tackle, more effective lures—and the fishermen themselves are much more knowledgeable and experienced. Things have to be getting tougher for the fish as a growing legion of anglers gravitates to saltwater fishing and the shallow flats. Many look to the marine scene as an escape from overcrowded streams and poor freshwater sport. Others come because the challenges of light tackle are greater in thin water than anywhere else.

No one can blame these fishermen for their decision; nor should any effort be made to limit flats fishing. The problem is that newcomers view the salt as an endless well. It is not endless and never was. Far-sighted people talk in terms of stocking oceans to support the increased fishing pressure. Trial balloons have already been sent aloft, and I suspect that more such efforts are on the drawing boards. But even if successful stocking techniques are developed and implemented, you can bet that it will be an expensive process.

If the tarpon, bonefish, or permit had commercial value and were sold as food fish, the situation today would be truly bleak. Fortunately, the saving grace is that most of these species are released unharmed and few people pursue them for food.

Development Challenges

Flats and estuaries are among the richest lands in the world. They should be treasured and protected, and yet they are not respected. Developers view an estuary as an unbuilt housing project or a barrier wall of condominiums. Systematic destruction of our coastal estuaries ranks as the foremost threat to fishing. Without an estuary, most gamefish and all of the flats species cannot survive. When populations diminish, it is often because the larvae and juveniles cannot grow safely. They require estuaries, and this habitat is being destroyed by uncaring people.

In the lower half of Florida, for example, mangroves are being eliminated at an incredible rate. The root systems of the mangroves actually filter the water and make it clear. These same roots are a haven for countless juveniles. Efforts are under way to stop this destruction and start a rebuilding process. However, when concrete seawalls replace the mangroves, there is no way fish are going to survive.

Florida is also plagued with water problems, especially the diversion of fresh water from its natural destination. The Everglades are really a broad, slow-flowing river that moves through the saw grass to Florida Bay. This influx of fresh water is vital to both bait- and gamefish species. Diversionary controls by water management commissions have upset the balance of nature and threaten the very existence of the Everglades and of fishing in Florida Bay. It is one of the great nursery grounds, yet it is being destroyed.

The conflict between sport and commercial interests will always be present. Concessions must be made on both sides, but when netters move in and virtually eliminate the bait supply, it is a problem that cannot be overlooked. Here is an example: After an absence of several years, grass started to take root on the bottom of Maryland's Susquehanna flats at the head of the Chesapeake Bay. This return of habitat brought striped bass back into the area. The netters were right behind. Not only did they take the rockfish, but they also tore up much of the new grass in the process, eliminating the habitat that held the fish in the first place.

Fortunately, there are some encouraging signs. Look at the policies of the guides in the Florida Keys, for example. A few years ago they brought in all kinds of fish caught in the ocean and either used them for food or hung them on racks to attract new customers. Today these same guides are in the vanguard, asking to have bag limits placed on delicate species and turning fish loose automatically. Now it is a matter of survival for everyone. Those who have fished barracudas in the same area for a few decades will tell you with sadness how the average size of the fish has decreased over the years. There was a time, however, when every barracuda was killed and dragged back to the dock and displayed before being tossed in a garbage can. These practices are now shunned. Every fish is becoming increasingly valuable in the water, because a dead fish can never spawn again.

If fly fishermen sound upset, it is because of our personal love for the flats and everything on them. We can remember what it was like and can only hope that fishing in the shallows will continue and even improve in years to come. Flats fishing is an unforgettable experience, and we would like every other angler to gain the same measure of enjoyment from it. It is only possible if all of us begin caring and become concerned.

Final Thoughts

We must all vow to protect the environment, because our ecosystem is extremely fragile. Above all, we should release every unwanted fish unharmed and take only what we need. As long as everyone is conscientious, government-imposed limits will not be necessary. If we are going to continue to enjoy recreational fishing as we know it today, we all must take part in protecting and enhancing the fish and the habitats that give us such great sport.

INDEX